Arthur G. Lippiatt
Graham G. L. Wright

THE ARCHITECTURE OF SMALL COMPUTER SYSTEMS

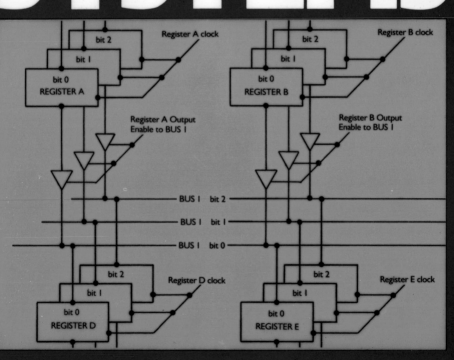

Second Edition

The Architecture of
Small Computer Systems

To: Karen
       Kevin
       Sonia
       David
       Richard
       Adrian
       Nicola
       Esta

A.G.L.

To the memory of my mother – triste ministerium.

G.G.L.W.

The Architecture of Small Computer Systems

Second Edition

ARTHUR G. LIPPIATT

Camelot Software and Systems; formerly The Hatfield Polytechnic

and

GRAHAM G. L. WRIGHT

The Polytechnic of Wales

Prentice/Hall PHI International

ENGLEWOOD CLIFFS, NEW JERSEY   LONDON   NEW DELHI   RIO DE JANEIRO
SINGAPORE   SYDNEY   TOKYO   TORONTO

**This edition first published in the
United States of America, 1986**

British Library Cataloguing in Publication Data

LIPPIATT, Arthur G.
    Architecture of small computer systems—2nd ed.
    1. Minicomputers
    I. Title   II. WRIGHT, G. G. L.
    001.64'04   QA76.5
ISBN 0-13-044736-6 (p)

Library of Congress Cataloging in Publication Data

LIPPIATT, Arthur G., 1936–
    The architecture of small computer systems.

    Bibliography: p.
    Includes index.
    1. Computer architecture.   2. Microcomputers.
    3. Minicomputers.   I. WRIGHT, Graham G. L.,
    1936–   II. Title.
    QA76.9.A73L56   1985   621.3819'582   85–3490
ISBN 0-13-044736-6 (p)

ISBN 0-13-044736-6

PRENTICE-HALL INC, *Englewood Cliffs, New Jersey*
PRENTICE-HALL INTERNATIONAL UK LTD, *London*
PRENTICE-HALL OF AUSTRALIA PTY LTD, *Sydney*
PRENTICE-HALL CANADA INC, *Toronto*
PRENTICE-HALL HISPANO AMERICANA SA, *Mexico*
PRENTICE-HALL OF INDIA PRIVATE LIMITED, *New Delhi*
PRENTICE-HALL OF JAPAN INC, *Tokyo*
PRENTICE-HALL OF SOUTHEAST ASIA PTE LTD, *Singapore*
PRENTICE-HALL DO BRASIL LTDA, *Rio de Janeiro*

Printed in Great Britain by A. Wheaton & Co Ltd, Exeter

10 9 8 7 6 5 4 3 2

Contents

Preface to the First Edition

The two major aims of this book are:

(1) To explain to computer science students what the hardware in a computer system does. Many computer scientists find difficulty in distinguishing what the electronic subsystems in a computer can do from what a program can make them do.

(2) To explain to engineers what a computer system does. The advent of the microprocessor and microcomputer has fairly rapidly brought the field of computer systems into the sphere of interest of many engineers who have previously had nothing to do with computers excepting perhaps as a tool in the design process. For them an understanding of the overall system is important. Experience in teaching engineers indicates that they find little difficulty in learning the new digital electronic techniques, many of which they probably have met in any case, but they do have difficulty in finding suitable reading to learn about the wider picture of the overall system.

The aim has been to satisfy these requirements in a volume small enough not to discourage the potential reader by its sheer bulk or its high price. Of necessity much detail has had to be omitted. As a result, however, the system's functions can be described without confusing the reader with details of minor alternatives and the minutiae of implementation techniques. It is hoped that the professional engineer wishing to know something of computer systems will find here a sound first text, and that the student of computer science or of electrical engineering will find sufficient material for an introductory course.

Computer architecture covers that area of knowledge and expertise which is equally of interest to the computer scientist and to the electrical engineer. It is really the common ground which both the hardware specialist and the software specialist should understand. These groups of people are increasingly being required to work together on projects in the design, production, testing and commissioning of equipment. Without a sound understanding of the architecture of computer systems, intelligent interaction between them, and an appreciation by each of the other's problems, becomes impossible.

An examination of the features of some commercially available computer and microprocessor systems leaves the impression that in some cases the engineers who designed them were not as aware as they might have been of how the software designers would wish to use the facilities provided. Consequently those facilities are not very easy or convenient to use. Equally it is clear from conversations with software specialists that it is at times difficult for them to appreciate what the hardware subsystems are really capable of achieving.

It was, of course, difficult to know what topics to include in the text and much more difficult to know which topics to omit. It was decided therefore to keep in mind the needs of the groups of people mentioned above, to aim at an introductory text, to limit the material to that which one may expect a student to cover in a one-year university or college course (when supplemented by suitable practical work), and not to cover material which is easily available from many other books. Numbering Systems have been omitted for that reason.

The principles explained in the text are related to the realities of the world of commercial computer systems in an appendix which contains a summary of the specifications of some popular small computer systems. The terminology used in the appendix is that of the rest of the text and may not correspond with that of the particular computer system manufacturer. It is important to relate principles and practice, to help the reader to understand the nature of the different compromises reached by various design teams in applying those priciples to real system designs.

Technical terms have been *italicized* and defined at their first appearance in the text. It is very easy for a specialist to use terminology which is either not understood by the newcomer to the subject or, much worse, which is misunderstood because the words used are familiar to the reader in another context in which their meaning is rather different. This often seems to be the case in the spheres of hardware and software.

The book is arranged in seven chapters, the first giving a superficial treatment of topics covered in greater detail later on, and introducing the basic terminology of the subject. The second chapter explains the type of instructions which a computer can obey, a topic which is the cause of some considerable difficulty to the newcomer, and gives some idea of the way in which those instructions are used. Chapter 3 tackles another area of computer architecture which provides students with some difficulty—the way in which information is coded into a computer system. A number of topics covered in this chapter are often treated as separate topics. They are covered together to emphasize that they are all to do with information coding and to help to dispel the misconception that they are hardly, if at all, related. Chapter 4 is a section on standard memory addressing techniques. The chapter is designed to help the engineer to understand why the programmer wishes to use these techniques and also to explain to the programmer the functions which the hardware performs to produce the different addressing modes. Chapters 5 and 6 cover the important topic of the Input/Output subsystem. Chapter 5 is devoted to an explanation of how data transfers are carried out in a computer system. This chapter will present no problem to the electrical engineer, but the computer science student may well find it rather difficult. Chapter 6 presents both the hardware and software aspects of interrupt handling. Chapter 7 considers computer arithmetic (not binary arithmetic) and the effects it has on the architecture of the system, particularly its effect on the instruction set. It includes discussions of floating point and BCD arithmetic. A number of uses of the condition codes (flags) are also considered in this chapter.

Preface to the
Second Edition

In writing the second edition of this book, the joint authors have endeavored to adhere to the stated claims of the first edition and to update the text in accord with currently-used systems.

The first three chapters and chapter 7 are substantially unchanged. Chapter 4 has been extended to include additional addressing modes and a discussion of addressing data on the stack.

Chapters 5 and 6 have been rewritten and extended. The I/O examples have been brought up to date by dropping the paper tape and teletype examples. Chapter 5 now includes an explanation of the workings of serial I/O. The approach to interrupts in chapter 6 has been changed to emphasize the need for interrupt-driven systems to implement realtime systems, and the section on DMA has been extended.

A new chapter 8 has been added, dealing with memory management techniques. The new microcomputers can address many megabytes of memory, and the management of that memory is now so fundamental that a discussion of memory management should not be left to more advanced texts.

The appendix has been modified in two ways; firstly, it contains architectural information on the more recent microprocessors and superminis, and secondly the systems included are those which are the most popular in their market sector, so that a reader may have the greatest chance of finding a system to which he or she has access described therein. The bibliography has been updated, and specific references to the systems described in the appendix have been added.

Acknowledgments

We wish to thank those readers who have written to point out errors in the first edition. Those errors have been rectified in this edition.

AGL would like to thank Pat Brazier who typed most of the second edition and provided constant encouragement to complete the work involved.

GGLW would like to thank Colin Bowring for his help in suggesting sources and material used in the appendix.

We would both like to record our appreciation of the perseverance of Giles Wright of Prentice-Hall International in encouraging and enabling the production of the second edition as a joint exercise between the two authors.

CHAPTER 1

Introduction to a Computer System

1.1 INTRODUCTION

To describe a computer system in a few words is impossible. Computer systems are intricate arrangements of sophisticated components, and it takes a lot of time and work with computers to generate a thorough understanding of them. Computer systems come in a large variety of shapes, sizes, capabilities and specialities. They range from small and relatively simple microcomputers to large and very complex mainframes, with a price range from about a hundred to a few million dollars. They have a large number of normal and special uses. This book deals particularly with small computer systems, at the lower end of the price and performance range occupied by the various types of microprocessors, microcomputers and minicomputers. Small computer systems are, by virtue of their lower cost, very widely used and available, particularly in schools and colleges; and they are also correspondingly accessible to the student. Larger computers are, on the other hand, fewer in number and increasingly remote and unapproachable, locked inside securely controlled computer rooms.

This book attempts to explain the fundamental principles of the architecture – the internal organization – of small computer systems, without generating confusion by explaining the many variations possible. Reference is made to real computer systems to show how the principles are applied in practice, and also to show some of the variations encountered commercially. Appendix 1 contains a more detailed description of some common computer systems within the scope of this book, among which the reader is very likely to find a machine, or its processor, to which he or she has access.

A large proportion of the book is also relevant to larger computers, but as might be expected, the range of variations and complexities are correspondingly greater. Also, for reasons which will be explained later in the book, the architecture of large computers that is evident to the student is often not their true architecture, and it is often very difficult to distinguish reality from appearance.

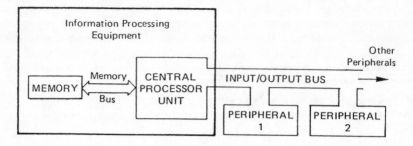

Figure 1.1 *Computer system block diagram*

What then is a computer system? Its major characteristics are:

1. It is an organized set of electronic equipment used to *process* information;

2. It is provided with information for processing by a range of *input* devices, such as keyboards, handsets, punched card readers, magnetic disk and tape drives, thermometers, pressure gauges, voltmeters, counters, weighing machines, speech analyzers, cash registers, telephone lines, timers, character and bar code readers and many others;

3. After it has processed the input information, it transmits the results of processing to one or more *output* devices of which there is again a large variety, such as CRT displays, TV monitors, magnetic tape and disk drives, valves, printing machines such as line printers, matrix printers, typesetters, typewriters and ticket printers, telephone lines, electric motors and other actuators, buzzers, speech amplifiers, traffic lights and many others.

A computer therefore consists of some electronic information processing equipment, a number of information supplying devices—the input devices—and a number of information receiving devices—the output devices. Their arrangement into a computer system is illustrated in Figures 1.1 and 1.2. The input devices and output devices are physically connected to the information processing equipment by a connection known as an

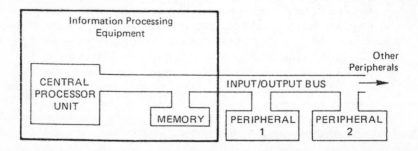

Figure 1.2 *Alternative system block diagram*

Input/Output (I/O) bus which allows information to be transferred between the devices connected to it. The characteristics and workings of this bus will be described in detail in Chapter 5. Input and output devices are collectively called Input/Output devices or *peripheral* devices, or often just peripherals.

The information processing equipment can conveniently be subdivided into two main subsystems, the information processor itself, usually called the *Central Processor Unit*—the CPU—or just the processor, and an information *memory*. A memory is required because the processor can process information much more quickly than the peripherals can supply it. Information from the peripherals is therefore put into the memory until all the information for a particular job is available in the memory. The CPU then processes the information and returns the resulting information to the memory. From here it is sent at a suitable (slow) rate to the output peripherals. The memory is an electronic system and can therefore provide the CPU with information at a suitably high rate. Figures 1.1 and 1.2 show the block diagram of two alternative computer systems using different ways of connecting the memory into the system. Both of these alternatives are used in different commercial minicomputer and microprocessor systems. The differences between the two systems arise because the system of Figure 1.1 has an independent connection between the memory and the processor whereas in the system of Figure 1.2 the memory shares the communication path to the peripherals. This latter system is found in most microprocessors and in some of the more recent minicomputers. The two systems are discussed in more detail later.

1.2 STORED PROGRAMS

A digital computer system is very versatile for two reasons. First, there is a very large variety of peripherals which may be connected to it. Second, and much more fundamental, the central processor can be programmed so that what the system does is determined not when it is manufactured but when it is used. The central processor of a digital computer system performs any task which can be defined by a list of instructions, called a *program*, which is stored in the information memory of the computer system so that the CPU can obey it. The power and flexibility of a computer system arise from the fact that programs can be stored and the computer system can decide which program to obey by testing external conditions. As a result it may change its actions to suit different circumstances as they arise. This is the principle of a stored program machine. Stored program machines are not necessarily computer systems, but all general purpose digital computers are stored program machines. All the programs in a machine are given the collective name *software*. It is because the software is readily changed that a computer system can be adapted to a great variety of tasks.

A computer system then, is manufactured so that the task it performs is determined after manufacture by:

1. The peripherals attached to it.
2. A program of instructions in the CPU, written by a person who may be called a *programmer*, and stored in the computer's memory.

1.3 CODING OF INFORMATION IN A COMPUTER SYSTEM

Whenever information is used by people it is received by them and/or transmitted by them in coded form. There are many codes in common use in the world and most people understand a few of them. Any of the human senses can be used to convey information between people; for example sight is used for written messages, sound for spoken messages, touch for braille messages. As people are equipped with systems for reading (eyes), for writing (hands), hearing and so on, it is these phenomena which are used for the exchange of information between people. Computers are equipped with subsystems which respond to electrical phenomena, such as voltages and currents; moving magnetic fields; light and sound waves. It is therefore not surprising that these are the means of communicating information between computer systems and between the subsystems which form a computer system. Coding of information is, however, not just a matter of finding a suitable medium for its transmission. It is also a matter of deciding on a set of conventions agreed by all concerned in the exchange of information. In human society universal agreement on a set of conventions for anything is a practical impossibility. A variety of conventions arises, each of which becomes a standard for a certain group of people. The most common example of coded information is a language. The sets of codes representing units of information are the words of the language. These are expressed in a number of ways—sets of sounds, sets of written symbols and so on. The English language uses 26 different written symbols—the letters A to Z—which can be combined in a number of agreed ways to make words. A different set of symbols is used to represent numeric information, the numbers 0 through 9. These extra symbols are not strictly necessary since there are also words to represent numbers, but they are very convenient when performing a particular type of information processing called numeric calculations. For this purpose a special set of manipulations is agreed to apply to the symbols 0 through 9 which do not apply to the symbols A through Z. For example, subtraction of symbols 0 through 9 is meaningful, but subtraction of the symbols A through Z is not. There are other sets of symbols allocated for special purposes, punctuation marks and numerical operators being two of them. Again, these are not absolutely essential but are very useful in assisting a receiver of a message to deduce the meaning of the message, or, to use computer terminology, to *decode* the message.

A computer system can be made to recognize words of a number of symbols. The symbols, however, are electrical phenomena, not writing on paper or sounds in the air. A most important characteristic of these electrical phenomena is that they have only two distinguishable states compared with the 26 distinguishable states of the English alphabetic symbols or the ten states of the numeric symbols of the decimal numbering system. These two distinguishable states form the alphabet of computer system language. Since there are only these two "letters" in the computer system alphabet it is to be expected that computer words will generally contain more letters than English words.

For convenience, so that people can understand the internal information manipulations of a computer system, the two letters of the computer alphabet are allocated agreed written symbols understandable to people. These symbols are 0 and 1. There are also words for them in the English language, zero (or nought) and one. So a computer word may be represented on paper by a string of symbols such as:

0010110101001101

which is a computer word 16 symbols long.

Now, any system in which there are only two objects or two states is called a *binary system*. The symbols chosen to represent the computer alphabet are the same as the binary digits 0 and 1 in the binary numbering system. Hence it is normal to refer to the letters of a computer word as BInary digiTS, or *bits*. Thus the example of a computer word shown above is a computer word 16 bits long. The computer word length is normally constant in any computer system and it should be noted that there is usually no direct translation possible between one English word and one computer word. Units of information in a computer system are usually smaller than an English word.

Microprocessors usually have a word length of 4, 8 or 16 bits. Minicomputers usually have word lengths of 16 bits although there are minicomputers with word lengths of 8, 12, 18, 24 and 32 bits. Large computer systems, the *mainframe computers*, have longer word lengths which may be 24, 32, 36, 48 or 60 bits.

1.3.1 Classification of Information in a Computer System

There are three classifications of information which help in the understanding of the working of a computer system. The three types of information which concern us here are:

1. Alphanumeric information
2. Numeric information
3. Contextual information

1.3.1.1 Alphanumeric Information
Alphanumeric information is the representation in computer words of the letters and other symbols of the languages of people. It is necessary for this information to be stored in a computer so that the computer can print messages to people. For example if a computer is used for calculating the pay due to the employees of a company, one of the end results of the information processing is the production of pay slips containing messages to the employees, informing them of the results of the calculations. These messages consist of the 26 letters of the alphabet as well as the numbers 0 through 9 and some other special symbols. Inside the computer each of these letters, numbers or symbols, collectively called *alphanumeric characters*, is represented by a computer word or part of a word.

There are many standard conventions in use for the representation of alphanumeric characters in computer language, i.e. in the form of groups of bits, but that in most common use is the 8-bit ASCII code (ASCII stands for American Standard Code for Information Interchange). Figure 1.3 shows a small selection of ASCII 8-bit codes, although their structure is beyond the

Alphanumeric Character	8-bit ASCII code								Bit number
	7	6	5	4	3	2	1	0	
0	0	0	1	1	0	0	0	0	
1	1	0	1	1	0	0	0	1	
2	1	0	1	1	0	0	1	0	
3	0	0	1	1	0	0	1	1	
4	1	0	1	1	0	1	0	0	
5	0	0	1	1	0	1	0	1	
6	0	0	1	1	0	1	1	0	
7	1	0	1	1	0	1	1	1	
8	1	0	1	1	1	0	0	0	
9	0	0	1	1	1	0	0	1	
A	0	1	0	0	0	0	0	1	
B	0	1	0	0	0	0	1	0	
C	1	1	0	0	0	0	1	1	
D	0	1	0	0	0	1	0	0	
E	1	1	0	0	0	1	0	1	
F	1	1	0	0	0	1	1	0	
G	0	1	0	0	0	1	1	1	
H	0	1	0	0	1	0	0	0	

Figure 1.3   *A selection of ASCII 8-bit codes*

scope of the present discussion (but see Chapter 3, section 3.3). In a computer system these codes are produced automatically by input peripherals such as typewriters or VDUs when a key on the keyboard is depressed, and are recognized automatically by output peripherals such as printers. If the letter A is typed on a VDU or typewriter connected to a computer system, the VDU or typewriter automatically sends the computer a set of electrical signals which can be represented by the code 01000001 (see Figure 1.3). If the computer sends a VDU or typewriter the code 01000001 then it automatically displays the letter A.

The binary alphabet of the computer's language can be represented by means other than the writing of the symbols 0 and 1 on paper. For example, a common input medium on small computer systems used to be punched paper tape. The characters of the English language can be coded onto paper tape in a form that makes them easily translated into electrical signals. The convention normally adopted is to punch a hole in the tape to correspond to the computer state which is also represented by a 1, and to leave paper where there is to be a 0. Characters are punched one to a line across a paper tape one inch wide. The characters are punched at a density of ten per inch along the tape and each character is represented by a code of eight 1 or 0 (hole or no hole) bits across the tape, coded in 8-bit ASCII code. Figure 1.4 shows the appearance of a punched paper tape containing the same codes as those in Figure 1.3.

Magnetic tape systems work in a similar way. The magnetic surface is magnetized so that a North pole represents a 1 and a South pole represents 0. Information is held on 8 or 9 magnetic tracks across a ½ inch tape, at 800, 1,600 or up to 6,250 8-bit codes per inch length of the tape. Cassette tape

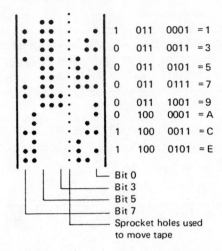

1	011	0001	= 1
0	011	0011	= 3
0	011	0101	= 5
0	011	0111	= 7
0	011	1001	= 9
0	100	0001	= A
1	100	0011	= C
1	100	0101	= E

Bit 0
Bit 3
Bit 5
Bit 7
Sprocket holes used
to move tape

Figure 1.4 *Punched paper tape showing ASCII encoded characters*

systems attached to small microcomputers usually have only one track, in which case the information is held serially, 1 bit at a time, along the length of the tape.

1.3.1.2 Numeric Information

Numeric information is necessary for the representation and manipulation of numbers, basically the ability to add and subtract them. In English a different set of symbols (0–9) is used to represent numbers from that used to represent words (A–Z), but in a computer system this is not done. The representation of numbers in a binary numbering system will be well known to those who have taken a course in modern mathematics. Those who have not are referred to a book on the subject or to a text on computer logic design (see the bibliography at the end of this book). Very briefly, any number may be represented by a string of zeros and ones in which the binary digits represent ascending powers of two starting from the right. In the decimal system the decimal digits represent ascending powers of ten starting from the right. All that is required in a computer system, therefore, to enable it to manipulate numbers is the conversion of numbers to their binary equivalent on input to the system, and the necessary electronic subsystems to perform the numeric manipulations. These electronic subsystems are standard items whose design is covered in many books on logic design.

1.3.1.3 Contextual Information

Much of the information content of a group of bits in a computer system is derived from its context—its environment. This is of course also true of words in the English language. The context of a computer word may be its use within a particular problem, its position within a string of words, or its physical position within the computer system. An example of each is given below.

The context within a particular problem usually, but not always, refers to the environment formed by the program and therefore generated in the first place by the programmer. Suppose a program has been written to compile some statistics on the employees of a company. It would be possible to store the information about each employee in *fields*—groups of bits—within a computer word in the manner shown in Figure 1.5. The program could be written to interpret the information coded in this way, but the coded words would be meaningless outside the context of this program. In other words the particular program employs a set of conventions which are standard within the program but not agreed for use elsewhere.

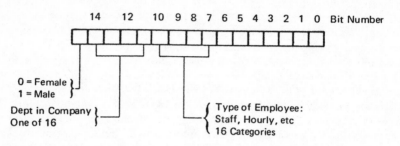

Figure 1.5   *Coding of information in fields in words*

It has been established that the pattern:

01000001

when used in the context of a string of alphanumeric *ASCII-encoded* characters, represents the letter A. However, in the context of a string of pure binary numbers that same pattern of bits represents the decimal number 65. If the same bit pattern were used in a set of numbers within a computer system using a decimal code it may represent the two-digit decimal number 41 (see Chapter 7). Its position within a particular string of words used to represent a known type of information is therefore crucial to its correct interpretation or decoding.

The importance of the physical context of a group of bits within a computer system will become more apparent later in the book. At this stage it can be simply illustrated by pointing out that if the pattern:

01000001

is in the output part of a printer then the printer is busy printing the letter A. If the same pattern is in the part of the computer system which manipulates numbers, then the system is operating on the number 41 or 65. Hence the effect of the pattern on the system, or the meaning of the pattern to the system, depends on the physical location of the pattern within the system. Context, then, is an important aspect of the interpretation of information within a computer system.

1.4 THE MEMORY

The memory is used to store the program (the instructions to the CPU) and *data*. Data is the non-processed input information, the processed information ready for output to the output peripherals and the partially processed information between those two stages.

In many computer systems there is a hierarchy of storage devices such as magnetic disks, magnetic tapes, magnetic bubble memories, semiconductor memories and ferrite core memories, which together form a memory system. Such memory systems are outside the scope of this text. The discussion here is restricted to the basic memories found in all computer systems and which often form the complete memory in small systems.

The memory is an electronic system which appears from the outside to consist of a number of separate *locations* each of which is identical to all the others. The information stored in each memory location is normally one computer word. Each location can be identified uniquely because the locations are all given a unique reference number, called the *address* of that location. The number of bits in every location of a minicomputer or microprocessor memory is therefore usually 8 or 16. In mainframe computers the memory may contain 24, 32, 36, 48, 60 or more bits per location.

1.4.1 Writing and Reading

The act of depositing a word in a memory location is called writing a word to that location, and the act of retrieving a word from a memory location is called reading that memory location. When a word is written to a memory location the word which was previously in that location is obliterated and cannot be retrieved thereafter. When a word is read from a memory location only a copy is produced by the memory, leaving the word still unaltered in the memory location. The word in a memory location may therefore be read any number of times without destroying it.

1.4.2 A Simple Memory System

The memory electronics may conveniently be considered to be divided into two major subsystems, the memory control electronics and the storage system (the actual memory locations) as shown in Figure 1.6. All communications between the memory and the rest of the computer system are via the memory control electronics, which in this text will be called the *memory controller*. Elsewhere it will be found to be called the memory manager, memory management unit (see Chapter 8), memory access controller and

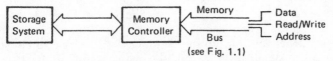

Figure 1.6 *Simple memory system*

other similar names. Whenever any device requires access to the memory, either for reading or for writing, it must send the memory controller the address of the memory location to which access is required. It must also inform the memory controller whether the access is a read or a write, and if it is a write operation it must send the word to be written. The memory controller performs the necessary action. Only one access to the memory can be in progress at any one time.

1.4.3 Interleaved Memories

Some of the larger minicomputer systems may have an interleaved memory system as shown in Figure 1.7. This requires a more complex memory controller than in the simple system. An interleaved system contains two independent storage systems. Half the locations are in one storage system and the rest are in the other. Thus access may be made to two locations simultaneously provided the locations are in different storage systems. Usually the locations with even addresses are in one system and those with odd addresses are in the other system. Data is normally stored by a program in an orderly fashion in sequentially addressed locations and an interleaved memory allows a block of words to be deposited in or copied from memory very rapidly.

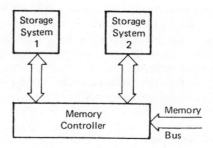

Figure 1.7 *Interleaved memory system*

1.4.4 Multiple Ported Memories

A multiple ported system is shown in Figure 1.8. In effect there are a number of access ports to the memory. Each port appears to the rest of the devices in the computer system to act as an independent memory controller of the simple type described above. Usually such memories have multiple storage systems but these storage systems may or may not be interleaved. Each port may work independently in any of the storage systems which is not busy with another port. A detailed study of these systems is outside the scope of this text.

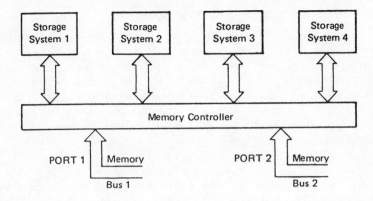

Figure 1.8 *Multiple ported memory system*

1.4.5 Parameters of Memory Systems

1.4.5.1 Memory Size

An important parameter of any memory system is its maximum size, the maximum number of locations which it can contain. The computer system must be able to refer to each individual location by sending the memory controller the address of the location. This address is a (binary) number and in a computer system binary numbers usually contain the same number of bits as a computer word. It is normal practice, therefore, to install a memory which has a maximum size such that all its locations can be addressed by a single computer word. Memory size is normally quoted as a multiple of 1,024 locations which can be addressed by a 10-bit word and which is called 1K of memory. Thus a 16-bit address can reference 64K memory locations. A computer using a 16-bit addressing system can therefore have a maximum memory size of 64K. Microprocessor or minicomputer systems using an 8-bit word, which can address only 256 words, usually use two computer words to give a 16-bit address.

Most minicomputer systems allow addressing of a memory system larger than that which can be addressed by a single computer word. The rather advanced addressing techniques required to achieve this are described in Chapter 8.

1.4.5.2 Access and Cycle Times

The access time of a memory system is the time between the acknowledgement from a memory controller that it has recognized a request for a memory read and the time when it signals that it has retrieved the word requested. In current computer systems time is measured in nanoseconds (nS) each of which is one thousandth of one millionth of one second. Access time in current memories is of the order of 10 to 500nS.

The cycle time of a memory is the time between requests for access to the memory for reading or writing when the memory is working at its maximum speed. This is between 1 and 3 times the access time as defined above.

1.4.6 Types and Properties of Storage Systems

The cheapest and most common type of storage medium is manufactured from semiconductor materials. These semiconductor materials retain information in the form of electric currents and charges. The information in semiconductor memories is lost when the electricity supply is switched off, because the electric charges leak away from the semiconducting material. If this is important a semiconductor memory can be provided with a battery to supply power when the mains supply is not available.

1.4.6.1 Random Access Memories

A random access memory is one in which the access time of a memory location is independent of the address of the location. The main memory of all computer systems is organized in this way. Devices such as magnetic tapes are not random access, they are serial access devices. The time taken to read a particular item of information from a tape depends on where that item is on the tape relative to the position of the piece of tape currently being read.

The name random access memory—RAM—is applied rather incorrectly in current semiconductor and computer jargon to mean a random access memory which can be read and written by the computer system of which it forms a part. This distinguishes it from random access memory which can be read but not written by the computer system. The latter is called Read Only Memory.

1.4.6.2 Read Only Memory

Read Only Memory—ROM—has recently become much used for applications requiring information which is constant. The advent of cheap semiconductor ROM and the application of microprocessors to small fixed program systems has provided a large market for read only memories. They are finding application in larger systems also. The information in a ROM is implanted during the manufacture of the memory and cannot be changed thereafter.

For small production runs there are devices available called *Programmable Read Only Memories*—PROMs—which are manufactured with each bit of each location containing a binary 1. The user can write the required information into these with a special piece of electronic equipment information called a *PROM programmer* into which the PROM is also plugged. Thereafter the information in the PROM cannot be changed.

There are also PROMs available which can have their contents reset to all ones, after programming, by exposing them to ultraviolet light for about 20 minutes. These devices are called *Eraseable Programmable Read Only Memories*—EPROMs. They may be reprogrammed after exposure to the ultraviolet light by using the PROM programmer. The exposure to ultraviolet light resets the content of each bit of each location to a binary 1, erasing the information which was previously in the memory. An *electrically alterable read only memory*—EAROM is yet another type of memory device in common usage. This device is written in much the same way as the ultraviolet erasable EPROM but its contents can be erased by supplying sufficiently high voltages to some of its connections for a relatively long period of time. These devices can be incorporated into the computer system as a peripheral to the system. It is possible for the computer system itself to write information into these ROMs although this does take some considerable time, a few seconds. They are widely used in computer peripherals, particularly in terminals (VDUs and printing terminals) in which they store the characteristics of the terminal device. A user may alter the characteristics by informing the computer of the desired characteristics, the computer then writes this information into the EAROM. The terminal retains those characteristics until such time as the user again alters them.

1.4.6.3 Stacks

A stack is a special type of serially accessed memory, illustrated in Figure 1.9. It can be filled only from the bottom up and can be read only from the top down. Thus if a string of words is written to the stack, the words can be read only in the reverse order. Writing to the memory is called *Pushing* a word onto the stack and reading the memory is called *Pulling* a word off the stack or *popping* the stack. The great advantage of this type of memory in certain applications is that a device wishing to write to it or read from it does not have to supply the address of the required information. The stack controller contains a pointer to the top location of the stack and that is the only location which can be accessed. Notice that the pointer appears to point to the next empty location if a push (write) operation is requested or to the topmost filled location if a pull (read) operation is required. In most modern computer systems a memory of this type is implemented using a random access memory, which is usually part of the main memory, by providing some special control electronics to give it the characteristics described.

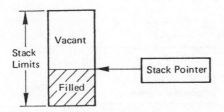

Figure 1.9   *Stack organized memory*

1.5 THE CENTRAL PROCESSOR UNIT

As its name implies, the central processor unit—the CPU—is the centerpiece of the whole computer system. The CPU obeys the programs of instructions, which enable the computer system to perform its tasks. All actions which take place within the computer system are initiated by the central processor unit but are not necessarily directly controlled by it.

The central processor is capable of storing, temporarily, a number of words which it has read from the memory. These words are stored in electronic subsystems called *registers*. In computer systems, a particular group of bits assumes a particular significance to the system only when it is resident in a register. It is the purpose of the register in the system which confers a particular significance on the group of bits. In general, the same group of bits assumes a different meaning as it is transferred from one register to another. This is an example of the context of a group of bits being dependent on its physical position in the computer system. Words in transit between registers and words resident in the memory have no particular significance to the computer system.

The significance or meaning of the words stored in the CPU therefore depends on the purpose of the registers within the CPU. The memory contains the CPU instructions and the data, which may be processed, partially processed or unprocessed. The CPU sorts out the instructions from the data by routing the instructions to a special CPU register called the *CPU instruction register* and by routing the data to the *CPU data registers*.

1.5.1 The Main CPU Timing Cycle

The CPU continuously executes the cycle of events depicted in the diagram of Figure 1.10. This cycle is often called the instruction cycle of the CPU. This cycle of events occurs automatically within the electronics, often called the *hardware* of the system, and enables it to retrieve the instructions one at a time from the memory and to obey them. The programmer has no control

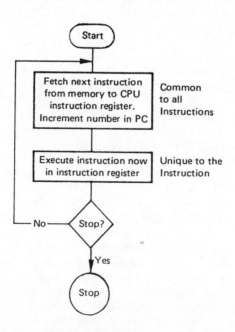

Figure 1.10   *CPU main timing cycle*

over this sequence of events, only over what instructions appear in the memory and the order in which they are executed (obeyed) by the CPU. Figure 1.10 displays the following features of the machine's instruction cycle:

1. The CPU executes a two-stage cycle, namely *fetch* the instruction, then *execute* it and test to see if a stop is required. If a stop is required then stop, else fetch the next instruction. The electronics can perform more than one task simultaneously. In a CPU the test for a stop condition is performed by the electronics while it is executing the instruction so that as soon as the instruction execute is complete the next fetch can begin.

2. The CPU cannot stop in the middle of an instruction. The importance of this will be shown later in the text. It can be intuitively appreciated that this must be the case, because an operator pressing a stop button should presumably bring the system to a tidy halt and not leave it suspended in the middle of its short repetitive cycle.

A fundamental convention in all computer systems is that the instructions forming the program are stored in the memory in adjacent locations, so that normally the address of the next instruction is higher than the address of the location of the current instruction by the *size* of the current instruction (the number of bytes or words which it occupies in memory). This allows the use of a very simple device for keeping track of the instruction locations in the memory. There is a special register in the CPU whose only function within the computer system is to hold the memory address of the next instruction to be fetched (and executed) by the CPU. This register is present in all processors and goes under a variety of names. In this text it is referred to as the *program counter (PC)* but it is called elsewhere the Instruction Address Register (IAR), the Control Register (CR), the Sequence Control Register (SCR), the Instruction Pointer (IP) and other such names.

When the CPU starts the fetch stage of its two-stage timing cycle it sends the memory controller the number in the program counter as the address of the location to be read. In most processors the CPU increments the number in the PC as soon as the instruction has been retrieved from the memory and before the instruction is executed. This leaves the PC in its correct state for the next instruction fetch. The "fetch next instruction" and "increment the PC" are common to all instructions, and this part of the cycle cannot be influenced by the programmer. The "obey the instruction" part of the cycle is automatic insofar as it will always happen, but the actual events which occur are dependent on the particular instruction and are therefore under the control of the programmer.

1.5.2 The CPU Instructions

The two main configurations of small computer systems were shown in Figures 1.1 and 1.2. The instructions which the CPU obeys are concerned with the movement of data between the registers of the major subsystems of the computer system. Hence in a computer system organized as in Figure 1.1, where the memory is connected to the CPU by its own data link, there are three major subsets of instructions. These cause:

1. Data transfers between the memory and the registers in the CPU.
2. Data transfers between registers in the CPU and registers in the peripherals, using the Input/Output bus.
3. Data transfers within the CPU among its own registers.

In computer systems organized as in Figure 1.2, where the memory is connected to the Input/Output bus, there are only two major subsets of instructions, those in (2) and (3) above with the memory included in the devices on the I/O bus.

Instructions causing data transfers between the memory and the registers of the CPU are usually called *memory reference instructions*. Those causing data transfers between registers in the CPU and registers in the peripherals are called Input/Output instructions, but those causing data transfers within the CPU are often not given a collective name. In computer systems where the memory locations are a subset of the set of registers connected to the I/O bus, the Input/Output instructions are indistinguishable from memory reference instructions, so the manufacturer's literature sometimes classifies instructions as memory reference or non-memory reference instructions. Figure 1.1 represents the actual physical method of connecting the memory, the central processor and the peripheral devices in some minicomputer systems. In some microcomputer systems, mainly those manufactured by Intel and Zilog, the memory is physically connected to the system as is shown in Figure 1.2, but the memory locations and the registers in the peripheral devices have to be accessed by separate instructions. The memory locations are accessed by memory reference instructions and the peripheral registers are referenced by Input/Output instructions, in exactly the same way as in systems which are physically organized in Figure 1.1.

The set of instructions causing data transfers within the CPU is usually subdivided into groups which perform certain types of data manipulation. These groups will be considered in more detail in Chapter 2.

It is worth noting that each peripheral device has an electronic controller, just as the memory has, and these controllers contain registers between which data transfers take place when the device is working. The CPU does not control those data transfers directly. All it does is read from or write to some of the registers in the peripheral controller as appropriate. Each peripheral controller contains a register which is in effect its instruction register. It is the loading of this register by the CPU which starts the peripheral action (e.g. the printing of a character). The CPU reads or writes the peripheral registers only if it is obeying an instruction which causes a data transfer between a CPU register and a peripheral register (an I/O instruction). In that sense therefore the CPU controls the peripherals, but notice that this really means that the CPU actually only initiates the actions of the peripherals.

1.5.3 The CPU Registers

Two of the CPU special purpose registers have already been mentioned, the instruction register and the program counter. For data transfers to occur between the CPU and the rest of the computer system it is necessary that the CPU contains one or more data registers. The programmer requires a number of locations in the system where data currently being worked on by the program can be stored temporarily. These locations are usually registers in the CPU. The existence of registers provides fast access to data and so increases the work throughput of the system. These registers are called the *general purpose (GP) registers* or the *accumulators*. In many small computers the GP registers and the registers required by the hardware for the data transfers are the same registers. In others, the GP registers are actually not in the CPU at all, they are in the memory, In these computer systems the CPU still contains data registers, but these are solely to enable the hardware to perform the transfer of data within the system. The software is totally unaware of the existence of these registers. Processors in common use contain 1, 2, 4, 8 or 16 accumulators. These registers must be allocated addresses for reference, just as the memory locations were given addresses otherwise it would be impossible for the CPU instruction to specify which register is to take part in a data transfer. Binary numbering of the registers is used and this leads to the choice of the number of registers being 2, 4, 8 and so on. In some computers the program counter and some other special purpose registers are included in the set of addressable registers. Although they can be used for general data storage their special function within the system clearly necessitates that this is done with great care on the part of the programmer.

1.5.4 The Arithmetic/Logic Unit—The ALU

This is the CPU subsystem which manipulates data in transit through or within the CPU. The details of its functions are discussed in more detail in Chapter 2. Briefly, however, this unit adds and subtracts computer words when they are being used as numbers, and it can perform logical operations on computer words as well, hence its name. It is normally a very high speed device, taking about 20 to 100nS to add two numbers. It has two inputs, each of which can receive a word from a CPU register, and an output which can send the resulting word to a CPU register. It does not normally contain its own registers as it uses the CPU registers.

1.6 THE COMPLETE CPU

The CPU as described so far could be that of Figure 1.11. Note the following points about the system shown in this Figure.

1. All the registers are the same length because they all provide temporary storage for one computer word.
2. The word read by the memory controller can be routed within the CPU to either the instruction register or to any of the GP registers.
3. The ALU receives its two input words from the CPU registers.
4. The result word from the ALU is routed to the GP registers.
5. The word in any one of the GP registers can be sent to the memory.

6. The origin of the memory address when a word of data is to be read or written is not shown.

The basic CPU in any system contains the subsystems shown in Figure 1.11, and all practical systems will contain rather more.

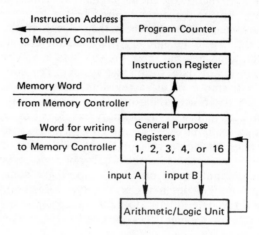

Figure 1.11   *A simple central processor*

1.7 SOFTWARE

A computer system is usually delivered complete with some software, some programs to help the user. A large minicomputer system will have a sophisticated suite of programs, called an *operating system*, which controls the system in many different environments. Small microprocessors may be provided with a very small suite of programs in a single ROM integrated circuit containing, say, 1K 8-bit words, which affords the user minimum help.

1.7.1 Preparing a Program for the Computer

A person setting about the writing of a program for a computer must:

1. Specify the method for solving the problem, the *algorithm* for the solution of the problem.
2. Write a program to execute the algorithm and translate the written program into machine language instructions for the computer being used.
3. Load the program into the computer memory.
4. Run the program, find its errors and correct them.

It is for steps 2, 3 and 4 that the software is required.

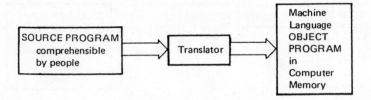

Figure 1.12 *Program derivation*

1.7.2 Writing and Translating a Program

The program may be written in the computer language (ones and zeros); in a high level language in which one statement translates into a large number of machine instructions; or in one of a number of intermediate languages. The most common language of interest to readers of this text is probably *assembly language*. Most assembly language statements translate into one machine instruction. People do not write in machine language because it is very difficult to understand and even more difficult to amend. Unfortunately machines cannot understand any language other than their own, so people write programs in a language they can understand and the program is translated into machine language. The machine language version is then loaded into the computer memory. The process is illustrated in Figure 1.12. The program written by the programmer is called the *source program* because it is the source of the program which is eventually loaded into the computer memory.

The translator of the source program is usually a computer program which uses the source program as its input data and produces the machine language program, called the *object program*, as its output data. If the source program is written in assembly language the translator program is called an *assembler*. If the source program is written in a high level language (such as BASIC or FORTRAN), which produces more than one machine instruction per statement, the translator is called a *compiler*. If the assembler or compiler program is written to run on a computer which is not the same as the computer for which the translation is being carried out, it is called a *cross assembler* or *cross compiler*. For the rest of this chapter it will be assumed, where necessary, that the source program is written in assembly language.

1.7.3 Loading the Object Program

When the source program has been assembled into the object program the latter must be loaded into the computer memory. This loading is achieved by a program called a *loader* which is already in the memory and is one of the standard programs provided by the computer system manufacturer. In small systems, or when a cross assembler is used, the assembly and loading are done at different times. They are completely separate procedures as illustrated in Figure 1.13. In stage 1 the assembler produces the object program on some intermediate medium such as cassette tape. In stage 2 the loader

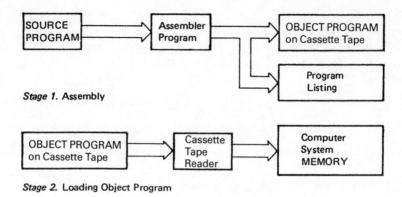

Figure 1.13 *Program assembly and loading*

reads the information on that medium into the computer's memory with the help of the appropriate peripheral, which is connected into the system as described in other chapters.

1.7.4 The Program Listing

An important function of the assembler is the production of a *program listing* as well as the object program. This listing is a printout of the source program, the machine language translation (usually in octal or hexadecimal notation), the address of the memory locations into which the loader will put the machine instructions and the comments written by the programmer in the source program. Figure 1.14 shows an extract from the listing of an assembly language program. The comments explain to the reader of the program listing the action which the instructions cause within the computer system for which the program is written. They do not provide an English language translation of the machine instructions.

The program listing is a most important document. It provides the person developing a program, or the engineer fault finding in the system, with the only means available of knowing what instructions are in the memory and what those instructions should cause the computer system to do.

1.7.5 Debugging the Program

When a program is first written it usually contains errors. These errors, or *bugs*, must be located and corrected, a process known as *debugging* the program. There are a large number of proprietary hardware and software aids for program debugging and only a few will be very superficially described here.

The suite of programs which is resident in the computer system includes the loader and a *debug* package. This is provided as a ROM in micro-

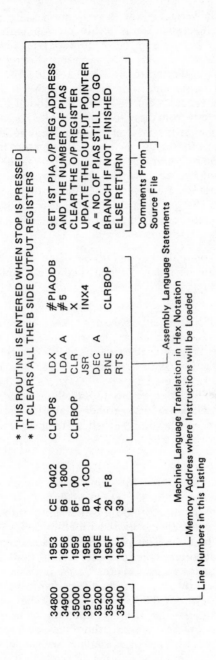

```
                                                 * THIS ROUTINE IS ENTERED WHEN STOP IS PRESSED
                                                 * IT CLEARS ALL THE B SIDE OUTPUT REGISTERS

34800   1953   CE 0402        CLROPS   LDX     #PIAODB     GET 1ST PIA O/P REG ADDRESS
34900   1956   B6 1800                 LDA   A #5          AND THE NUMBER OF PIAS
35000   1959   6F 00          CLRBOP   CLR     X           CLEAR THE O/P REGISTER
35100   195B   BD 1COD                 JSR     INX4        UPDATE THE OUTPUT POINTER
35200   195E   4A                      DEC   A             A = NO. OF PIAS STILL TO GO
35300   195F   26 F8                   BNE     CLRBOP      BRANCH IF NOT FINISHED
35400   1961   39                      RTS                 ELSE RETURN
```

Line Numbers in this Listing

Memory Address where Instructions will be Loaded

Machine Language Translation in Hex Notation

Assembly Language Statements

Comments From Source File

Figure 1.14 *Extract from a program listing*

processor systems and on paper tape, floppy disk or a similar medium for minicomputer systems. Communication between the programmer and the debug program is usually via a typewriter or visual display unit. The debug package provides facilities such as the ability to examine the content of the memory locations and registers in the computer system and the ability to change those contents. *Breakpoints* may be inserted into programs so that the program executes to that point and stops to allow the programmer to examine the state of the system, to determine whether if it is as expected. Suppose the program executes correctly to a breakpoint at location N but does not execute correctly from there to a breakpoint at location M. It can be deduced that a program error exists between the breakpoints. These can be made to approach one another and the error can therefore be pinpointed. If only a simple alteration is required to a single instruction, the debug program would allow the change to be made by the appropriate changing of the memory location contents. However, if a number of instructions require insertion this is difficult because all the following instructions in the program must be moved up to make room. This is where the assembler is appreciated, because the necessary insertion may be made in the source program and the new source program can be assembled to produce a corrected version of the object program for loading.

1.7.6 Simulators

It is sometimes possible to obtain access to a simulator program. This is a program which uses the object program as its data and can simulate the actions that the object program will cause in the real system. It does this by allocating memory locations in its computer to represent the registers and memory locations of the simulated system and performs the data transfers specified by the object program. It provides facilities such as the setting of breakpoints in the simulation. It also provides statistics on the performance of the simulated system which would be difficult to obtain in the real system.

1.7.7 Editors

The source program is generated by typing it into a computer system, in which it is stored. When an alteration is to be made to this program, either to correct a typing error when the program is first input or to effect a change because of an error detected during the program debugging, a program called an editor may be used. This program is a standard system program supplied by the manufacturer of the computer system on which the assembly is to be carried out. It allows a user to create a *file* in the computer memory which is data for the editor program. The file contents may be changed by typing commands to the editor. This data file may also be used as data by the assembler program and can be printed either on a line printer or on a typewriter by the programs which control those devices. The editor program therefore is a general purpose program used to generate and alter data files in the computer memory, but it has nothing directly to do with running or assembling a program. It has no comprehension of the meaning of the data which it is manipulating.

CHAPTER 2

The Instruction Set of the Central Processor

2.1 INTRODUCTION

Two conventions will be used throughout the rest of this book. They are:

1. The words "the content of" or "the word in" or "the number in" will be replaced by the square brackets [ ]. Hence [L] means the word in the memory location whose address is L.
2. It will be assumed that computer words are 16-bits long unless otherwise stated. Where there are significant differences in machines with a different word length these will be indicated.

So far in this text only a few obvious instructions have been mentioned in passing, namely add, subtract, load CPU register from memory and store the content of CPU register in memory. It is because there are so many other possibilities for instructions, depending on the architecture of the CPU and the rest of the system, that there are so many different commercially available computer systems. Each of them has a different instruction set and all of them are useful, viable systems. It is fortunately true that there are certain types of instruction common to most computer systems. This chapter introduces the types of instruction which will be found in most CPU instruction sets.

It is important to consider the effect of the architecture of the CPU on both the instructions which are possible and on the power of those instructions in a programming situation. Suppose the simple processor of Figure 1.10 is being used to perform some arithmetic calculations. Suppose further that it is necessary to add the number in the register whose address is X to the number in the memory location whose address is N, leaving the result in the memory at location N. This can be restated in a much shorter form, using the convention above, as:

[N] ← [N] + [X]
where ← is read as "becomes".
and X refers to a CPU register.

To execute this instruction the CPU must perform a number of data transfers which can be represented by the following set of statements:

[Y] ← [N]	/copy [N] into register Y
[Y] ← [Y] + [X]	/add [X] to [Y] and put the
	/result in register Y
[N] ← [Y]	/copy the result to memory location N

This, of course, assumes that register Y is free to take part in the calculation. If however all the registers contain words that are required later in the data processing, then it is necessary first to store the word in register Y in some spare location in the memory and to reinstate the word back in register Y after the calculation. This requires that the following data transfers take place:

[T] ← [Y]	/save the word in Y in location T
[Y] ← [N]	/
[Y] ← [Y] + [X]	/same steps as before
[N] ← [Y]	/
[Y] ← [T]	/reinstate the word in Y

Hence five data transfers, each requiring a CPU instruction, may be necessary to add a number in a register to a number in memory.

If the architecture of the CPU of Figure 1.11 is now modified to that of Figure 2.1 by the addition of two data paths (data highways) then it becomes possible to introduce into the instruction set of the CPU an instruction which causes the addition of a number in a CPU register to a number in memory and is equivalent to the five instructions above. This, then, is a powerful

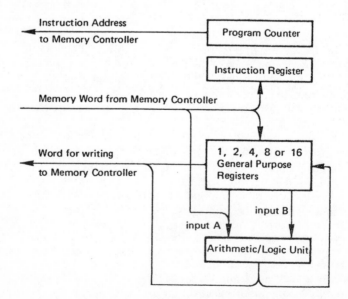

Figure 2.1 *Modified central processor*

instruction because it improves the CPU performance, if not fivefold, then at least by a factor of two or three when performing register-to-memory additions. The execution of such an instruction would involve the CPU in performing automatically the following sequence of data transfers:

1. Fetch the instruction into the instruction register and increment the program counter content;
2. Read the memory location whose address is N and route [N] to the arithmetic unit A input;
3. Route [X] to the arithmetic unit B input and instruct the arithmetic unit to ADD the numbers on its inputs;
4. Route the output of the arithmetic unit ([N] + [X]) to the memory and instruct the memory controller to write to location N.

These steps do not represent a sequence of CPU instructions but are a sequence of data transfers required for the execution of a single CPU instruction.

In the example above a fairly small change to the architecture of the CPU has allowed the expansion of its instruction set. Whether that expansion would be incorporated in practice would depend on the power of the extra instructions to improve the work throughput of the CPU weighed against the cost of the extra hardware involved. Instructions of the type used in this example, the addition of the content of a CPU register to the content of a memory location, and also the addition of the content of a memory location to the content of a CPU register, are found in the instruction sets of many minicomputers and microcomputers.

2.2 MEMORY REFERENCE INSTRUCTIONS

In general, memory reference instructions are of the type already discussed, for example, ADD [memory location] to [CPU register]. Such an instruction contains four units of information, one *operation* (add), the addresses of two *operands* (the data to be operated upon), and the address of the location where the result of the operation will be stored. Those addresses may be the addresses of either memory locations or of CPU registers but, by definition, in a memory reference instruction at least one of them must be the address of a memory location. In small computer systems the instruction word in the instruction register is not sufficiently long explicitly to contain the addresses of three memory locations. In practice, therefore, the location for the storage of the result is almost always implied to be the same as the location of one of the operands. Thus memory reference instructions usually contain not more than two addresses. If the two addresses are both the addresses of locations in the memory the instruction is said to be a *two address* instruction. If the addresses are of one memory location and one CPU register the instruction is called a *one and a half address* instruction. If the instruction contains only one memory address and no other it is called a *single address* instruction. In small computers the single and one and a half address instruction formats are the most common and are shown, for a machine with a

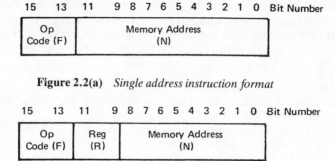

Figure 2.2(a)   *Single address instruction format*

Figure 2.2(b)   *One and a half address instruction format*

16-bit word length, in Figure 2.2. Single address instructions contain two meaningful sets of bits, called *fields*, the operation code field and the address field (N). One and a half address instructions contain three fields, the two in the single address type and a register address field (R). It can be seen from Figure 2.2 that:

1. A single address instruction can address a larger number of memory locations than the one and a half address instruction because there are more bits in the N address field.

2. When an operand is obtained from memory it is the number in the N address field of the instruction register which is sent to the memory controller as the address of the memory location to be accessed. This occurs only during the execution (not the fetching) of a memory reference instruction.

3. The one and a half address instruction may be more powerful than the single address instruction because it allows the possibility of operations between words in memory and those in the CPU registers.

A computer in which there is only one CPU register for general purpose use can use the single address format but still effectively be a one and a half address instruction. The R field in the instruction is unnecessary because the single GP register is implicitly addressed by the type of operation specified by the operation code field. For example, instructions of the type "add the contents of memory location N into the accumulator" do not explicitly state which accumulator because there is only one.

Computer systems with an 8-bit word length, and that includes many of the commonly used microprocessors, use a variable length instruction word. The instruction is then one, two or three words long. Usually an 8-bit word is referred to as a *byte* so these machines use one, two or three byte instructions depending on the requirement. The 24-bit instructions contain a memory address which is 16 bits long. This allows the addressing of a large memory and at the same time allows a large number of different operations to be specified. In practice, most computer systems with a 16-bit word length also use multiple length instructions. Such computer systems contain instructions which are 16 bits, 32 bits or 48 bits long. Modern 16-bit microprocessor-based computer systems require some 24 to 32 bits for the memory addresses, so that a 3-word instruction is necessary to contain the fields required for a one and a half address instruction.

Most CPU instruction sets contain both one and a half and single address memory reference instructions. The problem of allowing access to a large memory whilst simultaneously allowing the use of a large number of different operation codes and using only a 16-bit (or smaller) word is dealt with in Chapter 4.

2.2.1 Logical Operations on Data

So far only the arithmetic functions add and subtract have been mentioned. Manipulation of binary data and the extraction of useful information contained within fields in words requires not only the add and subtract operations but also the logical operations AND, OR, NOT. These operations are defined by the tables of Figure 2.3. Such tables are called *truth tables*. In general, they show every possible combination of the values of a number of binary variables and the corresponding value of the appropriate logical operation using those combinations.

2.2.1.1 The Logical AND Operation

For two variables A & B, the logical AND operation is defined by the table of Figure 2.3(a). From this table it can be observed that whenever a binary variable is *ANDed* with a one the result is the same as the variable being ANDed, and whenever a binary variable is ANDed with a zero the result is zero irrespective of the value of the variable being ANDed.

2.2.1.2 The Logical OR Operation

For two binary variables A & B, the logical OR operation, also called the *inclusive* OR operation, is defined by the table of Figure 2.3(b). From this table it can be observed that whenever a binary variable is ORed with a one the result is a one irrespective of the value of the variable, and that when a binary variable is ORed with a zero the result is the same as the value of the variable.

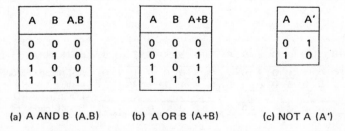

A	B	A.B
0	0	0
0	1	0
1	0	0
1	1	1

A	B	A+B
0	0	0
0	1	1
1	0	1
1	1	1

A	A'
0	1
1	0

(a) A AND B (A.B)   (b) A OR B (A+B)   (c) NOT A (A')

Figure 2.3   *Logical functions of two binary variables*

2.2.1.3 *The Logical NOT*

This is defined by the table of Figure 2.3(c). It is an inversion of the value of a variable.

2.2.2 Uses of the Logical Operations

Suppose the 16-bit word of a computer contains two 8-bit ASCII coded characters, and it is required to extract one of these into a GP register for transmission to a printer. Suppose the characters are assembled into the computer words by a program which reads characters typed in on a keyboard. Neither the programmer who wrote the program to assemble the characters nor the writer of the program to prepare the characters for printing will know in advance what the characters will be. So the programs must be written in such a way that, irrespective of what the characters are, they can be retrieved from the memory locations and put into the registers for printing. This operation can be achieved by using the logical AND function. The problem in general is to extract a field from a computer word even when the pattern in the word is not known. The property of the logical AND that is useful is that by ANDing the 8-bit ASCII code required with an 8-bit field of ones, the resulting 8 bits will be the same as the bits of the ASCII coded character. By simultaneously ANDing the other 8 bits of the 16-bit word with zeros the resulting bits in that field will all be zero. This operation is shown in Figure 2.4.

A different problem may arise when the characters are being assembled from the keyboard input. Suppose the typist makes a mistake which is not seen at once. Later the erroneous character must be changed. This involves removing from memory the word containing both the erroneous character and another correct character, deleting the incorrect character from the word and inserting the correction. One method by which this can be done is to remove the incorrect character from the word without destroying the half of the word containing a correct character, by ANDing the word with a mask, as explained in the previous paragraph and illustrated in Figure 2.4. The correct character code is then logically ORed into the vacant part of the word. Figure 2.5 illustrates the process. The first line in this figure is the last of Figure 2.4, the second is the ASCII code for the letter E correctly positioned in the space made by the mask. The third line shows the result of the logical OR operation.

The logical inversion is required in addition to the AND operation and the OR operation to allow more complex logical operations to be carried out by

15		13		11		9	8	7	6	5	4	3	2	1	0	Bit Number
0	0	1	1	0	1	0	1	1	1	0	0	0	1	1	0	ASCII coded 5 & F
0	0	0	0	0	0	0	0	1	1	1	1	1	1	1	1	Mask
																LOGICAL AND
0	0	0	0	0	0	0	0	1	1	0	0	0	1	1	0	Result (coded F)

Figure 2.4 *Use of the logical AND operation*

15	13	11	9	8	7	6	5	4	3	2	1	0	Bit Number
0 0	0 0	0 0	0	0	1	1	0	0	0	1	1	0	Result as Fig. 2.4
1 1	0 0	0 1	0	1	0	0	0	0	0	0	0	0	Correctly coded E
													LOGICAL OR
1 1	0 0	0 1	0	1	1	1	0	0	0	1	1	0	E ORed into word

Figure 2.5 *Use of the logical OR following logical AND*

programs in the computer system. Any logical function (Boolean function) can be evaluated by a machine with these three basic logical operations. In fact, only the inversion and one other operation are theoretically required to allow the realization of all logical functions.

2.2.3 Other Logical Operations

Although all other logical operations can be programmed using the basic logical operations, many machines provide some other operations as standard. For its internal functioning the ALU uses such logical functions as:

NAND	/AND–NOT
NOR	/OR–NOT
EXCLUSIVE OR	/(A AND (NOT B)) OR ((NOT A) AND B)

These operations are sometimes made available to the programmer. The *Exclusive–OR*, or XOR, is particularly useful at times. It is defined by the truth table in Figure 2.6, from which it can be seen that its other name, the *non-equivalence* function, is very appropriate. If two binary variables are XORed the result is a one if the variables are different and a zero if they are the same. A property of the XOR which is also sometimes useful, particularly in engineering applications, is that if a variable is XORed with a zero the result is the same as the variable but if it is XORed with a one the result is the inverse of the variable. It is also apparent, from Figure 2.6, that if the XOR function is performed between the variables in any two columns of the table the result is in the remaining column. Hence if:

	A XOR B = C
then	C XOR B = A
and	A XOR C = B

The above result has many applications. One of them is in checking the correctness of transmitted codes, see Chapter 3 section 3.4. Although it is

A	B	A XOR B	
0	0	0	A = B
0	1	1	
1	0	1	
1	1	0	A = B

Figure 2.6 *EXCLUSIVE-OR function table*

outside the scope of this book, it is interesting that the modern method of recording on magnetic surfaces (called *phase encoding*) uses this property of the XOR function.

2.2.4 Jump Instructions

Suppose a search is being made through a list of numbers, say account reference numbers, to find a particular number so that some action, such as updating the account, can be taken. Figure 2.7(a) shows what could be an extract from a program to carry out such a search. An account number A is brought into one of the CPU registers, say register R, tested to see if it is the number required and if not then a *jump*, or *branch*, occurs back to the point in the program where the next account number is brought into register R. Figure 2.7(b) illustrates the location of the instructions in the store. It is apparent from Figure 2.7(b) together with the fact that the CPU fetches its next instruction from the memory location whose address is in the program counter, that to perform a jump the CPU must change the number in the program counter. In the example given, when the instruction in location Q has been fetched the [PC] will be incremented to Q + 1 and the instruction will then be obeyed. If [R] is not the required number then [PC] must be changed to the number P else [PC] must remain unchanged at Q + 1. An instruction which performs a test on data and changes [PC] or not, depending on the result of the test, is called a *conditional jump* instruction or *conditional branch* instruction. The conditions tested vary considerably from one computer to another but usually include:

[GP register] = zero
[GP register] = non-zero
[GP register] = negative number
[GP register] = positive number

An explanation of how these and other conditions may be detected is given in Chapters 3 and 7.

The format of these instructions is usually that of a single address memory reference instruction as shown in Figure 2.2(a), in which the address field contains the address to which the jump must be made. In executing this type of instruction the CPU tests the condition and if it is true then a data transfer occurs from the address field of the instruction register to the corresponding field of the program counter. If it is not true, then the program counter content remains unchanged. This is an instance in which the data transfer in the computer system is not necessarily that of a complete computer word.

A common variation of this type of instruction is the *skip* instruction, the usual form of which is "skip (ignore) the next instruction in the program if the condition C is true". In this case, if the condition is true, the CPU increments the number in the program counter. Since [PC] was incremented immediately after the instruction fetch it will have received a double increment during the current instruction timing cycle so the next instruction is fetched from the memory location next but one from the location of the skip instruction. Notice that compared with a conditional jump instruction a test for a condition has to be performed the opposite way round if a skip

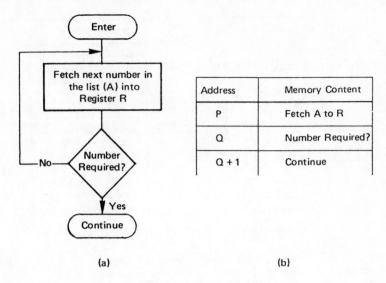

Address	Memory Content
P	Fetch A to R
Q	Number Required?
Q + 1	Continue

(a)   (b)

Figure 2.7   *Program jump*

instruction is used to obtain the same effect. This can be understood if the example of the search for a particular account number is considered again. The flowchart of Figure 2.7 contains a test for the required account number. This test can be carried out by subtracting the required account number from the number in register R and testing the result, which will be zero when the correct account is found. Using a conditional jump instruction a jump is required if [R] = NON ZERO. If a skip instruction is used a skip is required if [R] = ZERO. This is illustrated in Figure 2.8 which shows the program needed to perform the test and jump. Figure 2.8 also shows that, in the example chosen, the conditional jump is a better way of achieving the result because there is one less instruction in the program loop. The machine will, therefore, execute the program more quickly. If the instructions in the loop are executed often the time saved may be appreciable.

Using SKIP Instruction	Using JUMP Instruction
(1) Subtract Number of Required Account from [Reg R]	(1) Subtract Number of Required Account from [Reg R]
(2) SKIP next line if Result = ZERO	(2) Jump to (1) if Result = NON-ZERO
(3) Jump to (1)	
(4) Continue	(3) Continue

Figure 2.8   *Comparison of SKIP and JUMP instructions*

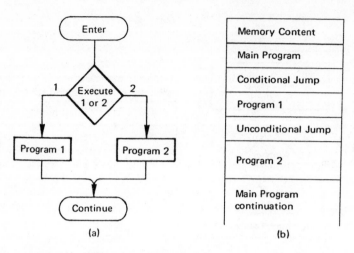

Figure 2.9   *Use of conditional jump*

It will be noticed that the instruction skipped in the example in Figure 2.8 is an *unconditional jump* instruction. This instruction is found in all CPU instruction sets, not just those which contain skip instructions. Another example of the use of an unconditional jump is illustrated in Figure 2.9. Suppose a program performs a test to decide which of two courses of action to take, each of which consists of a number of instructions and is therefore a program in its own right. Suppose also that the programs are arranged in the memory as shown in Figure 2.9(b). The test and jump to program 2 is carried out with a conditional jump or skip as explained above. If the test indicates that program 1 is to be executed, then when the end of program 1 is reached an unconditional jump is required to the rest of the program. Otherwise both programs 1 and 2 will be executed.

2.2.5 Subroutine Entry and Exit Instructions

A subroutine is usually a program which performs one small well defined task. In a small computer system it is not normal to find a multiply instruction in the instruction set, but multiplication of two numbers is a common requirement in small-computer applications. Suppose a program is written which performs multiplication. This small special program would probably be called a *routine* rather than a program because it would most often be embedded within a program to perform some much larger task. If the multiplication is required at a number of points in the larger program, it is possible to repeat the set of instructions forming the multiply routine each time it is required. In this case the arrangement of the program in the memory may be as shown in Figure 2.10(a). A better system is to write the multiply routine once only and to execute it whenever necessary. This saves memory space and makes the job of writing the program less tedious. A possible arrangement of this program in memory is shown in Figure 2.10(b) in which the multiply routine is called a subroutine of the main program.

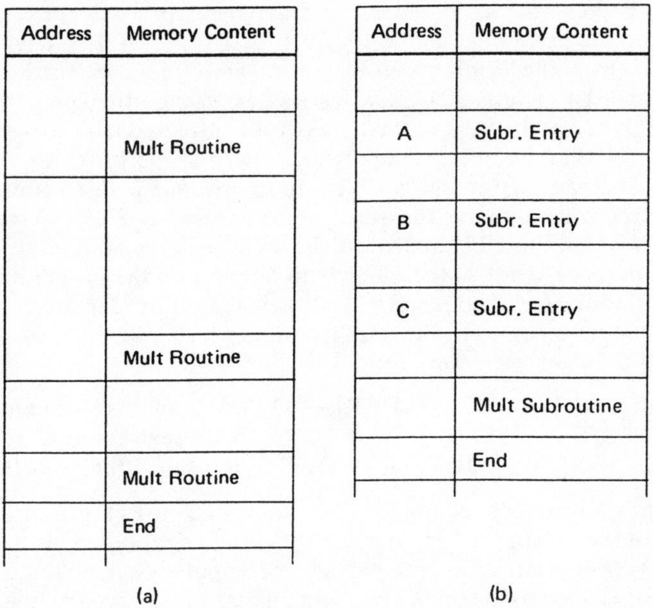

Address	Memory Content
	Mult Routine
	Mult Routine
	Mult Routine
	End

(a)

Address	Memory Content
A	Subr. Entry
B	Subr. Entry
C	Subr. Entry
	Mult Subroutine
	End

(b)

Figure 2.10   *Use of subroutines*

Entering the subroutine does not present a problem, an unconditional jump would do that. Returning from the subroutine to the main program at the correct address does present a problem. The programmer cannot know in advance what will be the return address at any particular pass through the subroutine, because, for example, the main program may branch and both branches may need to use the subroutine.

It is necessary, therefore, to include instructions in the CPU instruction set which enable a program to cause a jump to a subroutine and to return from that subroutine to the main program at the address next after the address of the instruction which caused the jump. There are a number of ways in which this may be achieved. Suppose the program has progressed to the jump to subroutine instruction in location A (see Figure 2.10(b)). During the execution of this instruction the program counter contains the number $A + 1$ which is the address to which a jump must be made at the end of the subroutine to cause a successful return to the main program. The number $A + 1$, is called the *return address* or the *link address* because it is the link between the subroutine and the main program. If a method can be devised for storing the return address in the memory at a location where it can be picked up by the subroutine and used for a jump, then return to the correct point in the main program is assured. This is what happens in all the methods used for subroutine entry and exit. The subroutine entry instruction, then, causes the following data transfers to occur within the computer system:

1. $[Q] \leftarrow [PC]$ /return address in location Q
2. $[PC] \leftarrow [N]$ /put start-of-subroutine address in PC

Step (2) is the same as for an unconditional jump. The return from the subroutine requires some method for instructing the CPU to fetch its next instruction from the location whose address can be found in location Q. This can be done by including such an instruction in the instruction set of the machine. When addressing of the memory is considered in Chapter 4, it will be apparent that an instruction of this type may be provided for other reasons. Such an instruction is called an *indirect jump* instruction and its format is the same as that of the other jump instructions. The difference in its execution is that the CPU interprets the address in the address field of the instruction register not as the number to be put into the program counter, but as the address of the memory location containing the number to be put into the program counter. The data transfers which take place to allow the return to the main program are:

1. [MEMORY CONTROLLER] ← Q   /send address to memory
                                        /with read request
2. [PC] ← STORE OUTPUT WORD   /put link address in PC

No mention has so far been made of how the CPU knows the number Q, the address of the location where the return address is stored. This is in fact a matter of convention within the particular computer system. Some systems store the link address in the location immediately preceding the first instruction of the subroutine. This is very convenient because then the subroutine entry instruction is of the form shown in Figure 2.11. The memory address (N) in this instruction is the address of the location where the link address is stored. It is assumed that the first instruction of the subroutine is in location N + 1. The data transfers which are required for the execution of this instruction are:

1. [N] ← [PC]   /store link in location N
2. [PC] ← N   /put the number N in the PC
3. [PC] ← [PC] + 1   /increment the [PC] (= N + 1)

The most widely used convention, especially in the modern computers which are all provided with a stack, is to store the content of the program counter on the stack when entering a subroutine. To effect a return to the main program the return instruction then has to pop the top number off the stack and put it in the program counter. The data transfers for a subroutine entry in this type of system are as shown below, where [[SP]] means the contents of the memory location whose address is in the Stack Pointer register. [[SP]] represents the contents of the contents of the Stack Pointer register.

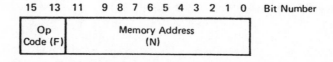

Figure 2.11   *One form of subroutine entry instruction*

1. [[SP]] ← [PC]   /store [PC] on the stack
2. [SP] ← [SP] − 1   /decrement [SP] because
                          /the stack grows downwards

When a return occurs the data transfers are:

1. [SP] ← [SP] + 1   /increment the stack pointer
2. [PC] ← [[SP]]   /load PC from top of stack

2.3 NON MEMORY REFERENCE INSTRUCTIONS

Instructions under this heading are those which cause data transfers within the CPU between the registers of the CPU.

2.3.1 Register–Register Instructions

Some of these are similar to some of the memory reference instructions. In particular, those instructions which perform arithmetic and logical functions between the words in registers with the result being deposited in a register are usually much the same in format as a two address memory reference instruction. The main difference is that the two addresses are the addresses of registers in the CPU and therefore the address fields in the instruction are smaller than in a memory reference instruction. A typical register–register instruction format is shown in Figure 2.12. Notice that in this Figure the operation code has been allocated more bits than was the case for the memory reference instructions. This is because the address fields do not need as much room in the instruction word. The instruction shown in Figure 2.12 would perform the operation specified by the data transfer:

[Y] ← [Y] (F) [R]

where (F) represents the ALU function specified in the F field of the instruction

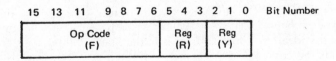

Figure 2.12 *Register–register instruction*

In computer systems using an 8-bit word it is usually found that the register–register instructions are one or two bytes long. The first byte is used for the operation code and the second byte for the two register addresses so the format is almost identical to that of Figure 2.12. If the CPU contains only a small number of registers, say one or two, then the instruction may be only one byte long, because the register addresses will be 0 and 1, which take up only one bit each. The remaining 6 bits are usually sufficient for the operation code.

2.3.2 Shift Instructions

There are many uses for shift instructions and they are provided in all CPU instruction sets. Usually shifts are carried out on the content of one register and the shifted word is left in the register. However, sometimes a shift instruction is used which causes the word in one register to be shifted and the result to be put in another register. This type of instruction is more commonly found in the instruction sets of the large machines than in the instruction sets of machines with a word length of 16-bits or less.

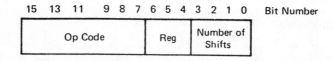

Figure 2.13   *Shift instruction format*

If the pattern of bits in a register represents a number, shifting that pattern one place to the left doubles the number, just as shifting a decimal number one place to the left multiplies the number by ten. Shifting a number right one place in a CPU register halves the number. These manipulations are useful in multiply and divide routines and for other arithmetic calculations. The shifts can also be used for pattern manipulation. For example, earlier in this chapter the logical functions were used to place two characters coded in ASCII 8-bit code into one 16-bit word (see Figure 2.5). It is usual for an 8-bit character to be placed in the right hand (least significant) end of an accumulator when it is obtained from the originating device. If the character is to be ORed into another word as in the example it must first be shifted to the left hand side of the word. A "shift left 8 places" instruction achieves this. The effect of a shift depends on the context in which it takes place. It is either an arithmetic operation or a logical operation depending on the significance of the bit pattern being shifted.

The format of the shift instructions is often that of Figure 2.13. Three fields in the instruction specify the type of shift, the register whose content is to be shifted, and the magnitude of the shift. In 8-bit machines the shift instruction is often only one byte long which does not provide room in the instruction for the "number of shifts" field. Consequently only one shift is implied and if more than one shift is required then the instruction must be repeated in the program. Single-shift-only instructions are also found in the instruction set of some 16-bit machines.

2.3.2.1 Logical Shifts

Logical shifts are defined as those shifts in which the end of the register being vacated is filled with zeros and the bits moving out of the register are lost.

7	6	5	4	3	2	1	0	Bit Number
1	1	1	1	0	0	1	1	Original state of register
0	0	0	1	1	1	1	0	Final state after right shift 3 places. Bits 2, 1, 0 (011) have been lost. 000 shifted into top end.
1	0	0	1	1	0	0	0	Final state after left shift 3 places. Bits 7, 6, 5 (111) have been lost. 000 shifted into bottom end.

Figure 2.14 *Right and left logical shifts of 3 places*

These shifts can be either right or left shifts and are illustrated in Figure 2.14 for an 8-bit word.

2.3.2.2 Arithmetic Shifts
Arithmetic shifts are normally right shifts. If the pattern in a register represents a number then that number may be either positive or negative. If the number is right shifted, the most significant bit of the number must not change. An arithmetic right shift shifts the most significant bit right into the next least significant position and at the same time leaves the most significant bit unchanged. Such shifts are illustrated in Figure 2.15 and are used normally only for shifting numbers, not for shifting patterns.

2.3.2.3 Circular Shifts
A circular shift, or a *rotation* as it is sometimes called, is one in which the register whose content is being shifted can be considered to be arranged in a

7	6	5	4	3	2	1	0	Bit Number
1	0	0	1	1	0	1	0	Number originally in register R
1	1	1	1	0	0	1	1	Number shifted right 3 places (divided by 8). Bits 0, 1 and 2 lost. Sign bit (1) propagated.

Figure 2.15(a) *Arithmetic shift on negative number*

7	6	5	4	3	2	1	0	Bit Number
0	1	1	0	0	1	0	1	Number originally in register.
0	0	0	0	1	1	0	0	Number shifted right 3 places. Bits 0, 1 and 2 lost. Sign bit (0) propagated

Figure 2.15(b) *Arithmetic shift on positive number*

15	13	11	9	8	7	6	5	4	3	2	1	0	Bit Number
1	1	1	1	0	0	1	1	0	0	0	0	1 1 0 1	Start
0 0 0 0	1	1	0	1	1	1	1	1	0	0	1	1	Finish, Bytes Exchanged

Figure 2.16   *Circular shift 8 places on 16-bit word*

circle so that its most significant bit is next to its least significant bit. A right circular shift causes the digit in the bit 0 position to shift into the bit 15 position (or the bit 7 position in an 8-bit machine). A left circular shift causes the digit in the bit 15 (or 7) position to shift into the bit 0 position. A circular shift of N places right has the same effect as a circular shift of L–N places left, where L is the register length. For this reason some small computer systems have a circular shift instruction for one direction only.

It is sometimes desired to shift a field in a word into a particular position in a register without losing the information in other parts of the register. For example, if characters for printing are stored in a 16-bit machine, with two characters in each memory location (assuming 8-bit ASCII characters), then it is normal to find that incoming characters are put in the least significant 8 bits of a register. One method of assembling such two-character 16-bit words is to use the logical left shift and OR in the second character as described in section 2.2.1.5. However this leaves each word with the first character that was input in the most significant half of the word and the second character input in the least significant half of the word. Since it is not normal to input messages with the character pairs reversed, the two halves of the 16-bit word must be interchanged before output, assuming that the characters are output from the least significant end of the word. This can be achieved by a circular shift of 8 places as shown in Figure 2.16.

2.3.2.4 Other Shift Instructions
The most common variation on the shifts already described are shifts involving a register extended by the carry bit. The latter is a single-bit memory. In the context of the present discussion it in effect forms an extra bit on the register whose contents are being shifted. Thus in a 16-bit machine a left shift apparently takes place in a 17-bit register. The carry bit is concatenated with the register to form bit 16 (8) for a left shift, and to form a less significant bit than bit 0 for a right shift. It is also sometimes interposed between bits 15 (7) and 0 in the circular shifts. This is useful in certain circumstances because the carry bit is a bit that can be tested and can cause a program branch in one of two directions according to whether it is set or not. It is also useful when double length shifts (see next paragraph) must be programmed in a machine in which the instruction set does not contain such instructions. The use of the carry bit in these circumstances is described in Chapter 7.

2.3.2.5 Double Length Shifts
A double length shift is one carried out on the content of two registers concatenated to behave as if they formed a single register with a length twice that of the machine word.

If the word length of the computer system is too short to hold a number which is required for a calculation, two (or more) words can be used to hold that number. Then all manipulations and calculations must be on the double length word. Multiplication routines, for example, are easier to program if a double length shift is available as a standard instruction.

2.3.3 Flag Instructions

Most CPUS contain a number of single-bit memories, called *bistables* (or *flip-flops*) by electronics engineers and *flags* by programmers. These single-bit memories contain a bit which is a one or a zero according to certain conditions in the machine. Most of these bits change from one to zero and vice-versa automatically as the hardware detects the conditions in the machine. The most commonly encountered flags are listed below and their uses are explained more fully in Chapter 7:

1. The Zero Flag
2. The Negative Flag
3. The Carry Flag
4. The Overflow Flag

Each of these monitors the condition of the output word from the ALU at the end of the execution of an instruction. If the ALU output is zero, the zero flag sets to one otherwise it unsets to zero. If the output is negative the negative flag sets to one otherwise it unsets to zero, and so on.

These flags are often considered to form a register, called the *condition codes register*, whose length may be less than the length of a machine word. Instructions are provided for the manipulation of the contents of the condition codes register. In addition to the conditional jump instructions which cause a jump if the flags in the condition codes register indicate the tested condition to be true, there are instructions for setting or unsetting the individual flags. In some computer systems the condition codes are treated as a register whose content can be manipulated in the ALU together with the content of another register. The contents of the condition codes register together with the contents of the program counter are sometimes considered to form a single word (longer than the standard machine word length) which is called the *program status word*.

2.3.4 Miscellaneous Instructions

Other miscellaneous instructions are to be found in the instruction repertory of most computer systems. One such instruction is "Do Nothing". This is useful for leaving spaces in a program during development and sometimes, particularly in small special purpose microprocessor applications, for introducing time delays before the CPU initiates some action in the Input/Output system.

2.3.4.1 Halt Instruction
This is found in some instruction sets but is often a privileged instruction. That is to say there is a flag in the CPU to indicate if the machine is in

privileged mode. If the flag is set the halt instruction halts the machine, otherwise it does nothing (or raises an interrupt – see Chapter 6).

2.3.4.2 Wait Instruction
This instruction is very useful if the CPU is used to drive a number of external devices which do not operate quickly enough to keep the CPU continually busy. This is often the case in control applications. The wait instruction causes the CPU to suspend activity until one of the peripherals signals that it requires some attention. Confusingly, in some computer systems the instruction which is called halt is the wait instruction described here.

2.3.4.3 Clear Register
It is sometimes useful to be able to set all the bits of a register to zero, and most machines include a clear instruction for that purpose. Some instruction sets also include a clear instruction in the memory reference instructions to allow clearing of memory locations.

2.3.4.4 Twos Complement
If a number is stored in the machine and for some reason it is required in its negative form, this instruction saves the effort of programming the negation using the other instructions. Most machines provide such an instruction. Twos complements are explained in Chapter 3, section 3.5.

2.3.4.5 Other Instructions
There are other instructions in the instruction sets of most machines but by the time the reader arrives at the point of using them reference to this document will probably not be a concurrent task. No more instructions will therefore be considered, but the reader is referred to the Appendix where some subsets of the instruction sets of some small computer systems are given.

CHAPTER 3

The Coding of Information in Computer Systems

3.1 INTRODUCTION

Information exists only in coded form. The code may be that of a language, or of a set of binary bits. The meaning of the code may depend on its position in a stream of information or its position within a system, i.e. on its context. It is often convenient to change the information coding from one code to another to make its manipulation easier, a process called either *encoding* or *decoding* but better called *code conversion*. This chapter considers the structure of some of the coding systems met in computers. These coding systems are often treated as separate topics, but they are treated here in the same chapter to emphasize that they are really different facets of information coding.

3.2 THE CODED REPRESENTATION OF BINARY PATTERNS

All computer words, such as the contents of the store locations and registers in the computer system, can be represented by a pattern of binary digits written as ones and zeros. For example:

0110010111101100

is a 16-bit computer word. This is a very clumsy representation because it is difficult to read or reproduce accurately. It is more usual, therefore, to break down the word into smaller groups of bits such as:

0 110 010 111 101 100

or 0110 0101 1110 1100

These are much easier to read and to reproduce accurately than the identical 16-bit word above.

The writing of computer words in binary form, even in small groups of bits, soon becomes tedious. It is much more convenient to allocate codes to the possible groups of bits. The two most common systems are to use groups of three bits and allocate codes in *octal* notation, or to use groups of four bits and allocate codes in *hexadecimal* notation.

3.2.1 The Octal Coding System

A group of three binary digits has eight possible arrangements as shown in Figure 3.1. If these groups are considered to be 3-digit binary numbers then the eight groups represent the numbers 0 through 7. These numbers are the digits of the octal numbering system. The 16-bit word

   0 110 010 111 101 100

can therefore be represented by the octal number

   0   6   2   7   5   4

the most significant digit of which can have only the values 0 or 1. It is conventional in the world of minicomputers and many mainframe computers to use the octal representation for the computer words. All the documentation for these machines is written with this notation to represent words.

000	0	001	1
010	2	011	3
100	4	101	5
110	6	111	7

Figure 3.1   *Octal numbers*

3.2.2 The Hexadecimal Coding System

Most microprocessor literature, the literature of 8-bit minicomputers and of IBM and IBM-like computers (which take an 8-bit byte as the unit for coding) use the hexadecimal system of coding shown in Figure 3.2. This system takes the binary digits in groups of four, rather than groups of three. As there are sixteen possible combinations of four binary digits these can be represented by the two-digit octal numbers 00 through 17, the decimal numbers 0 through 15 or the hexadecimal numbers 0 through F. The octal numbering system uses a subset of the ten decimal digits with which most people are familiar and the hexadecimal numbering system uses a superset of these digits. Instead of inventing a new set of symbols to represent the numbers above 9, the symbols A through F are used. These are not letters in this context, they are numbers and can be subjected to arithmetic processes such as addition, subtraction and so on which are not possible with letters.

   The hexadecimal representation of the 16-bit word which has been used as an example in this chapter:

   0110 0101 1110 1101

can therefore be written as:

   6   5   E   D

Binary	Hex	Octal	Decimal
0000	0	0	0
0001	1	1	1
0010	2	2	2
0011	3	3	3
0100	4	4	4
0101	5	5	5
0110	6	6	6
0111	7	7	7
1000	8	10	8
1001	9	11	9
1010	A	12	10
1011	B	13	11
1100	C	14	12
1101	D	15	13
1110	E	16	14
1111	F	17	15

Figure 3.2   *Coding of four bits*

The conversion between octal and hexadecimal notations is not easy to perform without writing the binary equivalent as an intermediate stage and therefore one tends to adhere to one system or the other when dealing with any particular computer system.

1	3	3	3	3	3	Octal 16-bit boundaries
8 Bits			8 Bits			
2	3	3	2	3	3	Octal 8-bit boundaries
4		4		4	4	Hex 8 or 16-bit boundaries

Figure 3.3   *Bit boundaries using Hex or Octal*

Computer systems using an 8-bit word require, of course, only two hexadecimal or three octal digits to represent one word. The hexadecimal system is favored in 8-bit machines because they often use multiple length words, for example they always use at least 16 bits for addresses. As shown in Figure 3.3, a 16-bit word can be expressed as the concatenation of the hex (adecimal) digits for its constituent 8-bit words, but if the octal system is used, then the bit boundaries are different in the 8-bit and 16-bit cases.

3.2.3 Arithmetic Using Octal or Hexadecimal Codes

To check the results of an arithmetic operation, as is often required during the development stage of a program, there is no need to convert from octal or hexadecimal to the binary equivalent. Arithmetic may be checked by direct manipulation of the octal or hex digits, because a carry occurs between the groups of binary digits at the same time as it occurs between the digits of the octal or hexadecimal systems. However, octal or hex arithmetic does not come easily to those who have not committed the octal or hex addition and multiplication tables to memory. The octal system is rather easier to manipulate in this respect and is favored by some for that reason.

3.3 THE CODED REPRESENTATION OF ALPHANUMERIC CHARACTERS

Many systems have been used to represent alphanumeric characters and many are still in use. The discussion here is mainly of the ASCII (American Standard Code for Information Interchange) coding system, which is one of the most commonly used codes.

The early coding systems used for the coding of alphanumeric characters were for the transmission of messages over telegraph networks, and the national and international teleprinter networks still use codes which were introduced some decades ago. These codes were used essentially for the transmission of the characters found on the standard typewriter keyboard. The earliest system, after the morse-type codes, was a *5-level code*, i.e. a coding system in which each character was represented by five binary digits. A 5-level code has the disadvantage that there are only 32 combinations of 5 bits. Around 64 combinations are required to represent the 26 letters of the alphabet plus the 10 decimal digits plus special characters for punctuation and message control. Hence in the 5-level system two codes are reserved for *shift codes*, i.e. upper case shift and lower case shift as on the typewriter keyboard. Thus there are 62 possible character codes plus the two shift codes. This system has fallen into disuse in computer systems mainly because the receipt of a code is not in itself sufficient to decide what the code represents. The system has also to examine the last shift code, which makes the decoding dependent on the recent history of the system. The falling cost of hardware has meant that the provision of more hardware to decode a code with more bits is no longer sufficiently expensive to offset the inconvenience of a 5-level code.

A 64-character set can be uniquely coded by using a 6-level coding system. The receipt of a code in this system then defines the character unambiguously without reference to the history of the system. The use of 6-level codes was the next logical stage in the historical development of widely accepted alphanumeric codes.

The cost of hardware is still falling and the current demand is for a coding system which allows the unique coding of both upper case and lower case

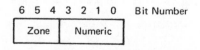

Figure 3.4   *Division of 7-bit code into two fields*

Zone	0	1	2	3	4	5	6	7
Numeric (Hex)								
0	NUL	DLE	SP	0	@	P	`	p
1	SOH	DC1	!	1	A	Q	a	q
2	STX	DC2	"	2	B	R	b	r
3	ETX	DC3	#	3	C	S	c	s
4	EOT	DC4	$	4	D	T	d	t
5	ENQ	NAK	%	5	E	U	e	u
6	ACK	SYN	&	6	F	V	f	v
7	BEL	ETB	'	7	G	W	g	w
8	BS	CAN	(	8	H	X	h	x
9	HT	EM	)	9	I	Y	i	y
A	LF	SUB	*	:	J	Z	j	z
B	VT	ESC	+	;	K	[	k	{
C	FF	FS	,	<	L	\	l		
D	CR	GS	–	=	M	]	m	}
E	SO	RS	.	>	N	↑	n	~
F	SI	US	/	?	O	_	o	DEL

Figure 3.5 *7-level ASCII codes*

characters plus the 10 decimal digits and special characters. The ASCII code is a 7-level code which allows the unique encoding of 128 different characters. The complete 128-character set is shown in Figure 3.5.

It is convenient to divide each 7-bit code into two separate fields and to represent these fields by their octal or hexadecimal equivalents as shown in Figure 3.4. The fields are a three-bit field, the most significant three bits in the code, which form the *zone field*, and the least significant 4-bit field which forms the *numeric field* of the code. All the 128 codes can be displayed in a table with the values of the zone field representing the columns, and the values of the numeric field representing the rows. This is shown in Figure 3.5, from which the following points may be observed:

1. The numbers 0 through 9 are represented by codes with zone bits equal to 3 and numeric bits equal to the number.
2. The codes for the letters of the alphabet exist in zones 4, 5, 6 and 7.
3. All characters in zones 2 through 7 with the single exception of the code 7F produce a printed output.
4. A letter in zone 4 or 5 is the upper case equivalent of the lower case letter in the corresponding position in zones 6 and 7. If the middle bit of the zone field is ignored, provided that the most significant zone bit is a 1, then zones 4 and 6 and zones 5 and 7 become indistinguishable from one another. This feature of the coding system is useful, for example, in printers with only one case. These devices may be sent both case letter codes provided they are designed to ignore the middle zone bit when the most significant zone bit is a one. They will then produce the single case representation of the letter whichever code is sent.

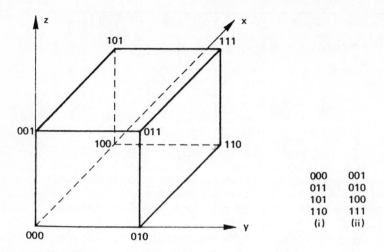

Figure 3.6 *(a) Unit cube code representation (b) Non-adjacent code sets*

5. The codes for the letters of the alphabet may be considered to be binary numbers, in which case it will be observed that these numbers are in ascending order and adjacent to each other. This is often useful in a program because

(Code for B) = (Code for A) + 1
(Code for C) = (Code for B) + 1

and so on. This is helpful, for example, when a program is required to sort a list of names into alphabetical order because the program uses the arithmetic instructions to sort the letter codes into ascending numeric order.

6. The special characters are in zones 0 and 1 and all of these characters are non-printing characters, i.e. a printer receiving ASCII characters in zones 0 or 1 produces no printed character in response to that code. These characters are normally used to control the operation of devices used in the transmission of characters and their effect is dependent on the particular devices in use in the system. The non-printing character codes in zones 0 and 1 can normally be produced on a keyboard either by depressing special keys such as Escape or Tab, or by pressing the Control key simultaneously with one or two other keys. The Control key forces bit 2 of the ASCII character (see Figure 3.4) to a zero. The characters in zones 0 and 1 can be produced by simultaneously pressing the key marked as shown in the corresponding position in zones 4 and 5. For example:

CONTROL + J   produces the line feed code (LF);

CONTROL + Z   produces the SUB code;

CONTROL + G   produces the BEL character which rings the bell in a teletype or bleeps the loudspeaker in a VDU (Visual Display Unit).

Current activity in the computer industry is creating a demand for even larger character sets. These are required so that computers may output and input information in languages which use characters not found in the Roman script. For example there is a large demand for computers with Arabic input and output. Some special applications require large characters sets. For example, in graphics applications there is a demand for symbols from which pictures and diagrams may be built, in addition to the alphanumeric characters required to annotate diagrams and produce text. In mathematical and scientific applications there is the need to represent the ASCII character set, some letters from the Greek alphabet and special symbols such as the integration sign. At present these character sets are encoded using the same codes as those used for the ASCII set. The ASCII code ESC (Escape) may be used to transfer from one interpretation of the codes to another. This is very much the same method as was used historically with small character sets, when the shift key fulfilled a similar function to that of ESC. With semiconductor memory prices still falling rapidly, a trend which is likely to continue for some considerable time yet, it would be surprising not to see new standard codes emerging over the next few years probably based on a 16-bit code.

3.4 CODED ERROR CHECKING

The subject of error checking in general is a very important and interesting one and the reader is referred to the bibliography for further reading. The discussion here is restricted to parity checking.

The 7-level ASCII code is transmitted and received as an 8-bit code, the eighth bit (bit 7) being a *parity check bit*. Parity checking is commonly used in computer systems when data is transmitted between units in the system. In the ASCII code *even parity* is used, in which bit 7 is a one or a zero to make the number of ones in the 8-bit code an even number. *Odd parity*, in which the parity bit is adjusted to make the number of ones in the code equal to an odd number, is used in many parity checking schemes. The parity bit is inserted by the transmitter and checked by the receiver. In the case of computer systems the insertion and checking of the parity bit may be either a hardware or a software function and in the cheaper and less sophisticated systems it is usually a software function.

Parity checking can be understood by considering a 2-level code, which could be used to transmit only four separate items of information. If a third bit is added, the error checking bit, there will be eight 3-bit codes available for transmission. These codes are illustrated in Figure 3.6(a) where they are represented as the eight corners of a unit cube called a *3-dimensional hypercube*. This is a particular case of an N-dimensional hypercube, which is used in the general case in which N bits are used to represent each code. The coordinates of the corners of the unit cube are the same as the eight 3-bit codes:

000 001 010 011
100 101 110 111

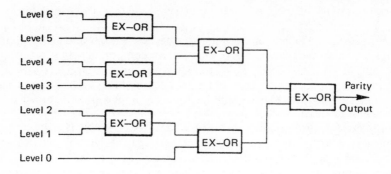

Figure 3.7   *7-level parity tree*

As only four items of information have to be represented by these eight codes, four of the eight codes can be chosen to be valid and the other four will be invalid. If the four valid codes are chosen to be the same as the coordinates of four nonadjacent corners of the cube then either of the two groups of codes shown in Figure 3.6(b) can be chosen to be the valid set of codes. Only those two groups of codes shown in Figure 3.6(b) meet the nonadjacent corner criterion. A property of each set of codes is that if a single bit of a code in one set is changed from one to zero or from zero to one, the resulting code is in the other set. If two bits in a code are changed, the resulting code is in the same set. This is really another way of expressing the nonadjacent corner criterion for the selection of the code sets. Parity checking systems make use of this property. A parity checking system assumes that the probability of a single bit error in a code is much greater than the probability of a multiple bit error. If this is not so in any system it is a waste of effort applying a parity check. There are other error checking methods applicable to such systems (see bibliography).

From Figure 3.6(b) it can be observed that to encode four items of information using either of the two sets of codes as the valid set, any two columns of the set of codes may be used as the information carrying bits since any pair of columns contains four unique codes:

00   01   10   11

The remaining column contains the check bit necessary to put the information code into the valid set. The check bit can be generated from the information because it will be noticed that the number of ones in each code is an even number in the set of Figure 3.6(b) (i) and an odd number in the set of Figure 3.6(b) (ii). These are the even parity and odd parity representations of the four items of information.

The reader may notice that the table of codes in Figure 3.6(b) (i) is identical to the XOR function table given in Chapter 2, Figure 2.6. Similarly, the set of codes given in Figure 3.6(b) (ii) has as its right hand column values which are the logical negation of the values in the right hand column of the XOR function of Figure 2.6. Thus the values in Figure 3.6(b) (i) are the values of a non-equivalence function, whereas those in the table of Figure 3.6(b) (ii) are the values of an equivalence function.

Checking of a received parity checked code for correctness is carried out, by hardware or by software, by modulus one addition of the bits in the received code. In hardware, modulus one addition is performed by a tree of XOR modules. Figure 3.6(b) shows that any one column of the three bit codes may be obtained by XORing the other two. In the checking of a 7-level ASCII code, the bits are grouped in pairs and XORed. The resulting outputs are then paired and XORed and so on until only one bit is the result as illustrated in Figure 3.7. Parity generation is carried out using the data code as the input to an XOR tree. Checking is often performed by using the same network and comparing the output with the received parity bit.

Parity checking can be used only for the detection of single errors. Automatic correction of the erroneous code is not possible because any one code of one set (in Figure 3.6(b)) can be generated by changing a single bit in more than one code of the other set. Hence detection of an error does not allow deduction of a unique code from which the incorrect code was produced. Error correcting codes are available but outside the scope of this discussion.

All error detecting systems rely on *redundancy*, the existence of unused codes, in the coding system. The parity system requires a 50 percent redundancy of codes, since only half the transmitted code possibilities are valid. The ASCII code uses even parity checking, which means that of the 256 possible 8-bit codes only the 128 codes with an even number of ones are valid. More secure coding systems, and those coding systems which provide error correction, use even higher redundancy rates.

3.5 CODING OF NUMBERS INSIDE THE COMPUTER

There are a number of ways in which numbers are coded for manipulation inside the computer system but only the most fundamental coding—the twos complement system—is described in detail here. It is probably easier to understand the principles of the encoding of numbers if at first the corresponding principles as applied to decimal numbers are explained.

Suppose one is faced with the problem of subtracting the number 59 from the number 27. It will not take the reader long to arrive at the solution −32.

Problem	Check
...0027 ...0059 subtract	...0059 ...9968 add
...9968 result	...0027 result
(a)	(b)

Figure 3.8 *Tens complement subtraction*

Unfortunately the method of arriving at this solution is not the method used by computers to solve the same problem. To obtain the answer −32 the reader, probably subconsciously, compared the two numbers, decided that 59 is the larger and so subtracted 27 from 59. This was not the problem to which a solution was required. By inserting a − sign in front of the answer to the calculation actually performed, the answer to the original problem was determined. A computer asked to subtract 59 from 27 would do as requested and apply the rules of arithmetic to the subtraction of 59 from 27. The result the computer would obtain is 9968! This is correct if one considers the following arguments. Any positive number is preceded by an infinite number of leading zeros so the calculation can be laid out as shown in Figure 3.8(a). Straightforward application of the laws of subtraction lead to the result, 9968, shown in Figure 3.8(a). The result can be checked by adding 59 to it, as shown in Figure 3.8(b), giving the answer 27. The number 9968 is called the *tens complement* representation of the number which is usually written as −32. The latter is the *signed magnitude* representation of the number.

The difference between the tens complement and signed magnitude coding systems is that the signed magnitude system uses the two symbols + and − for two different purposes. The first is to represent the sign of a number i.e. to indicate its direction from the number zero (see Figure 3.9). The second to represent the arithmetic operations of addition and subtraction. In the complementary number coding system the symbols + and − are unambiguously used to represent the arithmetic operations only. They are not required to indicate the position of a number relative to the number zero because all numbers have a unique representation as shown in Figure 3.9.

It is an agreed convention in the signed magnitude number coding system that leading zeros and the + sign are omitted for positive numbers but that the − sign is always included for negative numbers. In the complementary number coding system it is agreed that *at least one* of the leading digits 0 or 9 is written with every number. Hence in tens complement notation the numbers

098   and   98

are unambiguous. The first is ninety-eight and the second is minus two. It is conventional to refer to the leftmost digit in the number as the *sign digit* so in the tens complement numbering system any number with a sign digit of 9 is a negative number and any number with a sign digit of 0 is a positive number.

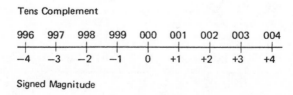

Tens Complement

996	997	998	999	000	001	002	003	004
−4	−3	−2	−1	0	+1	+2	+3	+4

Signed Magnitude

Figure 3.9   *Decimal numbers near to zero*

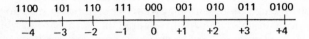

Figure 3.10 *Twos complement notation*

To convert from the complementary coding system to the signed magnitude system is a simple procedure. If the number is positive the systems are the same and if the number has a sign digit 9 then that number must be subtracted from zero and a − sign inserted in front of the result. For example:

$$000 - 998 = - 002$$

In the signed magnitude system special rules, which are very inconvenient to introduce into a machine, are applied to the manipulation of the + and − signs accompanying numbers. The importance of the complementary number coding system is that by strictly obeying the rules of addition and subtraction a correct and consistent set of results is obtained for all numeric calculations without the necessity of performing non numeric manipulations on non numeric characters, the + and − signs.

If numbers are represented in a binary numbering system they may still be represented in either signed magnitude or in complementary form, now called *twos complement* notation. In the twos complement coding system all positive numbers are preceded by *at least one* leading 0 and negative numbers are preceded by *at least one* leading 1. Thus in the twos complement numbering system a sign digit (*sign bit*) equal to 0 indicates a positive number and a sign bit equal to 1 indicates a negative number. Figure 3.10 shows the twos complement notation for some numbers close to zero.

The rules for conversion from twos complement form to signed magnitude form are similar to those used in converting from tens complement to signed magnitude. That is, if the (twos) complement number is preceded by a 0 it remains unchanged but if it is preceded by a 1 it must be subtracted from zero and a − sign must be inserted in front of the result.

From Figure 3.10 it will be observed that numbers on either side of zero and equidistant from zero are *complementary*, i.e. their sum is zero. This is true whatever notation is used to represent the numbers. Such pairs of numbers are said to be complementary pairs so, for example:

      − 4 is the complement of + 4
and   + 4 is the complement of − 4

or, in the twos complement system:

      1100 is the complement of 0100
and   0100 is the complement of 1100

The complement of a number N is, therefore, 0 − N irrespective of whether N is a positive or a negative number. In the twos complement notation, the complement of either a positive or a negative number is found by subtraction of that number from zero. It follows, since the complement of zero is $0 - 0$, that zero is its own complement in any complementary numbering system. Zero is therefore unambiguously represented in such a system, which is not the case in some other numbering systems where zero can have more than one representation. Further, as the leading digits for the number zero are 0s, the number zero is a positive number. This is important when writing programs containing conditional jumps in which a common error is to confuse the test for a positive number with the test for a number greater than zero.

3.5.1 Arithmetic Using Twos Complement Numbers

All modern computers use twos complement number representation and some use other notations as well. The two basic arithmetic operations are addition and subtraction. Addition of two numbers is straightforward. When twos complement notation is used for the numbers no special sign manipulation is required because the sign digit is a number 1 or 0 which is part of an infinite number of similar digits.

Subtraction of one number from another, say $(A) - (B)$ can be performed by addition of the complement of B to A because:

$A - B = A + (-B)$
where $-B$ $(= (0 - B))$ is the complement of B.

This statement is independent of the notation used for representing the numbers. A or B or both may be either positive or negative numbers. Computers usually perform subtraction by addition of the twos complement because a hardware adder is incorporated in the ALU and there is no point

---

Let $N = \ldots + r.\,(i) + \ldots + n(1) + n(0)$
where $n(i)$ is the binary coefficient of the nth term in a binary series

Then $N' = \ldots + n'(i) + \ldots n'(1) + n'(0)$
where N' is the logical NOT of N and n' is NOT n
so $N+N' = \ldots + (n(i) + n'(i)) \ldots + (n(1) + n'(1)) + (n(0) + n'(0))$
But since if $n(j) = 0$ then $n'(j) = 1$ and if $n(j) = 1$ then $n'(j) = 0$
it follows that $(n(j) + n'(j)) = 1$
So $N+N' = \ldots + (1)2^n + \ldots + (1)2^1 + (1)2^0$
i.e. $N+N' = -1$
so $N+N'+1 = 0$
or $N'+1 = 0-N$
But $0-N$ is the twos complement of N
Hence the twos complement of $N = N'+1$

Figure 3.11 *Showing two complement of $N = NOT\ N + 1$*

in providing a subtractor, although some machines have been made with subtractors. The conversion of a twos complement number into its complement is a simple logical and arithmetic operation which can be performed by the ALU. The subtraction from zero is equivalent to the logical operation NOT followed by *addition* of 1 as shown in Figure 3.11. The ALU hardware is capable of performing the function:

A + B′ + 1   where B′ is NOT B
which is the equivalent of A − B.

The hardware configuration required is shown in Figure 3.12.

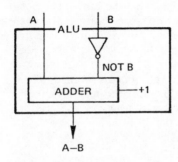

Figure 3.12   *Subtract hardware*

3.5.2 Machine Number Range and The Overflow Flag

The number range of a word in a computer is limited by the number of bits in the word and by the fact that at least one leading 1 or leading 0 must be included in the word. Thus in an 8-bit computer word the maximum number which can be stored in a single word is − 128 or + 127 as shown in Figure 3.13. All computers, whatever their word length, are limited in this way. The requirement for greater accuracy than can be provided by the use of one word to store one number leads to the use of multiple-length arithmetic in which two, three or more words are used to store a single number.

Suppose a computer with an 8-bit word length is used to add the number 96 to the number 120 (decimal). Figure 3.14 shows the calculation. If the addition is performed using a large number of bits it is, of course, correct, but

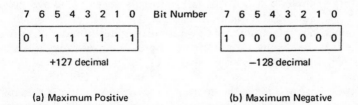

Figure 3.13   *Largest numbers in 8-bit word*

	8-bit word		
0	0110	0001	(+96)
0	0111	1000	Add (+120)
0	1101	1001	8-bit result negative 9-bit result correct

Figure 3.14 *Overflow*

the 8-bit computer can record only the least significant 8 bits of the calculation and it therefore appears that the sum of two positive numbers has given a negative result because the most significant bit of the result is a 1. This is a condition called *overflow* and it arises in a computer when the result of an arithmetic operation is a number outside the number range of the machine i.e. the result is a number larger than that which can be held in a single computer word. Overflow also occurs on the addition of two large negative numbers. Figure 3.15 illustrates the machine number range and overflow regions for a computer with an 8-bit word length. The overflow condition is detected by hardware in the ALU which causes the overflow flag (the V flag) in the condition codes register to set.

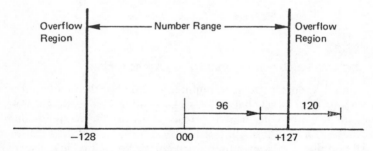

Figure 3.15   *8-bit number range and overflow regions*

If such a condition arises in the ALU during the execution of an arithmetic instruction in a program it is desirable that the hardware should remember that overflow occurred so that at the end of a series of calculations the whole set of calculations may be abandoned if overflow occurred at any point. It is very inefficient if the programmer has to insert a "test overflow" instruction after every arithmetic instruction and so usually once set the overflow flag remains set, even if subsequent operations give non-overflow results. The programmer may then test for overflow only once at the end of the program to verify that the results are not incorrect due to out-of-range results. The same effect is obtained in some machines by making the setting of the overflow flag cause an interrupt in the system (see Chapter 6). Special instructions are provided in the instruction set to allow the program to reset the overflow flag when it has been tested. A further discussion of the uses of the overflow flag can be found in Chapter 7.

3.6 THE CODING OF INSTRUCTION SETS

The instruction being executed by a CPU at any instant is the binary pattern in the instruction register. The hardware decoding system examines the operation code field of the instruction. From this it decodes the meaning of the rest of the instuction and performs the data transfers necessary to execute that instruction. The coding of information in the operation code field is normally logical to allow for simple decoding by the hardware. Consider the instructions discussed in Chapter 2. They fall into two sets, memory reference instruction and non memory reference instructions, each of which can be further subdivided into smaller sets. Suppose a 16-bit computer has about 16 memory reference instructions. Four bits are allocated for the operation codes. This allows 15 instruction codes plus one *escape code*, which indicates that the instruction is not a memory reference instruction, as shown in Figure 3.16.

The decoder distinguishes between memory reference and non memory reference instructions by examining the four most significant bits of the pattern in the instruction register. If they are all ones the instruction is non memory reference. The memory reference instruction is further decoded into subsets as follows:

1. If the Most Significant Bit (MSB) of the instruction is 0 the instruction is Arithmetic or Logical and therefore involves the ALU;

2. If the MSB is 1 the instruction is a jump type instruction and will involve data transfers to the PC.

15	14	13	12	Bit Number
				ARITHMETIC and LOGICAL INSTRUCTIONS
0	0	0	0	Not Used
0	0	0	1	Add [N] to [Accumulator]
0	0	1	0	Subtract [N] from [Accumulator]
0	0	1	1	AND [N] with [Accumulator]
0	1	0	0	OR [N] with [Accumulator]
0	1	0	1	NOT [N] into Accumulator
0	1	1	0	Load Accumulator from N
0	1	1	1	Store [Accumulator] in N
				JUMP INSTRUCTIONS
1	0	0	0	Jump to N if [Accumulator] is zero
1	0	0	1	Jump to N if Carry Set
1	0	1	0	Jump to N if [Accumulator] positive
1	0	1	1	Jump to N if [Accumulator] negative
1	1	0	0	Jump to N unconditionally
1	1	0	1	Jump to subroutine. Link in N, start at N + 1
1	1	1	0	Jump indirect through N
1	1	1	1	ESCAPE CODE from Memory Ref. Instructions

Figure 3.16 *Typical memory reference instruction set*

Within these two sets further subdivision is possible. For example, in set (b) if the two MSBS are 10, an access to the memory is required to load the PC or to store its contents. The instruction codes are thus seen to be arranged to allow for easy decoding for the hardware. To the programmer the binary codes are irrelevant because a programmer uses assembly language mnemonics to represent the operation codes and these are translated by the Assembler into the correct binary codes.

In the example under discussion, four ones in the most significant bits of the instruction constitute an escape code from the memory reference instructions. The instruction is then determined by decoding other fields in the instruction word. Non memory reference instructions can be subdivided into Input/Output (I/O) instructions and non I/O instructions in those computer systems in which the memory is not on the I/O bus (see Figure 1.2). This division into two subsets requires the use of one bit in the instruction, say bit 11, as shown in Figure 3.17. In each case, further fields in the instruction will then require decoding. I/O instruction formats will be considered in Chapter 5 and will not be discussed further here.

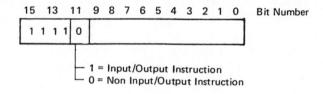

Figure 3.17   *One bit coding for two subsets*

Suppose bits 15 through 11 of the instruction are 11110, indicating a non memory reference, non I/O, instruction. The actual type of instruction is then coded into bits 10 through 0. The next major subset of instructions may be the shift instructions and if there are five of these instructions three bits can be used to code them, which leaves three of the eight possible 3-bit codes unused. One of these is required for the escape code into non memory reference, non I/O, non shift instructions. Figure 3.18 shows a possible coding for the five types of shift instruction. The coding structure here is *bit significant* coding, in which the bit usage is generally not very efficient but which is easily understood by people and easy to decode by hardware. Bit significant coding is frequently used in such places as the condition codes register of the CPU and in the status registers of peripherals. The coding of Figure 3.18 uses bit 8 to code the shift direction, bit 9 to code the arithmetic (1) or logical (0) shift type, and bit 10 to code for circular (1) or non circular (0).

Another way of explaining the coding of Figure 3.18 is to consider that bits 10 and 9 define four sets, of which three are the Logical Shifts, the Arithmetic Shifts, and the Circular Shifts while the other is the escape code 11. Within each of the Shift sets bit 8 codes the direction of the shift. The Arithmetic left shift is not used.

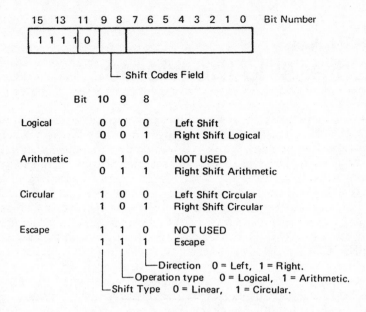

Figure 3.18 *Example of shift instruction coding*

The coding structures of the more recent computers is not necessarily as structured as that of earlier machines. This is because modern integrated circuit decoders can decode all combinations of N bits, whereas this was an expensive operation using earlier technologies. For example, if a 4-bit field in the instruction is decoded into 16 lines, only one of which is a 1 at any time, then it really is immaterial which of the 16 lines is chosen for any particular operation. Thus only the definition of the fields is really important. If not all the 16 combinations are used, then a 4-line to 16-line decoder will still be employed for the decode in modern machines because that is a standard integrated circuit or subset of an integrated circuit. In older technologies it was possible to economize on decoding circuits (and cost) by structuring the decoding appropriately.

The instruction code structure of some computer systems is described in the Appendix.

CHAPTER 4

Addressing the Memory

4.1 INTRODUCTION

Memory reference instructions are usually concerned with storing the content of a register in the memory, with causing a program to execute a jump to a memory location, or with obtaining an operand (the data to be operated upon) from memory for transfer into a CPU register. The operand may be combined with the content of the register en route, as in "add to register" instructions.

It is generally accepted that a viable general purpose computer system must be capable of addressing a memory of 64K words, requiring a 16-bit address for each memory location. In a small computer system in which the word length is short and in which the instruction is a single word, the instruction is not sufficiently long to contain an operation code, a register address and a 16-bit memory address. A problem which faces a computer system design team, therefore, is to devise methods which allow the CPU to access a memory which requires more bits for each address than can be accommodated in the address field of the standard memory reference instruction.

In the discussion which follows it is assumed that the machine word length is 16 bits. This allows specific examples to be given, but the addressing techniques are in no way restricted to 16-bit computers. The techniques are used in most mainframe computers, more for the convenience of the programmer than of necessity for memory addressing. In computers with word lengths shorter than 16 bits, the necessity for some of the techniques becomes even greater than in a 16-bit machine.

There are many techniques available which allow a 64K store to be addressed by a machine having a word length of 16 bits or less. They all involve the addition of hardware to the basic CPU. Most of the techniques increase the execution time of the memory reference instructions because these instructions now provide information from which the CPU can calculate the required memory address, called the *effective address*, instead of providing the effective address directly. It is the time required for this calculation which increases the execution time of the instruction. In some cases the extra time is negligible because the calculation is trivial. In other cases the extra time is a significant proportion of the execution time of the instruction. Often, however, the extra execution time is irrelevant because the use of the technique allows one instruction to be used in place of two or more instructions so that a saving in program execution time is achieved. The techniques to be discussed are not all mutually exclusive, and most computer systems allow the use of a variety of them either in different instructions or in combination in the same instruction.

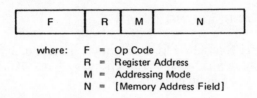

Figure 4.1   *Memory reference instruction format (16-bit)*

Memory reference instuctions in 16-bit computers usually have a format similar to that of Figure 4.1. This is a one and a half address instruction in which there is an additional field, the *addressing mode* field. The addressing mode field contains a code (M) indicating which of the techniques of effective address calculation are to be employed. M is not usually more than 3 bits long, allowing for 8 addressing modes. In instructions with this format, the N address field is about 8 bits long, meaning that only 256 words of memory may be addressed from the instruction. Consequently addressing of memory directly from the instruction is rarely used. Programs written for such a machine use memory reference instructions in which the effective address is calculated by the CPU by adding N to a 16-bit number as explained in the following paragraphs. In these computers the number N is more often referred to as the *displacement* or *offset* than as the memory address.

4.2 IMMEDIATE MODE ADDRESSING

This is a mode of addressing in which the operand required by the CPU is stored as part of the instruction, not in a separate memory location. Hence no effective address calculation is performed by the CPU because the operand is the number N and was fetched with the op code during the instruction fetch. N is called a *literal* or an *immediate operand*. This mode provides a useful means of storing small constants. For example, it is sometimes required to add a small number such as 2 to an accumulator. Instead of storing the number 2 in a memory location in a data area outside the program area it may be stored in the address field of the instruction, which contains sufficient bits to store numbers up to 255. This makes economical use of the memory, allows easier programming and gives more rapid execution of the program.

4.3 DIRECT ADDRESSING

In this addressing mode the number N in the address field of the instruction is the effective address. No effective address calculations are therefore required by the CPU, but location N has to be accessed to obtain the operand. This is the mode of addressing implicit in the explanation of memory reference instructions earlier in this text (see Chapter 2, section 2.2).

4.4 INDIRECT ADDRESSING

When the number N in the address field of the instruction is the address of the memory location which contains the effective address of the operand, the operand is said to be indirectly addressed.

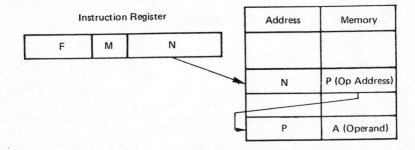

Figure 4.2   *Indirect addressing via memory*

This addressing mode is illustrated in Figure 4.2, which shows how an operand A may be accessed indirectly via a memory location N containing the address of the operand. Often the number N is referred to as a *pointer* which points to the memory location containing the effective address. The effective address calculation required of the processor in this case is the retrieving of the effective address from the memory location pointed to by N.

Indirect addressing via hardware registers is an alternative technique employed in some computer systems. In this case the number in the address field of the instruction is the address of a register in the CPU. It is this register which contains the effective address of the operand as illustrated in Figure 4.3.

Figures 4.2 and 4.3 show indirect addressing taken to one level but some computer systems allow more than one level of indirect addressing. One such machine is the Data General NOVA minicomputer which uses the system illustrated in Figure 4.4.

The word retrieved from memory when indirect addressing is specified in the instruction is assumed to be of the format shown. The most significant bit is an indirect bit and the other 15 bits are a memory address. If the indirect

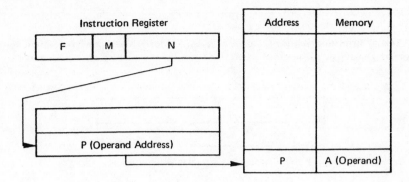

Figure 4.3   *Indirect addressing via registers*

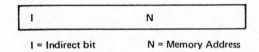

I = Indirect bit   N = Memory Address

Figure 4.4   *Indirect memory word, NOVA computer*

bit is a 0, the word is taken to be the address of the operand. If the indirect bit is a 1, the remaining 15 bits are taken as a memory address where another word of similar format is to be found. Thus the hardware automatically continues to search the memory until it retrieves a word with a zero in the most significant bit position. The disadvantage of this system is that it allows addressing of a memory with a maximum size of 32K locations, addressed by 15 bits, instead of 64K locations. This disadvantage can be overcome using other techniques described in this chapter.

Indirect addressing techniques usually cause instruction execution to be slower than that of direct addressing. In the case of indirect addressing via the memory this extra time is equal to the time taken for the extra memory cycles required to retrieve the effective address. However, indirect addressing allows the writing of more powerful instructions than does direct addressing. Programs using it tend to contain less instructions than equivalent programs which use only direct addressing, so that program execution time is less and the work throughput of the computer system is greater. Indirect addressing via the CPU registers generally does not give slower instruction execution time than direct addressing, because in both cases the CPU obtains the effective address directly from a CPU register—the instruction register in the case of direct addressing and a general purpose register in the case of indirect addressing via the registers.

4.5 MULTIPLE LENGTH INSTRUCTIONS

The technique of using multiple length instructions is introduced at this point because it can be regarded either as an extension of direct addressing or as indirect addressing via the program counter, i.e. a special case of indirect addressing via the CPU registers.

As an example consider the case of a double length jump instruction of the format shown in Figure 4.5.

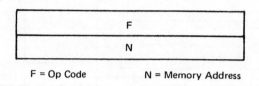

F = Op Code   N = Memory Address

Figure 4.5   *Double length jump instruction format*

A 16-bit jump address could be obtained by using an indirect jump instruction but that requires the programmer to set up a memory location or a CPU register with the jump address. In practice the most convenient place to store the jump address is in the memory location next to that containing the instruction. In this case the instruction can be considered to occupy two consecutive memory locations and is therefore a double length instruction. When the program runs, the instruction fetch, part of the machine main timing cycle (see Chapter 1, section 1.5.1) fetches the first word (the F bits) into the instruction register and increments the content of the PC. The CPU hardware interprets (decodes) this word as an instruction to access the memory using the number in the program counter as the effective address i.e. an indirect access to the store via the program counter. As the program counter was incremented at the end of the instruction fetch the memory location accessed to obtain the jump address is the next sequential one to that containing the instruction. The word retrieved from memory is put in the program counter to cause the jump. This is a case of single level indirect addressing via a CPU register.

If the double length instruction is a "Load Register from Memory Location N" instruction, the hardware performs a two-level indirect access to the memory, first using the (incremented) number in the program counter to obtain the number N and then accessing the memory again at address N to obtain the operand which is loaded into the register.

For the execution of double length instructions, therefore, the hardware provided to perform indirect addressing via the CPU registers and via the memory is used to obtain the operand, but the special position in the computer system of the CPU register containing the pointer (the Program Counter) gives an effect which is worthy of a special name.

If the instruction is considered to be a double length instruction rather than an indirect addressing instruction it is reasonable to call the technique direct addressing since the address of the operand is part of the instruction. But it should be borne in mind that, although this is a convenient way of describing the technique, the hardware cannot think and it is in fact performing its indirect addressing routines.

Microprocessors and minicomputers with 8-bit word lengths usually use single length instructions for register–register instructions. The memory reference instructions are double or triple length. A direct addressing memory reference instruction in an 8-bit machine may have the format shown in Figure 4.6.

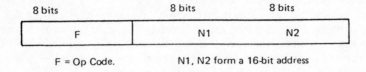

Figure 4.6 *Memory reference instruction in an 8-bit machine*

Although these multiple length instructions are conveniently classified as direct addressing instructions, they are in fact obeyed by the hardware performing multiple indirect accesses to the memory via the program counter to obtain the required number of 8-bit words from the memory (in an 8-bit machine the memory is only 8 bits wide). After each memory access the number in the program counter is incremented just as it is after an instruction fetch. The manufacturer's literature for these computers often refers to the machine's "variable length instructions". This is a correct description of course, but the hardware required to provide this facility is not complex in its function—it simply does the required number of indirect accesses to the memory via the program counter. This hardware is probably supplied in any case for the indirect addressing capability of the machine. The only extra hardware required is that which assembles the 8-bit words into three registers which together form the instruction register for three-word instructions.

4.6 EFFECTIVE ADDRESS CALCULATION USING REGISTERS

There is a set of techniques for calculating the effective address which is a set of variations of the same technique. The content of a 16-bit register in the CPU, say the A register, is added to the content of the N address field in the instruction, as illustrated in Figure 4.7.

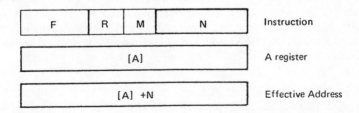

Figure 4.7 *Effective address calculation using register content*

The effective address is 16 bits long and can therefore be used to access the whole of a 64K memory. The individual names given to the techniques arise from the special function of the A register in the CPU. It is the combination of this special function and the use of the register in calculating the effective address which gives rise to what appears to the machine programmer to be a technique of memory addressing worthy of reference by a special name, as was the case with double length instructions. As far as the hardware designer is concerned these techniques are all much the same, addition of the content of a register to the number N from the instruction register. The extra hardware required in the CPU to support this addressing mode is the electronics to select data from the correct register.

4.6.1 Use of an Index Register

Indexing is a technique employed by the programmer to access an ordered block of data in the memory. It is used, for example, when the program must perform the same operations repeatedly on different items of data. Normally this data would be stored in memory locations, say, D, D + 1, D + 2, . . . D + M. Clearly one does not wish to write the program T times for T items of data. The program is, therefore, designed to loop back through the same set of instructions, but at every pass round the loop the data addresses are changed.

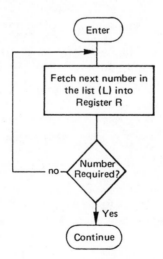

Figure 4.8   *Indexing situation*

Figure 4.8 is a flowchart of such a program. One way of changing the data addresses is to write the program so that the instructions referencing the data use an address which can easily be incremented (or decremented) using the machine instruction set. If the address is incremented each time the program passes round the loop, the address indexes through a data table in memory.

If the addressing mode calls for indexing, the effective address is automatically calculated by the hardware to be:

N + [X]   /where [X] is the number in a special register
           /called the *index register*.

As the index register is 16 bits long the effective address is also 16 bits long, and the data accessed may be anywhere in a 64K memory. The N address in the instruction has been extended to 16 bits by adding the 16-bit index to it.

On simple way to index through a data block is to write a program at the beginning of which the index register is loaded with the address of the first word of the data block. Every time a word is fetched from the data block the number in the index register is incremented. Thus, if an accumulator is to be loaded with the words from the data block, the "load accumulator" instruction is written in the format shown in Figure 4.9, where the number N in the displacement field is zero.

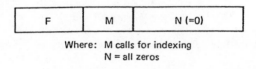

Where: M calls for indexing
        N = all zeros

Figure 4.9 *Indexed load instruction*

After this instruction has been obeyed the index register is incremented so that the second time the "load accumulator" instruction is obeyed the data will be the second word from the data block, and so on. In this case the index register is being used as the operand address register and this address is being incremented every time an operand is accessed. As N = 0, the content of the index register is the effective address and the technique is effectively indirect addressing via the index register.

The index register may be a special register in the CPU or it may be one of the GP registers. If it is a special register there will be special instructions to load it from memory, to store its content in the memory and often instructions to increment or decrement its contents. In some computers the index register can be used as the source of one of the operands for instructions which cause a data transfer through the ALU; Arithmetic operations between the index and the content of the other registers can then be performed. If the GP registers are used for indexing then clearly all the instructions which affect the GP registers can be used to manipulate the content of the index register.

4.6.2 Multiple Index Registers

Anyone who writes programs for a machine with only one index register soon finds that it would be very convenient if there were more than one index register. For example, it is fairly common to find oneself writing a program to take data from a table, to operate on it and then to put the result into a different table. This requires indexing of two tables in the same program loop, a job which is easily done if there are two separate index registers. However, even though a facility is very convenient in some circumstances it will not necessarily be provided. There are attendant disadvantages, in this case the fact that the index register must be addressable to distinguish one index from another. This makes it necessary to restrict even further the direct addressing capability of the memory reference instructions, because bits must be allocated in the instruction for the address of the index register. The instruction format for such instructions is that shown in Figure 4.10.

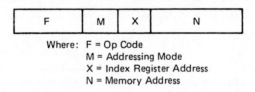

Where: F = Op Code
        M = Addressing Mode
        X = Index Register Address
        N = Memory Address

Figure 4.10   *Indexed memory reference instruction format*

Eight-bit computers have an advantage in some respects over 16-bit computers because they use a 24-bit memory reference instruction, so there are more bits available to specify the various addressing modes and index register addresses.

4.6.3 Autoincrement and Autodecrement

When an index register is used to index through a table of data it is necessary to increment or decrement the index after every access to the data table. This can usually be achieved by using an increment or decrement instruction. However, because it is such a common requirement, some computers incorporate special hardware which automatically increments or decrements the contents of the index register after a data access. This requires special instruction operation codes or special addressing modes and is called autoincrementing or autodecrementing of the index.

Indexing is a form of indirect addressing via a register. In situations when a large number of tables is being kept in memory, an equally large number of indexes may be needed. In practice it is more convenient to keep these indexes in memory and to access the tables they point to by indirect addressing instructions. In this case it is the content of the memory locations in which the indexes are stored which require autoincrementing or autodecrementing. It is also in circumstances such as these that an autoincrement or autodecrement will save most CPU time. This addressing mode is therefore more often applied to indirect addressing than to indexed addressing.

4.6.4 Relative Addressing

If the program counter is the register whose content is added to the N address field of the instruction register in the calculation of the effective address, the addressing mode is said to be the relative addressing mode. This mode of addressing is most often used in jump instructions. It is used to calculate the address of the next instruction rather than to access data. In a carefully designed program most jumps are to a point in the program not far from the current instruction. It is useful, therefore, if the instruction set contains instructions which cause a jump to a location N locations from the current instruction. The skip instruction has already been discussed in Chapter 2 section 2.2.4, and it can be seen that a jump to a location N distant from the current instruction is a more general case of the skip. Relative addressing allows a jump to be made without the necessity of using a register to store the jump address or of using indirect addressing. The CPU hardware is required to add the content of the program counter to the number in the N address field of the instruction register. Usually the number N in the instruction address field is treated as a signed twos complement number (see Chapter 3 section 3.5) so that jumps may be made either forward or backward in the memory from the current position. The hardware extends the sign bit of the number N through to the most significant bit of the word before adding the number in the program counter. It should be noted that the obeying of this type of instruction occurs after the [program counter] has been incremented, so that the jump is in fact relative to the address of the next instruction in the program. The block of memory which is accessible to relative jumps is sometimes called the Current Page of the program.

4.6.5 Address Extension Registers

Some computers employ address extension registers which contain the most significant 4 bits (say) of the memory address. In such computers it is convenient to consider the memory to be divided into 16 blocks each having 4K locations. These blocks can be considered to be numbered 0 through 15 (binary 0000 through 1111) and the address extension register contains the current block number. The effective address is calculated by concatenating a 12-bit address obtained by the other techniques described in this section with the 4 bits in the address extension register, as shown in Figure 4.11.

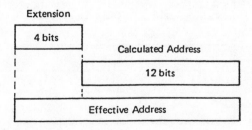

Figure 4.11   *Use of address extension register*

This system is useful for memory protection when it is a requirement that one program shall not interfere with any other program in the system. Each program is allowed access to certain restricted areas of memory determined by the setting of the extension register. Special privileged instructions are required to change the setting of the extension register and the machine executes these instructions only if it is running the executive program (the operating system). The 4K blocks are sometimes called pages and have fixed addresses in the memory. A similar system is employed in some 16-bit computers to allow them to use a memory of up to 256K words (= 4 × 64K). The extension register is then two bits long. Its contents are concatenated with a 16-bit address, calculated by one or more of the techniques described in this chapter, to produce the 18-bit address required to access a 256K word memory (see Memory Bank Switching later in this chapter).

4.6.6 Base Register Addressing

It is very convenient for a programmer to write programs as if they all start at location zero in the memory. When the programs are eventually loaded into the computer system they are located upwards from some memory locations whose address is called the *base address*. Thus the base address must be added to all memory references in the program. Some systems achieve this by using a special register called a base register which is loaded with the base address of the program currently being run. More detailed discussion of this technique in applications such as memory protection systems is beyond the scope of the present discussion, but it can be seen that the technique is similar to that of extension registers, excepting that the register length of a base register is normally longer than that of the extension register and it is necessary to *add* the content of the base register to the number N in the instruction rather than to concatenate it.

4.6.7 Based Indexed Addressing

This mode of addressing, which can be found, for example, in the recent 16-bit microprocessors, does not use indexing as defined above, in which the

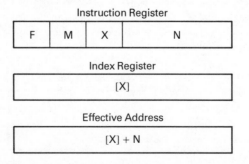

Figure 4.12   *Based-indexed address calculation*

index can be changed by the program when the program is running. In this addressing mode, a CPU register is nominated in the instruction to be the base register. The displacement which is to be added to the content of the base register is explicitly stated in the instruction. Figure 4.12 shows the calculations performed by the hardware to calculate the effective address.

This method of operand address calculation may be useful in accessing the ith element of an array. For example, a high level language program may reference variables I(4), J(8) etc. Based Indexed Addressing is the machine level addressing mode which corresponds to this method of specifying variables. The address corresponding to the start of array I is put into the base register, and the index, the value in the bracket, is used as the displacement in the instruction.

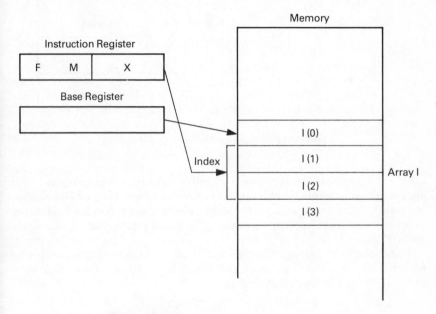

Figure 4.13   *Based-indexed addressing*

A more flexible type of based-indexed addressing is that in which the index is contained in a CPU register rather than in the Instruction register. This enables access to arrays of variables established dynamically during the running of the program.

It also allows access to a variable such as I(X) specified in the program, where X is a value held in a CPU register and calculated by the program. That is, it enables the programmer to write programs which calculate to which element of which array access is required.

4.6.8 Combined Indirect and Indexed Addressing

Suppose a program is being written which can take a number of different courses depending on some external events such as the operation of one of a number of switches on a control panel. Very rapid access to the program which deals with the particular switch may be obtained by the combined techniques of indexing and indirect addressing.

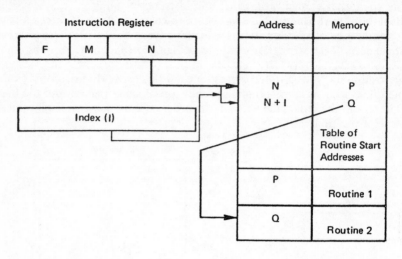

Figure 4.14 *Indirect addressing, pre-indexed*

Figure 4.14 shows the situation. A number corresponding to the switch is used as the index into a table of the addresses of the start of the various programs. An indirect jump via the start address of the table, indexed by the number of the switch, causes a jump to the appropriate routine in a single instruction.

Some computer systems give the choice between *pre-indexing* (indexing before indirect addressing as in the example of Figure 4.13) and *post-indexing*, which is illustrated in Figure 4.15.

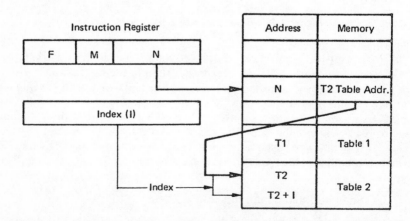

Figure 4.15 *Indirect addressing, post-indexed*

Post-indexing gives access to an entry in a table pointed at by a number used as an indirect address. For example, Figure 4.15 shows a number of tables in memory. Access is required to only one table whose start address T2 is in location N. An indirect addressing instruction "load register indirectly through address N, post indexed" fetches into the register the data memory in table T2, using the number in the index register as the index into table T2. Thus pre-indexing is the normal requirement when indirect, indexed addressing is used to effect jumps in a program. Post-indexing is usually required when indirect, indexed addressing is used to access the memory at data locations.

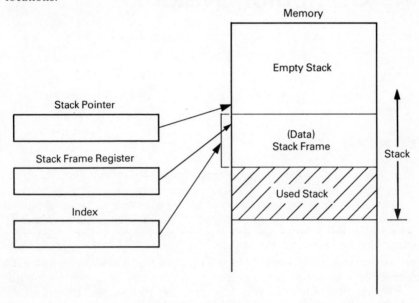

Figure 4.16   *Stack frame*

4.6.9 Addressing Data on the Stack

In some circumstances it is advantageous if data is held on the stack rather than in the CPU registers or in fixed memory locations. A block of data on the stack is said to comprise a *stack frame*. Data held in this way may be readily manipulated in a computer system which allows indirect addressing of the memory through a register. A stack frame may be established by pushing data onto the stack, and if necessary, decrementing the stack pointer to make room for data still to be calculated. Figure 4.16 illustrates such a stack. If the number in the stack pointer register is now copied into a base register, that base register points at the stack frame. The data can be readily manipulated using the stack frame register as a base register and invoking the based-indexed or indirect indexed modes of addressing. Subroutines which use this technique can be used recursively, which is to say they can call themselves. Such subroutines often result in considerable simplification in the coding of a program and considerable savings in program execution time.

CHAPTER 5

Data Transfers within
the Computer System

5.1 INTRODUCTION

The architecture of the computer system will now be examined from the viewpoint of the subsystem used to accomplish the data transfers between registers. This chapter is concerned with data transfers within the computer system itself (including the I/O subsystem), i.e. up to a distance of about 20 meters. A computer system which communicates with another device over a longer distance than this has a peripheral called a communications adapter or a similar name, connected to its I/O bus. The function of this peripheral is to transfer information between remote devices and the computer installation. As far as the computer system is concerned this peripheral is not special in any way—it provides input and output to and from the computer as do all the other peripherals.

5.2 COMMUNICATIONS WITHIN THE CPU

Data transfers in the CPU are transfers of the contents of the registers. These transfers occur along Data Highways or Data Buses, which are physically just bundles of wires or printed circuit tracks. In a 16-bit machine a data bus is 16-bits wide and consists of 16 wires or 16 printed circuit tracks.

A CPU can be considered to be a system of data buses, rather like a road system, into which the various registers are connected and along which the register contents can travel. Data transfers occur by the opening of the appropriate registers to the data bus system.

Figure 5.1 shows a CPU with two GP registers and three data buses. Two data buses are connected to the ALU to provide the two input words required by the ALU, and the third bus is used to provide input to the registers. The ALU output is connected to the third bus so that the ALU result may be routed to a register. Even the simple CPU shown in

Figure 5.1 is capable of performing a number of instructions. For example any ALU operation may be performed between the contents of registers 0 and 1 and the result can be deposited in any of the registers, including the PC, the instruction register, the memory address register, or the memory data register. This CPU can therefore perform register–register instructions, jump instructions, and some register–memory instructions.

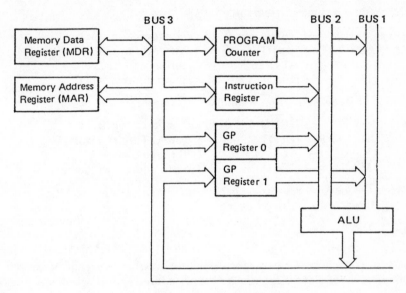

Figure 5.1 *A simple 3-bus CPU*

The data transfers required for these instructions are shown below where the meaning of the square brackets notation introduced in Chapter 2 is extended to include [BusN], meaning the data on BusN.

To Fetch an Instruction:

(1) [Bus1]   ← [PC]   /put fetch address on Bus1
     ALU O/P= [Bus1]   /set ALU to transmit [Bus1]
     [Bus3]   ← ALU O/P   /put fetch address on Bus3
     [MAR]   ← [Bus3]   /send fetch address to memory

When the memory has retrieved the instruction from the fetch address the following data transfer is carried out:

(2) [Bus3]   ← [MDR]   /instruction on Bus3
     [IREG]   ← [Bus3]   /put instruction into the
                                 /instruction register
     [PC]   ← [PC] + 1   /increment the [PC]

At this stage the instruction fetch is complete.

To execute a register–register add instruction:

(1)	[Bus1]	← [REG 0]	/register 0 to ALU I/P
	[Bus2]	← [REG 1]	/register 1 to ALU I/P
	ALU	= ADD	/set ALU to add
	[Bus3]	← [ALU O/P]	/sum to register input Bus
(2)	[REG1]	← [Bus3]	/result to register 1

To execute a jump instruction:

(1)	[Bus1]	← [IREG bits 0–11]	/N address on Bus1
	ALU O/P=	[Bus1]	/set ALU to transmit [Bus1]
	[Bus3]	← ALU O/P	/through to Bus3
	[PC]	← [Bus3]	/jump address to PC

To Load Register 1 From Memory:

(1)	[Bus1]	← [IREG bits 0–11]	/N address on Bus1
	ALU O/P=	[Bus1]	/set ALU to transmit [Bus1]
	[Bus3]	← ALU O/P	/through to Bus 3
	[MAR]	← [Bus3]	/send address to memory

When the memory has retrieved the data from the data address the following data transfers are carried out:

| (2) | [Bus3] | ← [MDR] | /data on Bus3 |
| | [REG1] | ← [Bus3] | /put data in register 1 |

A system such as this is very attractive to a system designer because it is simple, effective and elegant. All memory addresses during both instruction fetch and instruction execution are sent to the memory by the same route. This route is also used to send data to the memory. Notice that in the CPU of Figure 5.1 all data transfers occur through the ALU. This is a normal arrangement in a CPU and has implications for the ALU functions required. For example, the ALU must be capable not only of performing operations between words as discussed previously in this text but must also be able to transmit the word on one of its inputs directly through to its output without alteration. It also implies that the ALU operation performed on operands does not affect the time of execution of the instruction.

A system such as that of Figure 5.1 tends to minimize the control circuitry required. This reduces the cost of the system or allows the inclusion of circuits to perform other system functions on the same chip. Real computers, of course, contain more than three data buses to allow the bypassing of certain parts of the system under special circumstances.

Many of the instructions discussed in Chapter 2 can be executed by the system of Figure 5.1. By including a single bit shift, both right and left, within the set of operations which the ALU can perform (the instruction set of the ALU), then even the shift instructions can be obeyed provided the hardware can execute a number of cycles automatically.

By focusing attention on the system of data buses in the system it is possible to postulate a number of ways in which the system could perform the instructions which the instruction set requires. Further, it is apparent which instructions the system is incapable of executing. For example the CPU of Figure 5.1 cannot use register 0 as an index register because connections are not provided to separate buses for register 0 and for the instruction register. It is, therefore, impossible for the ALU to add the content of register 0 to the N address field of the instruction register. It would be necessary to add further connections to some of the buses if the CPU were required to execute such instructions.

5.2.1 Data Bus Hardware

The system of data buses in a computer system is of great importance because all instructions cause data transfers between registers. In modern computer systems most data transfers take place on a system of data buses. A look through the catalog of any semiconductor manufacturer will show a large number of components which can be connected directly into bussed systems. Most of these devices are Three-State (tri-state) devices. This does not mean that they cannot be used in binary systems. They are specially designed to work in binary systems! They have the very useful property that their output may be either 0 or 1 or it may be switched off—the third state—so that for all practical purposes the device is not taking part in the

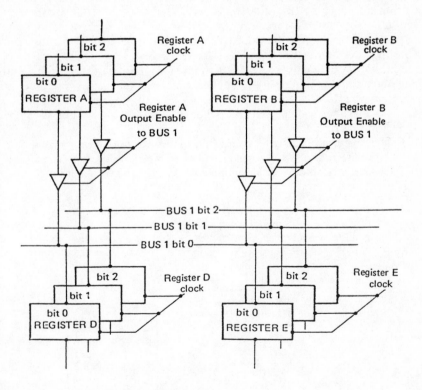

Figure 5.2 *Connection of registers to one system bus*

functioning of the system. The output may be switched on or off by an *enable* signal. When the enable signal is a 1 the output of the device is either a 1 or a 0 depending on the state of its input. When the enable signal is a 0 the tri-state device is switched off. That is, the device is disabled. A large number of these devices may be connected together to form a bus as in Figure 5.2, which shows the connections for three bits of a single data bus.

Two registers, the A and B registers, are shown with output connections to the bus and two registers, the D and E registers, are shown with input connections from the bus. This system can be used to transfer the contents of either of the A or B registers into registers D or E.

To perform a data transfer from register A to register E, the hardware enables the tri-state devices connected to the outputs of the bits of register A and disables the tri-state devices connected to the outputs of register B. The logical states of the bus lines are then determined by the contents of register A. This is the mechanism used by the hardware to output the contents of register A on to the bus. The contents of the bus are transferred into register E when the *clock* signal on register E becomes a 1. While the clock is a 0 no data is allowed into the register. This is the function of the clock signal. Normally all the register clocks are held at 0, thus preventing data from entering the registers and so preserving the contents of the registers. Thus by clocking register E (setting the register E clock from 0 to 1 then back again to 0), but not clocking the other registers, the data on the bus enters only register E. It would be normal for the system to disable the tri-state outputs of register A soon after the clock on register E returns to 0. The transfer of data from register A to register E is then complete.

The system shown in Figure 5.2 is simple for the sake of clarity. In a real computer system the output of a register may be connected to a number of buses, in which case there is a "Register R Output Enable to Bus" signal for each bus and a separate tri-state output device for each connection, as will be shown in Figure 5.4.

Each register input may be connected to more than one bus so that data can be transferred into that register from a number of different buses. This requires a selection device, a *multiplexor*, on the input of each bit of each

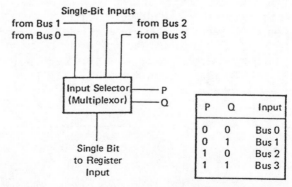

Figure 5.3 *Input data selector on each bit of each register*

register. A multiplexor is a device which connects one of a number of data inputs through to its output. The data inputs are numbered so that they can be addressed. The data input connected through to the output is the one whose address appears on the *select* control inputs of the multiplexor.

Figure 5.3 shows a multiplexor for selecting an input from one of four buses. The select signals, P and Q, cause the appropriate bus line to be switched through to the register input according to the table in Figure 5.3.

In a more elaborate system than that of Figure 5.2, a single register bit would have controlling inputs to decide

(a) the destination bus for its output
(b) the source bus for its input

and (c) when to clock the input into the register.

This is shown in Figure 5.4 where a single bit (Bit n) of one register is shown with output connections to four buses—Bus0 through Bus3. Figure 5.4 is a combination of one single bit of one register as shown in Figure 5.2, together with the input multiplexor as shown in Figure 5.3. In practice, each bit of each register in Figure 5.2 may be as shown in Figure 5.4. The Bus to which the output of the register is connected is selected by the output enable controls "Output Enable to Bus0" through "Output Enable to Bus3". The input to the register can be from any of the four buses selected by appropriate signals on the P Q select lines, accompanied by a clock signal. In such a system it is possible to output to one or more buses simultaneously. Provided that the electrical characteristics of the register devices are suitable it is also possible to transfer the content of one register out on one bus to a second register and simultaneously to transfer the content of a third register into the first register using a different bus. In the case shown, the same four buses serve as both the output buses and the input buses for the registers.

The control of data transfers in the CPU is vested in the control hardware whose function is to produce the appropriate register output enable signals, the register input select signals and the register clock signals at the correct times. It is the content of the instruction register (the CPU instruction) in combination with the current point of progress through the main CPU timing cycle, the Fetch–Execute cycle (see Chapter 1 section 1.5.1), that determines which data transfer must take place within the CPU. The control hardware, therefore, accepts its inputs from the instruction register and from the machine timing circuits and produces the appropriate enable signals and clocks to allow the correct data transfers to occur at the correct times. Thus the instruction register is a part of the control hardware of the machine, which is, of course, why the instructions control the machine.

Each of the sets of data transfers which specifies how the computer system executes one machine instruction is called a *microprogram*. Each data transfer specified within the microprogram is called a *microinstruction*. The control hardware of most modern computers is *microprogrammed*. That is to say, the control hardware is itself designed to be rather like a CPU system. The microinstructions are contained in a microinstruction register, and the outputs of this register are the signals which control the data transfers in the main CPU. Since there are a large number of control signals in the main CPU, the length of a microinstruction word is usually longer than that of a

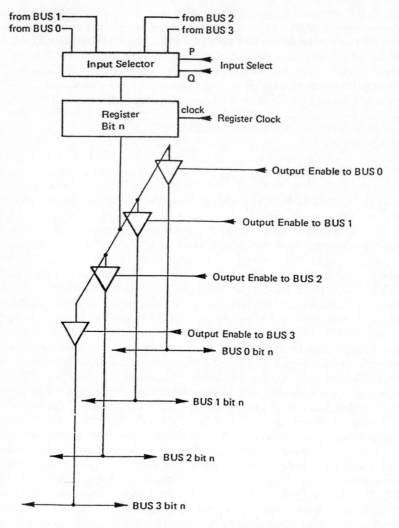

Figure 5.4   *One bit of one register in a 4-bus system*

word in the main CPU. Typically a minicomputer microinstruction is some 50 through 80 bits long. The microinstructions are stored in a special memory system, called the *control memory*, from which they are retrieved sequentially into the microinstruction register. Each microinstruction fetch is followed by a microinstruction execute, which causes a data transfer within the computer system. The control hardware sequences through different microprograms, depending on the instruction in the CPU instruction register. It is these different microinstruction sequences which give the differences in the system actions during the CPU instruction execute portion of the machine cycle.

It is through the use of microprograms (microcode) that the same instruction set can be provided on physically and technologically different computers; for instance, the instruction set originally devised for the IBM System/360 in 1965 is still the set provided on the current IBM 3080, although the systems are fundamentally different in nearly every way. The view that "architecture is the machine as seen by the assembler programmer" is not very helpful to the student of mainframe computers.

The topic of microprogramming is covered in the literature, and the reader is referred to the bibliography for further reading.

Much of the complexity of the hardware in a computer system can be seen to arise from the large number of connections of similar devices into a complete system requiring selection of a few devices under the particular circumstances at any moment, rather than from the aggregation of a large number of different devices into a coherent system.

5.3 THE INPUT/OUTPUT SYSTEM

5.3.1 Introduction

The connection between the peripheral devices and the CPU is called the Input/Output bus—the I/O bus. In some respects it is much the same as the internal CPU data buses. For example, it has a set of data wires to which are connected the inputs and outputs of registers in the peripheral devices. In other respects it is rather different from the CPU data buses. The most important difference is the method by which data transfers are controlled. The registers connected to the CPU data buses are all registers within one small autonomous system, the CPU, whereas the registers connected to the I/O bus are registers in different autonomous systems, the peripheral devices. These systems act quite independently of one another and there is no central control over them. The CPU initiates their actions, but does not exercise any control once their actions have been initiated. If the peripheral action requires the transfer of data between one peripheral and another, the CPU takes no part in that data transfer.

The I/O bus, then, is a bus connecting a number of autonomous systems. Each system requiring use of the bus, including the CPU, must make a request to do so and must observe certain protocols to ensure the correct transmission of the data along the bus. The bus is equipped with its own control system to allocate the use of the bus to devices requesting its use, and to monitor—but not to control—the progress of data transfers along the bus. The I/O buses of different computer systems differ from one another in detail and it is possible to trace an increasing sophistication in computer I/O bus systems over the years.

5.3.2 Principles of Data Transfers in I/O Systems

A simple system consisting of two devices which can communicate with one another is shown in Figure 5.5. There are two devices and a connection between them which contains some data wires and some control wires or

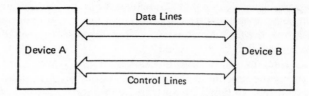

Figure 5.5 *Simple two-device system*

lines. Suppose device A can communicate with device B and suppose further that device A is the master device and B is a slave device, i.e. B responds to all requests made by A. If there are to be two-way data transfers in this simple system at least two control lines are necessary. One line is required to specify the *direction* of the current data transfer. Another is required to specify the *time* during which the data transfer is taking place. This second line is necessary because if A and B are devices which normally perform tasks independently of each other they do not normally act in synchronism, but they must synchronize their activity during the data transfer. The second control line is, therefore, a *synchronizing* line which enables the two devices to synchronize their activity for the period of the data transfer. The logical states of the two control lines for two data transfers, one in each direction, is shown in Figure 5.6.

The data being transferred will be on the data lines throughout the time when the SYNC line is at a logic 1 level. For a data transfer from A to B it is A which asserts (puts the data on) the data lines. For a transfer from B to A it is B which asserts the data lines in response to the SYNC signal. In both cases it is A which asserts the control lines.

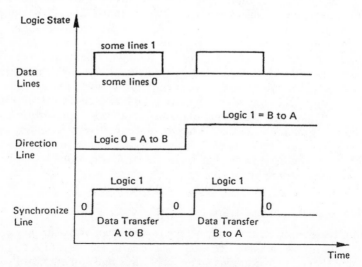

Figure 5.6 *Control line states during data transfers*

If the data lines are driven from tri-state devices like those connected to the CPU data buses the combination of:

(DIRECTION Line = Logic 0) *and* (SYNChronize Line = Logic 1)

causes the tri-state devices in A to turn on and those in B to remain off. The combination of:

(DIRECTION Line = Logic 1) *and* (SYNChronize Line = Logic 1)

cause the tri-state devices in B to turn on and those in A to remain off.

A synchronizing system rather like that just described is used in a number of minicomputer and microprocessor systems. In the microprocessor systems it is common to find that the synchronize signal is one of the clock signals which is used to time the CPU. In these systems the CPU is always in control of the bus, transfers of data between the peripherals being an unusual activity and requiring special hardware. In some of the minicomputers which have been on the market for some time a slightly elaborated version of this system is used in which the CPU is the master device and the SYNC signal is accompanied by a number of other SYNC signals on extra control lines. These extra signals subdivide the period of the main SYNC signal into a number of shorter periods and they are used to simplify the hardware design of the peripheral devices. These methods of synchronizing the activity of two devices are referred to in this text as *single-ended synchronizing*.

5.3.2.1 Handshaking

The single-ended-synchronize control system suffers from a number of disadvantages which can be overcome by a double-ended synchronizing system known as handshaking. The disadvantages of single-ended synchronizing become more marked as computer systems become more complex. One disadvantage of the single-ended method is that the time taken for a data transfer is fixed, so that if a computer system manufacturer develops a faster version of a peripheral device the computer system may not give a corresponding increased work throughput because of the fixed data transfer time. Often the manufacturer produces a faster version of the CPU which should mean an increase in work capability. In a single-ended synchronizing system this may require the installation of a set of new peripherals which can work with the faster synchronizing. To obtain the maximum work throughput in a computer system it is necessary to work every device at its maximum rate, and if the data transfer time between devices is fixed, new faster devices may not be fully used. The solution of scrapping the slow devices and buying new fast devices is often uneconomic, so some way must be found of allowing each device to transfer data at the maximum rate possible for that device. This implies that both devices involved in a data transfer must actively participate in the timing of the data transfer. A system in which that happens is called in this text a double-ended synchronizing system and is achieved using handshaking.

Handshaking is a system where two communicating devices respond to one another to effect synchronization. The system is an extension of the single-ended one and is illustrated in Figures 5.7 and 5.8.

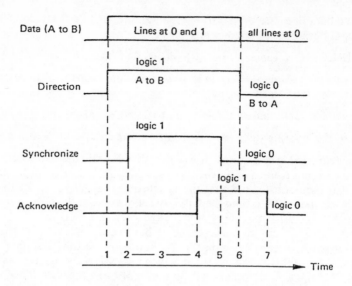

Figure 5.7 *Control sequence, handshaken synchronizing*

Suppose device A is sending data to device B. Device A first asserts the data lines and the direction line (1 on the time axis of Figures 5.7 and 5.8). It then asserts the synchronize line (2 on the time axis). When device A sends the SYNC signal, there is a waiting period (3) until device B responds via another control line as soon as it has received the data being sent to it. This signal is an ACKnowledgment by B that it has done what was requested by A, i.e. it has accepted the data being sent to it. On receipt of this ACKnowledgment A removes its request (5 and 6), i.e. it removes the SYNC signal followed by the data. When the SYNC signal is removed B removes its ACKnowledge (7) and the data transfer is complete. This system allows A to work with fast and slow devices, because the time required for each data transfer is now dependent on the response time of each device.

If the data transfer is from B to A a similar sequence of events occurs. Device A asserts the direction line and sends the SYNC signal. Device A now waits and B responds as quickly as possible by placing the data on the data lines. Only then does B send A the ACK which indicates that the required data is on the line. When A has accepted the data it removes the SYNC signal. In response to the removal of SYNC, the data and ACK are removed by B. The data transfer is now complete.

A system such as this is very secure because the successful completion of a data transfer relies on active participation by both devices. If one of the devices is faulty (or not switched on) the data transfer will not be completed. It is an easy matter to make the system aware of such conditions by building a *time-out* into device A so that if the data transfer is not completed within a predetermined time an alarm is raised in the system. Device A then releases its request for the data transfer. It is interesting to note that although the

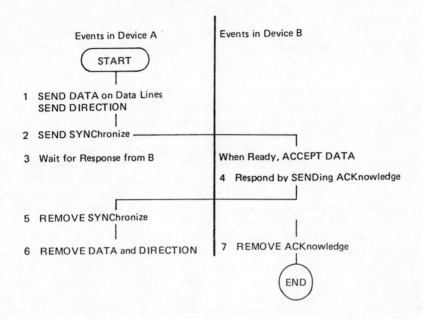

Figure 5.8 *Event diagram version of Figure 5.7*

implementation is different, the technique of handshaking is used in the transfer of data between programs using a data area in memory as a common area, data terminals in a computer network and elsewhere when data is transferred between one system and another.

5.3.2.2 Multiple Device Bussed Systems
The simple two-device system so far discussed will now be extended to a system in which there are a number of devices on a bus. In this system all data and control lines are bussed. There is a bus controller whose functions will be described. The system is that shown in Figure 5.9.

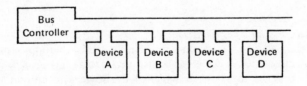

Figure 5.9 *Bus organized multiple device system*

This is the system used in computer input/output arrangements, where the devices A, B, C, D are the peripherals on the I/O bus. In most computers the CPU is considered to occupy a special position on the bus. This is because the system would not exist without the CPU and because the CPU is not connected to the bus in quite the same way as the other devices. None the less the CPU is only another device as far as the bus controller is concerned and if the CPU wishes to use the bus it may have to wait for a short time while another device completes a data transfer.

Data transfers on the bus take place between registers in the various devices connected to the bus, most often between a register in the CPU and a register in a peripheral device. Once a link has been established between two devices on the bus the data transfers occur according to one of the systems previously described, i.e. either by single ended or by double ended synchronizing. Most modern systems use some form of handshaking, at least when the bus is extended outside the CPU cabinet. Some minicomputers have a bus totally inside the CPU box. Circuit cards containing the peripheral controllers plug into the bus in the same box as the CPU. These machines are often provided with bus extender circuit boards as an optional extra (to be paid for!) if it is required to extend the bus outside the CPU box. Most microprocessor I/O buses are not capable of being extended outside the immediate vicinity of the CPU integrated circuit (chip), and most of the available microprocessor systems are provided on a circuit *board* which contains special chips to buffer the I/O bus lines. In general, a buffer is any device which is interposed between two dissimilar systems in order to match the different characteristics of those systems. The two dissimilar systems may then work together. In the particular case under consideration here, the buffers are electronic circuits interposed between the CPU I/O bus lines which must be short, and the long I/O bus lines connected to the peripherals.

There are now a number of problems which arise in addition to those which were encountered when only two devices existed in the system, although it is emphasized that the problems of the two-device system still exist and the solutions to them are the same in two-device and in multiple-device systems. The main additional system problems to be solved are:

1. Addressing of the devices
2. Sending of commands (instructions) to devices
3. Device priorities for use of the bus
4. Methods of implementing the system.

The first two are considered below, and the latter two are dealt with in Chapter 6.

5.3.2.3 Addressing of Bussed Devices

Consider the 4-device system illustrated in Figure 5.9. Suppose the bus is not being used and device A wishes to transfer data to a register in device C. If A puts the data on the data lines, to which all the devices are connected, then all the devices could accept the data. This is not normally desirable, so provision must be made in the system for device A to indicate that it is device C to which the data is being sent. In other words device A must be able to address device C. This can be achieved in a number of ways. The simplest to understand is the addition of more lines to the bus, the address lines. To achieve a data transfer to device C, device A asserts the direction line, the data lines, the address lines—on which it places a binary pattern which uniquely points to device C—and the synchronize line. Only the addressed device responds according to the single ended or handshaking protocol used in the system.

5.3.2.4 Sending Commands to Devices on the Bus

Suppose the CPU is sending data to a magnetic tape unit controller which is controlling four magnetic tape handlers (the devices onto which the reels of tape are mounted). The CPU must send data to the tape unit controller and must also inform the controller what to do with that data. The tape controller has to be told, for example, for which tape handler the data is destined. One method for doing this, used in commercial machines, is to add yet more lines to the I/O bus—the Command or Instruction lines. When a device transfers data to another device it also sends a command indicating what is to be done with that data. The direction line previously discussed is one such line, because it commands the receiving device to accept or to send.

So far, then, each bus is expected to contain lines on which there will be data, control signals, an address, and a command. The number of lines in such a bus is shown in Figure 5.10. The I/O bus of many commercial minicomputer systems is very similar to that of Figure 5.10.

Line Type	Number of Lines
Data Lines	One for each bit of the computer word Typically 16 for minicomputers 8 for microcomputers
Control Lines	Direction — one Synchronize — one Acknowledge — one
Address Lines	Typically 6. Allows for up to 64 devices
Command Lines	Typically 5. Allows 32 commands per device

Figure 5.10 *I/O bus lines – system with memory on a separate bus*

5.3.2.5 Another Solution to Addressing and Commands

There is another commonly used solution to the problems of addressing and commands. The internal organization of the peripheral controllers is designed to resemble that of the CPU. Each controller has an instruction register, some data registers and a status register rather like the condition codes register of the CPU. A command is passed to the peripheral controller by sending a word to the peripheral instruction register. Data is sent to or from the peripheral data registers. In a system like this the command lines of the I/O bus are not required because commands are sent to a register just as data is sent, only the register address is different. This system is very much like the working of a CPU which is sent a command by the transfer of data from the memory to the instruction register in the instruction fetch phase of the machine cycle, followed by the transfer of data which is the result of executing that command. The more recent minicomputers and micro-processors use a system which is rather like this. The system leads to a very flexible total computer system, in which the peripherals are not limited to, say, 32 commands each. The number of registers in any peripheral is not limited and this allows the memory system, which is a large number of registers, to be connected to the I/O bus. Every register in the I/O system has its own unique address rather than every peripheral having its own unique address. The number of address lines in the I/O bus is increased compared with those shown in Figure 5.10 because, although the command lines have been dispensed with, there has been an increase in the number of address lines. The computers which use this I/O system usually use 16 address lines giving a maximum of 64K possible peripheral registers. This number of peripheral registers is never required in practice. Computers in which the memory is connected to the I/O bus usually use the system of peripheral register addressing just described, where the peripheral registers have addresses which are indistinguishable from memory addresses. The loca-tions addressed are physically either within a peripheral controller or physi-cally within the memory system. The maximum size of the memory system is then not 64K locations but some lesser number. In practice the maximum memory size is around 60K in these systems, which is not a significant disadvantage compared with the benefits conferred by the use of this system. From the programmer's point of view, as peripheral registers are not distin-guishable from memory locations, this system allows all the memory refer-ence instructions to be used to manipulate the data in the peripheral registers. This is a powerful asset when writing programs to control the peripherals. There are no special I/O instructions in these systems. Memory reference instructions in such systems would probably be more aptly named if they were called "I/O bus register addressing instructions".

The bus lines required in such a system are shown in Figure 5.11, from which it can be seen that the number of lines in the I/O bus is more than, not less than, that of the system shown in Figure 5.10.

Line Type	Number of Lines
Data Lines	One for each bit of the computer word Typically 16 for minicomputers 8 for microcomputers
Control Lines	Direction — one Synchronize — one Acknowledge — one
Address Lines	Typically 16. Allows addressing of up to 64K locations in memory and in the peripheral controllers.

Figure 5.11   *I/O bus lines – system with memory on I/O bus*

One of the tradeoffs for the increased flexibility of this system is that commands and data are not now sent simultaneously—data must be sent to a peripheral's data registers and finally a command is sent to its instruction register. This does not slow the system appreciably because the time taken to send data along the I/O bus to the peripheral is usually very small compared with the time taken by the peripheral to execute its instruction. With the increasing sophistication of peripherals it is also true that the instructions they obey are becoming ever more complex. This system is, therefore, well suited to the current trends in computer system evolution.

5.3.2.6 Narrow Buses Requiring Multiple Transfers

Some machines take the principle of multiple transfers rather further than the data-followed-by-command system just described. This method is used in some of the more recent microprocessors, such as the Intel 8085 and the Zilog Z8000 because one problem with such devices is the provision of sufficient pins on the package to provide the connections to the I/O bus. These buses are commonly called *multiplexed* buses.

Instead of using separate address lines and data lines the multiplexed bus uses the same set of lines to serve both functions. There are two control lines for synchronizing, the address strobe line and the data strobe line. To output to a peripheral the CPU puts the peripheral address on the data lines and a logic 1 on the address strobe line. Synchronization occurs as before, either single ended or handshaken. At the end of the address transfer the CPU sends the data on the data lines and puts a logic 1 on the data strobe line. Synchronization occurs again. The trade-off, of course, is a reduction of cost due to the narrowness of the bus, versus an increase in the time required to perform a transfer to the peripheral devices. As was pointed out previously, this time penalty may not be severe. The data transfer time on the bus is measured in microseconds whereas most peripherals work on a time scale of milliseconds, so the bus time is a very small percentage of the total peripheral action time. Only systems with a large number of peripherals will in practice be adversely affected.

5.4 PROGRAMMED DATA TRANSFERS ON THE I/O BUS

5.4.1 Introduction

As was stated at the beginning of Chapter 1, data from a peripheral is usually put into the memory before it is used by a program. Data processed by a program is also normally put into the memory before being output to a peripheral. The simplest way in which the data can be transferred between peripheral and memory is along the I/O bus to a CPU register and thence to the memory or vice versa. This route is used a great deal in practice rather than using a direct connection between the memory and the peripherals. The data transfers between the CPU registers and the memory have been discussed in detail previously and will not be discussed here. The data transfers which are now of interest are those which occur between the CPU registers and the peripherals along the I/O bus.

A transfer of data from the CPU to a peripheral occurs when the CPU obeys an *output* instruction. No data is transferred along the I/O bus from a CPU register to a peripheral register under any other circumstances. Similarly data is transferred from a peripheral to the CPU if and only if the CPU is obeying an *input* instruction. Data transfers along the I/O bus cannot take place at the whim of a peripheral if the source or destination of the data is the CPU.

5.4.2 Input/Output Formats

Suppose the I/O bus is the type summarized in Figure 5.10 containing data, command and address lines. The data lines will be connected to the output of a CPU register or to the input of a CPU register depending on whether input or output is required. In a machine with an internal bus oriented architecture this means that the I/O bus data lines must be connected into the bus system in much the same way as an internal register, as shown in Figure 5.12.

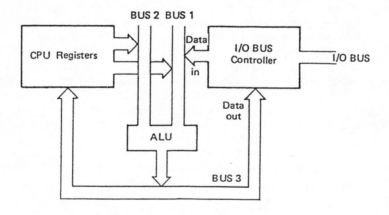

Figure 5.12   *I/O bus data line connections to CPU buses*

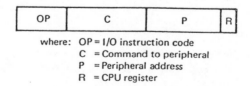

where: OP = I/O instruction code
         C = Command to peripheral
         P = Peripheral address
         R = CPU register

Figure 5.13   *I/O instruction format*

The Command and Address are part of the instruction to the CPU. This instruction is of the type "Send the data in register R to peripheral device P and command it to use it for purpose C". This instruction is an output instruction and has the 4-field format illustrated in Figure 5.13. The first field is the code which indicates an I/O instruction, the second is the peripheral command, the third is the peripheral identification—its address—and the fourth is the CPU register involved in the data transfer. As this instruction resides in the CPU instruction register when it is being obeyed by the CPU, the I/O bus command and address lines are logically connected to the instruction register during the execution of an I/O instruction. The sequence of events which takes place in the CPU during the execution of an I/O instruction is shown in the flowchart of Figure 5.14.

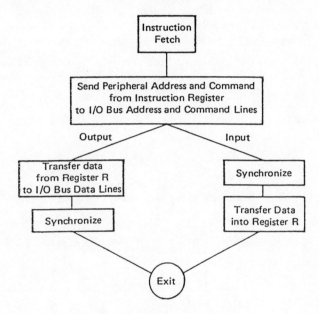

Figure 5.14 *I/O instruction execution*

It will be noticed that the number of command and address lines in the I/O bus is restricted by the number of bits in the instruction register. Buses and I/O instructions of this type are found in a number of minicomputers.

5.4.3 Input/Output Data Transfers

The word peripheral has been used rather loosely in this text so far to describe a device connected to the I/O bus of a computer system. Most peripherals are a mixture of electronic and electromechanical devices linked to form a small system. The electronics is usually called the peripheral controller and it is this controller which is connected to the computer system I/O bus as shown in Figure 5.15. Peripheral controllers range from very small electronic systems such as that controlling a keyboard such as may be used in a VDU terminal to complex systems such as that required to control, say, eight magnetic tape handlers. However because all controllers have to

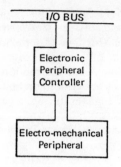

Figure 5.15 *Connection of a peripheral to the I/O bus*

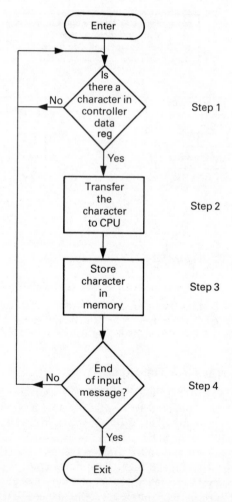

Figure 5.16 *Flowchart of keyboard input program*

communicate with the same CPU over the same I/O bus they have certain features in common and so do the programs which control the *CPU-peripheral* communications. The following discussion is confined to a simple device—a keyboard—used as an example and emphasizes only those features of the system which are applicable to I/O communications in general.

Suppose a program is to be written to enable the computer to transfer the data from a keyboard into the memory. A flowchart for such a program is shown in Figure 5.16. To understand how to convert this flowchart into a program of computer instructions requires a slightly closer look at the structure and functions of the peripheral controller.

STEP 1 of the flowchart requires that the program waits for a character from the keyboard to appear in the keyboard controller data register. The character is placed in this controller data register automatically when a keyboard key is pressed. The program must determine when a character has been transferred to the controller data register. The system must therefore allow the keyboard to send *status* information to the CPU so that the program running in the CPU can determine what is happening within the peripheral. This status information is held in a special purpose register in the peripheral controller—the Status Register. Once the status information has been transferred to a CPU register, the tests can be carried out by the standard shift, mask and conditional jump instructions discussed in Chapter 2.

The flowchart of Figure 5.16 can be converted into a program as follows, using I/O instructions with the format shown in Figure 5.13 and assuming that the keyboard controller contains a status register and a data register.

Step 1. This is an input instruction in which the C field is the code for "Put the Status Register Content on the I/O bus Data Lines and synchronize with the CPU", P is the keyboard address and R is the address of the CPU register into which the peripheral status data will be transferred. This instruction is followed by a set of instructions to determine the content of register R, branching back to repeat Step 1 if the controller has not yet read the character or continuing on to Step 2.

Step 2. This is a single input instruction in which the C field is the code for "Put the Content of the Data Register on to the I/O bus Data Lines and synchronize with the CPU", P is the keyboard address and R is the address of the CPU register into which the data will be transferred.

Step 3. This is a single memory reference instruction.

Step 4. This is a set of instructions to test whether the character just read is a special end-of-message character, such as ETX or EOT (see Figure 3.5).

Some computer systems allow simple tests, such as the keyboard status test in Step 2 of the program above, to be carried out by a single input instruction. For example, some instruction sets include an instruction of the type "Skip the next instruction if the peripheral whose address is in the address field of this instruction, is busy". This is an input instruction whose execution requires the keyboard controller to input its status for interpretation by hardware instead of by software. This is usually achieved by including another line in the I/O bus—the SKIP LINE. In this case the command field of the input instruction means "put the skip line at logic one if you are busy or at logic zero if you are not busy". The peripheral controller responds accordingly and the CPU hardware increments the content of the Program Counter if the skip line is at logic one. Only simple tests are conducted in this way. Complex tests must be carried out by a program which examines the status register as described above.

In computer systems in which the memory is attached to the I/O bus all data transfers on the I/O bus are initiated by memory reference instructions. The hardware is designed to determine whether the data transfer is to the memory system or to a peripheral register. Translating the flowchart of Figure 5.16 into a program of CPU instructions in systems such as these is a matter of programming exactly as if the peripheral registers were locations in the memory system. Once the function of the peripheral registers is specified, programming of the peripherals is carried out using memory reference instructions to perform data transfers between the CPU registers and the peripheral registers. The input instructions are memory reference instructions which transfer data from memory to a CPU register. Output instructions are memory reference instructions which transfer data from a CPU register to memory. The fact that these systems require no special I/O instructions is one of their advantages.

5.5 SERIAL COMMUNICATIONS

5.5.1 Characteristics and Working Description

Probably the most common form of communications encountered by the computer user are those between the user's terminal, the keyboard/VDU or hardcopy device, and the computer. These communications are normally achieved over an *asynchronous serial communications line* connected to the

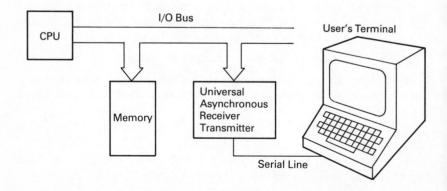

Figure 5.17   *Connection of user's terminal to computer*

computer I/O bus via a device known as a UART—Universal Asynchronous Receiver Transmitter. Figure 5.17 shows the terminal communications system. The UART is a peripheral device connected to the I/O bus.

The serial line consists of two wires along which characters are transmitted from the computer to the terminal and two wires along which the characters are transmitted in the opposite direction, from the terminal to the computer. Normally the earthed wire of each pair is not taken separately, so that there are three wires, transmit (from UART), receive (into UART) and the common earth wire.

Transmission of data between the computer and the terminal occurs in two stages. Firstly the computer transmits an 8-bit character along the I/O bus to a transmit data register in the UART. The UART, which controls the serial line then automatically transmits the 8-bit character one bit at a time to the terminal. Transmission one bit at a time is called *serial transmission* or data as compared to the parallel transmission of the 8 bits of the character on the I/O bus. The UART is, therefore, mainly a parallel to serial converter when transmitting data to the terminal.

A program which outputs a character to the terminal sends the 8-bit ASCII character to the UART transmitter data register using a suitable OUTPUT instruction. The electronics in the UART transmit the 8 bits to the VDU, one bit at a time, along the serial line connecting the VDU to the UART. In the reverse direction, the terminal transmits an 8-bit ASCII character one bit at a time to the UART, which collects the 8 bits into a single register, the receiver data register. When the receiver data register is filled, i.e. the ASCII character has been received by the UART, the program waiting for the character reads the character from the UART data register into a CPU register, using a suitable INPUT instruction.

In practice, the terminal device also contains a UART to control its end of the communication line. The connection is as shown in Figure 5.18. Notice that the transmit (Tx) wire from one device is the receive (Rx) wire for the other.

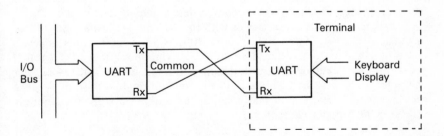

Figure 5.18   *Complete 3-wire serial connection*

The communications along the serial line are not handshaken in the way that communications on the I/O bus are handshaken. Synchronization of communications is achieved character-by-character not bit-by-bit even though the communication is bit-by-bit. Synchronization is achieved by the

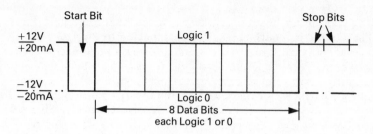

Figure 5.19 *Serial transmission conventions*

presence of *start* and *stop bits* which are transmitted before and after the 8-bit character. Figure 5.19 shows the voltage difference between the common wire (0volts) and the Tx/Rx wire during the transmission of a character.

When there are no characters being transmitted, the line is, to use communications jargon, *marking* (at logic 1 level) which is the idle state. When a character is to be transmitted the line is put to the logic 0 state for 1 bit-time. This period is called a *start* bit. When the UART receive circuits sense the start bit they prepare to receive the next 8 bits which are the data bits. At the end of the 8th data bit, the line returns to the idle (marking) state for a least one bit-period. This period is called a *stop* bit. If the line does not return to the marking state for this single bit period, the system detects an error and signals accordingly, normally by setting an error bit in the UART status register.

The transmission of an 8-bit ASCII character thus requires the transmission of at least 10 bits.

1. a *start* bit (logic 0)
2. 8 *data* bits (logic 1 or logic 0)
3. a *stop* bit (logic 1)

The bit rate measured in bits per second is determined locally by the UART. The *baud rate*, usually synonymous with the bit rate, is normally set to one of: 110, 150, 300, 600, 1200, 2400, 4800, 9600, 19200 bauds and is a constant of the particular line. Usually the maximum number of characters per second which can be transmitted is one tenth of the baud rate (10 bits per character). The case of 110 baud lines is conventionally different because the 110 baud lines are normally set up to require 2 stop bits, thereby requiring 11 bits per character.

5.5.2 Terminal Operating Modes

A terminal really consists of two independent devices. The keyboard is used to send information to the computer and is an input device. The VDU screen or the terminal printer is an output device. These devices are connected to the two halves of the terminal UART as shown in Figure 5.20.

Notice that there is no electrical connection between the keyboard and the screen/printer. In most situations, when a key is pressed on the keyboard the

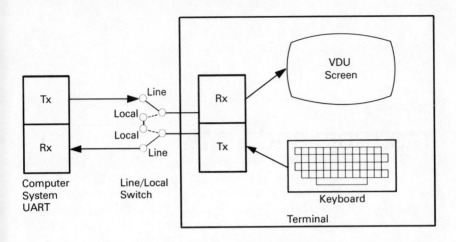

Figure 5.20 *Terminal organization*

terminal UART transmit section sends it to the CPU UART receiver. The computer program which receives the character by reading the CPU UART receiver data register into the CPU data register then outputs that character to the transmit data register of the computer UART. The character is transmitted back to the terminal UART receive section, which causes it to be displayed on the screen. Thus the computer program *echoes* the character which it receives.

The independence of the keyboard and the display device (the screen or printer) in the terminal, allows simultaneous transmission to take place in both directions. This arrangement is called a *full duplex* line and is the normal terminal operating mode.

Most terminals are fitted with a *line/local* switch. When connected to the *line*, the terminal is connected to the computer via a full duplex line as described above. When in *local* mode, the receive and transmit lines to the computer are disconnected, and the output of the terminal UART transmitter is connected directly to the input of the terminal UART receiver. Hence no information passes between the computer and the terminal, but the pressing of a key on the keyboard causes the character to be transmitted locally to the display device.

CHAPTER 6

Interrupts and DMA

6.1 INTRODUCTION

In a computer system in which input/output is programmed, as described in Chapter 5, it is the program running in the CPU which determines when data transfers occur between peripherals and the CPU. To achieve control of the system, the CPU must run a program which scans all the peripherals of the system, examining the status register of each peripheral to determine whether there is any activity within the device. In practice this is entirely the wrong way to design a system for efficient operation. The majority of peripheral devices are autonomous devices. Events which are not immediately under the control of the CPU happen within the device and the CPU is then required to take some action. If the CPU is designed so that it responds to a peripheral device only when some event occurs within the peripheral device, two major system advantages are realized. Firstly, the CPU does not regularly have to run a program scanning the peripherals to examine their status. The CPU can then be used to run other programs which enable it to cope with other work. Hence the CPU can be used more efficiently by spending its time on useful work rather than wasting time scanning peripheral devices. Secondly, if the CPU can be made to react quickly to an event in a peripheral device, it can effect some measure of *real time control* over the peripheral.

Consider first the efficient utilization of the CPU. A computer system run on the lines discussed in previous chapters would be very inefficient. That is to say, the amount of work it could cope with would be small compared with the amount it could potentially get through. That is because most peripheral subsystems operate very slowly compared with the rate at which the CPU operates. While data is being read into the machine the CPU spends most of its time in a nonproductive program loop (Step 1 of Figure 5.16)—testing to see if the peripheral is ready to input another data word. If it is assumed that the memory cycle time is one microsecond the program of Figure 5.16 will take probably about 20 microseconds to execute from the time it emerges from the loop of Step 1 to the time at which it reenters that loop. In an interrupt driven system, the CPU will not spend any time in a program loop testing the peripheral status. When the peripheral is ready to input a character the CPU will interrupt whatever it is doing to execute steps 2 and 3 of Figure 5.16. The CPU will then continue with the interrupted program. Thus, provided that there is useful work to do, the CPU will execute useful work programs whilst waiting for input from a peripheral rather than executing a time-wasting loop.

A *real time system* is one which responds to external events on a timescale comparable to that in which the events occur. Thus a computer system controlling a serial printer working at 200 characters per second, may be required to respond to events in the printer at a rate of 200 responses per second. The same system controlling the volume of water in a large reservoir may be required to respond to level changes within a few minutes, since in that period of time the change in level of the water will be very small. The required response time of a real time computing system is therefore determined by the external system, not by the computing system. Interrupts are fundamental to the operation of a real time system because they enable the CPU to suspend the program which it is currently executing and to jump rapidly to a program designed to respond to events in the peripheral device.

An interrupt driven system is fundamentally different from a noninterrupt driven system. In the latter the software determines the order in which the CPU responds to events in the peripheral devices. In an interrupt driven system, events in the peripheral devices determine the order in which the CPU runs the peripheral controlling software modules. Such a system can be considered to consist of a number of antonomous devices operating asynchronously, that is each device has its own time reference which is independent of the time reference of the other devices. At certain times determined by events within a peripheral subsystem, the peripheral requests that the CPU run the program which services that peripheral. This program is called the peripheral *service routine*. Thus, when the software which controls the computer system is written it is impossible to predict the order in which that software will be run. Software for such systems must be written as selfcontained modules to cope with events which occur within the hardware peripheral subsystems, and the whole system requires organizing in such a way that the modules do not interfere with one another.

All this does not violate the principle established in earlier chapters, that the CPU and its software controls the whole system. Although the devices in an interrupt driven system are asynchronous, they cooperate to perform the functions for which the complete system is designed. It is the CPU and its software which provide the coordinating function. Thus the CPU initiates some action by a peripheral device and then leaves the peripheral to communicate back to the CPU when that action is completed. In the case of the printer mentioned above the CPU obeys an output instruction to initiate the printing of a character. The CPU then continues with the running of other programs until the printer communicates back to signal that the character has been printed. At the time when the printer controller wishes to communicate with the CPU the latter will be busy running a program which has nothing to do with the printer, so if the CPU is to attend to the printer it must interrupt the program which is currently running. In a computer system designed to operate in this way, and that includes all modern computers, the CPU would spend a few microseconds attending to the printer and then it would continue with the program which was interrupted. Therefore, apart from the time overhead involved in actually changing from the running program to the printer program, the CPU is being usefully employed 100 percent of its time. Further, the response of the CPU, being only a few microseconds, is very fast on the timescale of the printer. Control of the printer thus occurs in real time and if the system is properly designed the printer movement will be always at maximum speed. Figure 6.1 shows a simplified flowchart of the printer service routine which will be executed 200 times per second whilst the printer is printing. The CPU is thus exercising supervisory control of the printer by determining what shall be printed whilst simultaneously continuing with other work.

Suppose the CPU is running a program, which we will refer to as P1, when it receives a request from a peripheral to interrupt the program to attend to the peripheral. This involves the CPU in switching to another program, say P2, which is the program written to control that peripheral. The program P2 is the peripheral service routine. For a printer this service routine could be the program flowchart in Figure 6.1. After executing the service routine the CPU must return to program P1. For the interrupt system to be efficient

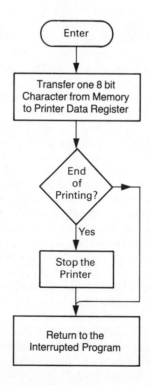

Figure 6.1 *Simple printer service routine*

there must be a mechanism for rapid and error free switching from P1 to P2 and back again. To devise such a system is not an entirely straightforward task, and has repercussions throughout the computer system.

It is impractical to require programmers to insert "Attend to any peripheral device requiring attention" instructions throughout their programs just in case some peripheral device should require attention when the program is running, and it would extend the execution time and space in memory of all programs written. The interrupt mechanism, therefore, must be entirely automatic and handled by the hardware. The hardware mechanism may be designed to obtain assistance from special software in the system to ensure that the interrupt occurs without errors. The problem of switching from program P1 to program P2 and back is much the same problem as was encountered in Chapter 2 with the subroutine entry and return. The switch into the routine must now be performed automatically by the hardware, not as a result of the CPU obeying a subroutine entry instruction but as a result of its receiving a signal from a peripheral device. To the hardware the origin of the request is of little importance, so it is not very difficult for the hardware designer to incorporate this extra feature although the further requirements discussed later on in this chapter make the complete system design task far from trivial. Although the hardware causes the entry without any help from the software the return to the interrupted program is performed by the execution of a return instruction similar to the return from subroutine instruction.

6.2 THE CPU STATE

This is a convenient point at which to introduce the idea of the state of the CPU which is defined at any point in time by:

    1. the contents of all the registers in the CPU
and 2. the state of all the control signals in the hardware.

After a program has been interrupted and the device service routine has been executed the CPU must return to exactly the same state that it was in when the interrupt occurred. Only if this happens will the interrupted program be able to resume exactly as if nothing had happened.

The contents of all the registers can be saved by storing them in a memory system, and it is convenient to reserve part of the computer system memory for this purpose. No program is allowed to use this part of the memory, so to all intents it does not exist within the computer system as the normal program sees that system. The state of the machine control signals cannot be saved, however, because the action of saving them would itself destroy them. Fortunately these signals return to a defined state at the end of the execution of every instruction, at the time when the machine cycle is between the end of an instruction execution and at the beginning of the next instruction fetch. It is therefore at this time that the CPU recognizes that an interrupt is required. The fact that the peripheral has to wait for the completion of the current instruction before its request for an interupt is acknowledged implies that the communications between the CPU and the peripheral relating to interrupt requests must be handshaken and cannot be of the single ended synchronizing type.

6.3 THE CPU REACTION TO INTERRUPTS

A closer examination of the computer system's reactions to an interrupt request will give an insight into the actions which must be undertaken by the hardware and those which may optionally be performed by hardware or software. First consider a computer system with only one peripheral which, although an unreal situation, will lead to an understanding of the basic principles involved. The complications which arise when there are more peripherals in the system will be considered later in this chapter. Figure 6.1 is a flowchart of the CPU main timing cycle, also called the instruction cycle. It is an elaboration of Figure 1.10 which showed that the CPU hardware may stop at the end of the execution of an instruction.

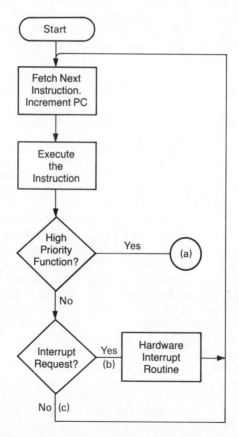

Figure 6.2   *CPU main timing cycle (ref Fig 1.10)*

Address	Memory Content
0	N
1	S
	Program P
N−1 N	
S	Printer Service Routine

Figure 6.3 *Interrupt program memory map*

In practice, very few CPUs are designed to be stopped. Even if there is no useful work for the CPU to execute, the CPU program normally loops until a peripheral device needs attention. The Halt or Wait instruction available in some computer systems is normally just a Halt or Wait until an interrupt request is received. It can be seen from Figure 6.2 that at the end of execution of an instruction, the CPU hardware has a number of possible courses of action. These are shown as:

(a) Execute higher priority functions than an interrupt request
(b) Attend to interrupt request
(c) Execute the next instruction

Actions in category (a) will be discussed later. The actions in category (b) are those currently under examination. These actions are shown in the diagram as the hardware interrupt routine and, as may be expected, they vary in detail from one computer system to another. However, the objectives of this hardware activity do not vary considerably from one machine to another. The following paragraphs are, therefore, a discussion of the objectives and some pointers as to how these objectives may be achieved.

The main objective of the hardware interrupt routine is to cause a program switch from the program currently running to the program which services the peripheral device.

Suppose a program P, see Figure 6.3, is running and that the peripheral device requests an interrupt when the CPU is obeying the instruction in location N−1. At this stage the program counter contains the number N which is the address of the next instruction to be executed in program P. At the completion of the current instruction the hardware interrupt routine must cause a jump to location S, the start of the interrupt service routine. To achieve this jump, the number S is placed in the program counter and used as the address for the next instruction fetch. As this would destroy the number N currently in the program counter, the system must save the content of the program counter as the return address or link address. This is much the same as the obeying of a subroutine entry instruction. The action taken by the hardware at the end of the instruction which is being obeyed when the interrupt request is made is, therefore, to store the content of the program counter in the memory system, to load the program counter with the number S and then to start an instruction fetch. All modern computers store the content of the program counter on the stack, for that is a part of memory which will not be accessed by the program which starts at location S (provided that program is bug free!).

The saving of the program counter content on the stack is the minimum action which the hardware must take. It is necessary for the system to preserve the state of the CPU across the execution of the peripheral service routine, so that the interrupted program may be continued without corruption. Preservation of the CPU state may be achieved by saving the state, executing the service routine, then restoring the CPU to its previous state. The time taken to save the CPU state and to restore it after the peripheral service is a time overhead during which the CPU is "housekeeping" rather than performing useful work. Furthermore, the time spent in saving the CPU state is time during which the peripheral device is kept waiting for the response it requires from the CPU. It is, therefore, very important to minimize the time required to save and restore the CPU state. In some computer systems, it is the responsibility of the programmer to save the content of any CPU register before using the register in the service routine. The programmer is also responsible for restoring the content of that register at the end of the service routine. In other computer systems, the hardware interrupt routine pushes onto the stack not only the content of the program counter, but also the content of all the other CPU registers as well. When saving and restoring of register content is the programmer's responsibility, the service routines are usually of the form:

```
PUSH      R1          ;      save contents of working
PUSH      R2          ;      registers R1,R2,R3 on the stack
PUSH      R3          ;
. . . . .
Service Routine instructions
. . . . .
POP       R3          ;      restore contents of working
POP       R2          ;      registers R1,R2,R3 from the stack
POP       R1
RET                   ;      return to interrupted program
```

In general terms the hardware must store the contents of the program counter and any other nonaddressable registers in the CPU, which often includes the Condition Codes Register or the CPU Flags and Status Register (see Chapter 7). Either hardware or software may be used to save the contents of the addressable registers of the CPU. Generally the software method is more flexible, but it may be slower in a machine with only a few addressable registers because an instruction fetch is required for each Save instruction. In machines with a large number of addressable registers the software method is more flexible and usually quicker because only a badly written service routine requires the use of a large number of registers.

6.4 INTERRUPT LINES IN THE I/O BUS

If the CPU is interruptable there must be an Interrupt Request line in the I/O bus. A peripheral may use this line to signal to the CPU to indicate that the CPU should interrupt its current program to attend to that peripheral. There is also an Interrupt Acknowledge line in the I/O bus, used by the CPU to indicate to the peripheral that the interrupt request has been recognized. These are the two lines used for handshaking. Usually the peripheral ceases to request an interrupt when it receives the acknowledge, and the CPU hardware causes the device service routine to run using one of the methods described elsewhere in this chapter. The interrupt request line and interrupt acknowledge line are the two basic lines required in the I/O bus of any computer system which allows interrupts. Other I/O bus lines will be described in the ensuing text as the need for them becomes apparent.

6.5 INTERRUPTS IN A MULTIPLE PERIPHERAL ENVIRONMENT

The interrupt mechanism will now be extended to allow for more than one peripheral device in the I/O system. The principles of the system reactions are just the same as described above, but there are added complications because the system must decide which device is requesting an interrupt and then find the correct service routine for that device. The system must also resolve the problem of which device to service if more than one device requests an interrupt at a given time.

6.5.1 Interrupting Device Recognition

First the problem of which device is requesting an interrupt, assuming that only one device is doing so. There are basically two approaches to the solution of this problem. One is to use special software and the other is to use special hardware. In computers designed, say, at the middle to end of the 1960s when hardware was relatively expensive, a software solution was generally favored. More recent designs have shown a tendency to use special hardware to perform at least some of the functions required, because hardware costs are decreasing while software costs are increasing. It is also generally true that software solutions are slower in execution than hardware solutions. Speed is important to reduce the time overhead involved, which increases the efficiency of the system and decreases the response time of the CPU.

6.5.2 Device Recognition by Software

It is assumed that the interrupt request bus line is a single line attached to all devices just like any other bus line. When a device requests an interrupt by signalling on this line, the hardware causes entry to a service routine using one of the methods described earlier, in section 6.3. In the earlier discussion the service routine was assumed to be the device service routine, but in a multiple peripheral system the routine is an *interrupt service routine*. This is a program whose function is to identify the interrupting device and cause a jump to its service routine. This is the purely software solution to the recognition problem. The interrupt service routine is usually a *device polling* program, which is a program to interrogate each device in turn to find out if it is requesting an interrupt. The interrogation can be carried out either by using skip instructions or by reading the content of the status register of each device, the device status, into a CPU register and then examining the interrupt request bit of that status.

A system in which there are skip instructions normally uses a polling routine containing two instructions per device polled. The first instruction is skip the next instructions if the device is not requesting an interrupt. The second instructions is an unconditional jump to the device interrupt service routine:

```
SKN    001        ;skip if device 001 not interrupting
JP     SRV001     ;jump to device 1 service routine
SKN    002        ;same for device 2
JP     . . . . .
```

The instructions for the saving of the register contents are assumed to be in the device service routines. The skip line, see Chapter 5 section 5.4.5, in the I/O bus is the hardware contribution to this system of device recognition. It saves the time involved in transferring the status to a CPU register, testing a bit in the CPU register and jumping if the status bit is set. Such a program may be very time consuming. A skip instruction is, of course, an input instruction with a command code indicating that the device shall put the skip line to logic 1 if the device is requesting an interrupt.

In computer systems in which the peripherals are memory mapped and in which there are no separate I/O instructions it is necessary for the status register of each device to be interrogated. The status register of the peripheral controller will contain one bit which is, say, 1 if the peripheral is requesting an interrupt and 0 if the peripheral is not requesting an interrupt. If the CPU instruction set contains a bit test instruction (as in the Z80, Z8000, LSI–11) then the device polling routine tests the interrupt bit of the device status registers and jumps if the bit is set to the device service routine. This requires two instructions per device:

```
BIT    P,STS001   ;test interrupt bit, device 001
JNZ    SRV001     ;jump to service routine if set
BIT    P,STS002   ;same for device 002
JNZ    . . .
```

Often, since the interrupt request is so important, the interrupt request bit is the most significant bit of the device status register. In computers such as the Motorola 6800, in which there is no bit test instruction which tests a single bit of a memory location, loading a general purpose register with the content of the status register allows the next instruction to cause a jump if the content of the general purpose register appears to be a negative number, i.e. if the interrupt request bit was set:

```
LDA    A,STS001    ;status to register A
BMI    SRV001      ;jump to device 1 service if negative
LDA    A,STS002    ;same for device 2
BMI    . . .
```

Notice that in all the above cases, the polling takes two instructions per device.

6.5.3 Device Recognition by Hardware

Device recognition by hardware occurs in systems using a *vectored interrupt* system. This means that a peripheral controller requesting an interrupt is designed so that when the CPU acknowledges the interrupt request the peripheral controller puts on to some special bus lines a vector (a binary pattern). This enables the CPU to find the peripheral device service routine very quickly.

One method of using the device vector is illustrated in Figure 6.4. For each peripheral device in the system there exists one reserved memory location which contains the start address of the peripheral service routine. Such a set of addresses is often called a *jump table*. The peripheral device vector is used to generate a memory address which is the address of a location in the jump table. The content of that location is loaded into the program counter. The next instruction to be fetched is, therefore, the first instruction in the

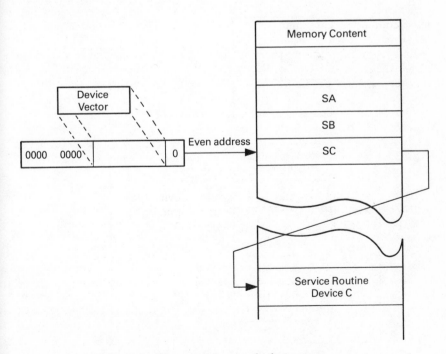

Figure 6.4 *Illustrating the use of a device vector*

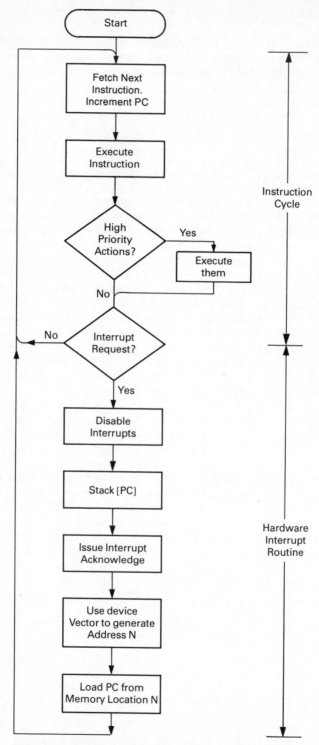

Figure 6.5 *Machine cycle with hardware interrupt routine*

peripheral device service routine. Hence the hardware interrupt routine (see Figure 6.2) activated at the end of the instruction cycle performs the following functions, as shown in Figure 6.5.

(a) Disable interrupts (see section 6.5.4.6)
(b) Stack the content of the PC
(c) Issue interrupt acknowledge signal to the peripheral devices
(d) Use the vector to generate a memory address N
(e) Load the PC from memory location N

The hardware then starts an instruction fetch, the instruction being the first in the peripheral device service routine. This action takes place very rapidly, requiring a memory access to stack the PC, a short delay for issuing the interrupt acknowledge and receiving the device vector, plus a second memory access to load the PC from memory location N. Current 16-bit memory systems in common use require only some 0.1–1.0 microseconds for this double access. Such a system provides much faster access to the device service routine than does a software polled system. The system overhead in accessing the device service routine is in this case just the time taken to execute the hardware interrupt routine, whereas in the polled system it includes the execution of the instructions of the polling routine. The hardware vectored system has the further advantage that the time required to access the peripheral service routine is independent of the number of peripheral devices in the system. In the software polled system, the average time required to access a peripheral device service routine is very nearly proportional to the number of devices in the system.

There are many variations of the vectoring technique described above, but in principle the system just described is very widespread. The most common variation is probably the use of two or more consecutive memory locations for each peripheral device. The first location contains the address of the service routine as described above, and the second location contains the content of the processor condition codes register to be used on starting the service routine. More than two locations may be required to contain the necessary information. For example, a 16-bit machine with 32-bit addressing requires two locations for the service routine address.

The device vector lines in the I/O bus may be a set of lines used only for that purpose, in which case there will probably be around six lines allowing for up to 64 devices. More often they are the data or address lines of the I/O bus, in which case the vector may be up to 16 bits long.

6.5.4 Device Priorities

6.5.4.1 Simultaneous Interrupt Requests
In a system containing more than one peripheral device (all real systems) it is conceivable that two or more devices may request an interrupt while the CPU is executing one instruction. At the end of the execution of that instruction the CPU hardware has two interrupt requests to deal with. Such requests are called simultaneous requests even though they may not have occurred at exactly the same time. They are simultaneous in that they are

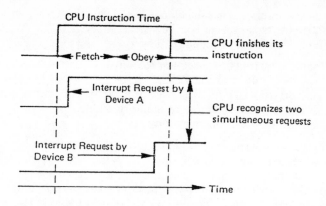

Figure 6.6   *Extreme case of simultaneous interrupts*

present together when the CPU is in a state to recognize an interrupt request. This is illustrated in Figure 6.6. The system must be able to resolve the problem of which device to service and which device to keep waiting, i.e. some *device priorities* must be established.

6.5.4.2 *Priority Allocation by Software*

The software device recognition system, the device polling method described earlier, has an inherent priority assignment because the devices are polled in sequence. This sequence confers a priority on the devices polled earlier over those polled later. It is interesting to note that the device which first requests an interrupt may not be the one which is serviced first. Suppose a low priority device raises an interrupt request and the machine switches to the device polling routine. Now suppose that a high priority device raises an interrupt request. The high priority device is polled first, is found to be requesting an interrupt, and is therefore serviced. The device which first requested an interrupt will be serviced after the high priority device service routine has been completed.

The great advantage of software allocation of priorities is that the priorities are under the control of the programmer and may therefore be changed dynamically to suit the prevailing conditions in the computer system. A device with a very high priority may be polled more than once, if necessary, during the polling routine.

6.5.4.3 *Priority Allocation by Hardware*

There are two important methods for allocating priorities by hardware. The first method is by *daisy chaining* the interrupt acknowledge line from the CPU, as shown in Figure 6.7.

When the CPU issues an interrupt acknowledge, this is sent only to the highest priority device, device A in Figure 6.7. If this device is not requesting an interrupt it passes on the acknowledge to the next device in the chain which reacts similarly. Only if a device is requesting an interrupt does it

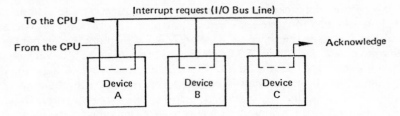

Figure 6.7 *Daisy chained interrupt acknowledge*

intercept the acknowledge and prevent its transmission further down the daisy chain. An interrupting device both intercepts the acknowledge and responds according to the system rules, for example by putting its interrupt vector on to the bus data lines.

The second hardware method is the use of multiple interrupt request lines. If each device is connected to the CPU by its own individual interrupt request line, a simple hardware circuit can be used to ensure that only the highest priority request is passed to the CPU. The fact that each request now comes over an individual wire also means that device recognition is inherent in the system, unlike the daisy chain system, so that device recognition vectors are not necessary.

In practice, computer systems often use a combination of the two hardware techniques, as shown in Figure 6.8. Such systems use, say, eight or sixteen interrupt request/acknowledge line pairs.

The interrupt request lines are allocated a priority level by a special hardware circuit and the interrupt acknowledge line corresponding to each priority level is daisy chained through the peripherals on that level. This is usually called a *multilevel interrupt* system. The daisy chaining at each level means that every device connected to the system has a unique priority within the system. As there is, in general, more than one device at each priority level, vectoring is used to switch the CPU into the peripheral service routine. For example, most microprocessor CPU chips contain only a single Interrupt

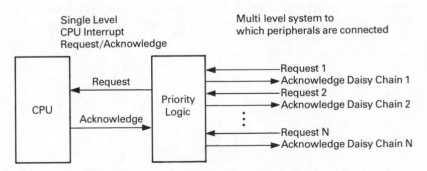

Figure 6.8 *Multilevel system derived from single level*

Request/Interrupt Acknowledge line pair. Consequently these systems are single level interrupt systems. However, many microcomputer systems are sold not just as a microprocessor, but as a microcomputer containing a microprocessor and other circuits all on a printed circuit board. Such board level systems may contain multilevel interrupt systems. The logic for the multilevel interrupt handling is contained on the microcomputer board, external to the microprocessor chip. Interrupt prioritizing chips are available for this purpose from a number of semiconductor manufacturers. Figure 6.8 shows the derivation of such a system. The CPU interrupt request line becomes active should any of the peripheral interrupt requests become active. The priority logic transmits the CPU interrupt acknowledge signal only to the acknowledge line for the highest priority level on which an interrupt request is being received from peripheral device. The highest priority device requesting an interrupt at that level responds according to the system rules, probably by asserting its vector on the I/O bus data or address lines.

6.5.4.4 Priority Allocation by Software and Hardware
The biggest disadvantage of hardware priority systems is that once priorities are allocated, by wiring, they are virtually fixed. In an attempt to obtain the flexibility of the software systems and the speed of the hardware systems a number of combined systems have been developed. Basically these systems use two registers, an *interrupt register* and an *interrupt mask register*, as shown in Figure 6.9.

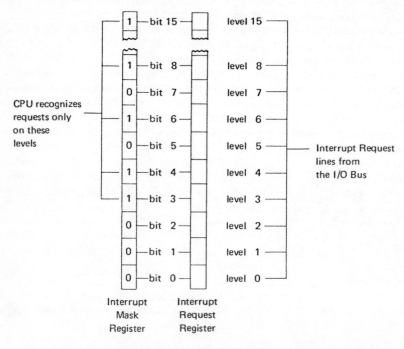

Figure 6.9 *Multilevel interrupt system*

The hardware system external to the CPU is the same as the multilevel interrupt hardware described above. The interrupt request lines terminate in the interrupt register. An interrupt request by any device connected to that level causes the appropriate bit in the interrupt register to set to a 1.

The interrupt mask register is a register which is addressable so that its content may be changed by an instruction in the CPU program. The corresponding bits of the two registers are logically ANDed. Hence only if there is a 1 in the appropriate bit of the mask register can an interrupt request be recognized by the CPU. At any time the program can disable interrupt requests at any level by writing a zero to the appropriate bit in the interrupt mask register. In Figure 6.9, levels 0, 1, 2, 5 and 7 are shown disabled. By disabling, say, level N and enabling level N–1, interrupts on level N–1 may be given priority over those on level N. Software is thus used to set up the hardware which controls the priorities. The use of software to set up hardware which controls a system is a growing trend in modern systems, in which the complexity of hardware is increasing rapidly.

In a multilevel system the devices on each priority level may be polled by software. This removes the need from the peripheral to generate a vector. The polling routine for a particular level may be accessed by hardware. The hardware priority circuits generate a vector, probably 4 bits long in a 16-level system. This vector is the number of the highest priority level at which there exists an interrupt request. The vector is used by the hardware to access the polling routine, the interrupt service routine, for that priority level. There are usually only a few peripherals on each level in a multilevel system. The polling routine for each level is, therefore, executed in a short time compared with the time taken to poll all the peripherals. This system is faster than the software system described earlier in this chapter, but slower than the vectored hardware system.

6.5.4.5 Nesting Interrupts

For some peripherals in a computer system there may exist a certain critical time within which an interrupt request must be answered to prevent a system error. For example, a disk system transferring a word at a time into the memory via the CPU may be able to transfer one word every 20 microseconds. It is essential, therefore, that the disk be serviced at least every 20 microseconds during the transfer of information from disk to memory. Suppose a much slower device, such as a keyboard, requests and obtains an interrupt service. Suppose further that just after the CPU starts to run the keyboard service routine the disk requests an interrupt. If the keyboard service routine can be finished within 20 microseconds there is no problem, but if it cannot then it is necessary to allow the disk to interrupt the servicing of the keyboard. This causes no difficulty with the keyboard, which stops between characters for a long period. Further there is nothing unusual in this as far as the interrupt system is concerned, because the CPU is running a program, which happens to be a device service routine (but the CPU does not know that), and a request has been made by the disk controller for an interrupt. If the request is allowed, all the systems described so far for handling interrupts will allow a return to be made, at the end of the disk service, to the keyboard service routine. But will they allow a return after the completion of the keyboard service to the program which the keyboard interrupted? Nesting of interrupts, as this is called, requires an interrupt handling system which can store a number of link addresses in the correct order to allow the progression back through the service routines to the original program. As long as each device has a unique location in which to store the link address back from its own service routine, then the interrupting of an interrupt service routine can be allowed. A device service routine can never be interrupted by its own device, so only one location is required per device. In computer systems using a stack, the link address is pushed onto the stack when an interrupt occurs. A jump is then made to a device service routine or an interrupt service routine. If that routine is interrupted, the PC content is again pushed onto the stack. This does not destroy the other information in the stack and, provided that the stack is big enough, service routines may be nested indefinitely.

6.5.4.6 Enabling and Disabling Interrupts

Three levels of interrupt enabling and disabling are encountered in computer systems. At the first level there is a blanket disable of all interrupt requests. At the second level, interrupts can be disabled from any one or more levels in a multilevel interrupt system by clearing bits in the interrupt mask register. At the third level, individual peripherals may be inhibited from raising an interrupt request to the CPU by the clearing of an interrupt enable bit in the status register of the peripheral controller.

Most computer systems provide special hardware within the CPU which puts the CPU into an uninterruptible state during the critical part of the interrupt recognition sequence. As soon as an interrupt is recognized, the hardware not only stores the link address as described previously but also puts the CPU into an uninterruptible state, see Figure 6.5. This may be done by the clearing of an interrupt enable bit in the CPU status register (the condition codes register or program status word), or by the clearing of the interrupt mask register, or just as a temporary hardware function. If the inhibition of interrupts is achieved by the clearing of an interrupt enable bit or by the clearing of the mask register, the inhibition lasts until the program changes the state of the appropriate bits. If the inhibition is a temporary hardware function it usually lasts for one instruction after the recognition of the interrupt. In that case it is up to the programmer to ensure that the first instruction of the interrupt service is a "forbid interrupts" instruction if the machine is required to run uninterrupted for more than one instruction.

In machines which use a multilevel hardware system with device polling at each level, the polling routine sets the interrupt mask register so that the routine runs uninterrupted by devices of the same or lower priority levels but may be interrupted by devices of a higher priority level. In machines which use a single level interrupt system with device polling, the polling routine runs uninterrupted, because an interrupt would serve only to restart the polling program.

Peripheral devices do not interrupt only when some event happens within them. They also interrupt when they are idle, to inform the CPU that they are available for work. If no work is available, the CPU disables that peripheral to prevent it from constantly interrupting to indicate that it is idle.

This is most simply done by the provision of an interrupt enable bit in the device controller status register. When the CPU program decides that the device interrupt requests should be ignored, the program clears the interrupt enable bit in the device status register. No more interrupt requests will be issued by this device until the program again sets the interrupt enable bit. The interrupt requests from the peripherals can therefore be disabled individually.

Typically, a complete operation by a peripheral device is accomplished by software in the CPU in three stages:

(a) At Stage 1 a CPU program requires that the peripheral perform say, a multistep operation. The program set up the control registers in the peripheral so that the device starts those operations, then sets the peripheral interrupt enable bit. The CPU continues with another program, which may be nothing to do with the peripheral.

(b) At Stage 2 the peripheral device interrupts the CPU, at the end of a step in the multistep operation, and the service routine runs. This performs the actions required at the end of the current step in the peripheral multistep operation. This stage is repeated for each step in the multistep operation.

(c) At Stage 3 the peripheral device interrupts the CPU to indicate that it has finished the multistep operation, and is available to perform another operation if required. The CPU then clears the interrupt enable bit in the peripheral controller and reactivates the program which required the peripheral operation. That program may then soon cause a repeat of the three stages in requiring another operation of the peripheral device.

6.6 TYPES OF INTERRUPT

So far only interrupt requests from normal peripheral devices have been considered. The vast majority of interrupts in an operational computer system are of that type. However, interrupts do arise from other sources and without such interrupts most systems could not function satisfactorily. In general, computer systems recognize interrupts from:

(a) External peripheral devices. These interrupts can be masked, i.e. inhibited by clearing the interrupt enable bits.

(b) Software running in the system.

(c) External nonmaskable sources. These raise interrupts for which there is no interrupt enable bit. Hence interrupt requests from such devices cannot be ignored by the CPU.

(d) Error detecting systems, such as power failure detection circuits and memory parity error detection.

Apart from any prioritizing of interrupt requests within each type of interrupt, there is a priority associated with each type of interrupt. The interrupt types are listed above in what is usually the reverse order of priority. Hence any interrupt of type (b) will take higher priority than any interrupt of type (a). Further, should an interrupt of type (a) be in progress when an interrupt of type (b) arises, the system will suspend the current action to deal with the type (b) interrupt. The four types of interrupt will be very briefly examined here in the reverse order of priority. It should be noted that the relative priority of the various types of interrupt varies between systems, depending on the details of the system interrupt structure and the types of interrupt available.

6.6.1 External, Maskable Interrupts

These are the lowest priority interrupts in any computer system. They are the interrupts which have been the subject matter of this chapter, and as such will not be further discussed here. Some computer systems can be operated in more than one of the modes described previously in this chapter. Thus there may be an interrupt request/acknowledge for vectored interrupts and an interrupt request/acknowledge for nonvectored interrupts. All vectored interrupts take precedence over nonvectored interrupts. Hence this type of interrupt may be subdivided into two priority groups. Each group may be further subdivided into priority levels as described earlier.

Maskable interrupts are characterized by the availability of a mechanism, usually a bit in the CPU condition codes register, for enabling the CPU to be set up by software so as to totally ignore interrupt requests from all the external devices.

6.6.2 Software Interrupts

A detailed discussion of this type of interrupt is outside the scope of this book. The reader should, however, be aware that software running in the system may raise an interrupt request. Such interrupt requests usually arise in the more complex systems in which the user writes software which runs under the supervision of other software (the operating system) provided by other agencies. Often a user program raises an interrupt request to gain the attention of the operating system software. It does this by raising an interrupt request, which causes the CPU to interrupt the requesting program and to run a service routine. The latter causes the user program to be suspended and the operating system runs.

In a privileged/nonprivileged system, one or more of the bits in the CPU condition codes register is used to indicate the privilege of the currently running software. If a program is not privileged certain instructions in the CPU instruction set will not be obeyed by the CPU. These are frequently instructions which perform input/output. A user requiring access to peripheral devices must therefore request access to those devices. The user program must specify what it wishes to be done, and then raise a software interrupt request to gain the attention of the operating system software which performs the input/output for the user. If the unprivileged program inadvertently contains a privileged instruction, the CPU hardware normally causes a system trap to occur. The service routine for this interrupt usually causes the offending software to be suspended and suitable error reports to be given to the user. These interrupts are internal to the CPU and do not require a special I/O bus line.

6.6.3 External, Nonmaskable Interrupts

A nonmaskable interrupt (NMI) request, as its name implies, cannot be ignored by the CPU unless a higher priority type is in progress. There is no enable/disable mechanism for the control of this type of interrupt. NMI requests are conveyed to the CPU by a separate pair of NMI request/acknowledge lines in the I/O bus. Usually there are very few devices connected at this level. NMI requests are usually provided by some important piece of hardware which is in use to guarantee the integrity of the system in the event of some unforeseen problem. For example, computer systems in which there is a power fail/restart mechanism often use the NMI line as the power fail indicator. If the power failure electronics detects imminent failure of the computer system power supplies (because the main supply has failed, for example) then the NMI interrupt routine saves all necessary data in nonvolatile memory and shuts the system down in an orderly fashion so that data are not corrupted by the power failure. When power is reinstated the system can then recover and continue without corruption. Clearly in such a situation all peripheral data transfers must be aborted because power will fail before they can be completed. Hence, power fail is higher priority than every peripheral data transfer, and must be acted upon even if a peripheral service routine for a very high priority peripheral has disabled interrupt requests to the processor.

6.6.4 Interrupts Raised by Error Detecting Hardware

The more secure computer systems contain built-in error detecting hardware. If such hardware detects a system fault, it raises an interrupt request. This may or may not be of a very high priority, but errors detected in critical parts of the system, such as the memory, are given very high priority.

Included in the highest priority level, and in many systems it is the only high priority interrupt, is the system hardware reset. This becomes active on power-up or on the pressing of the system reset (or system boot) switch. System reset is used, in an operational system, only in the most dire circumstances, such as if the system software contains errors (bugs) which have caused the system to "crash". The reset interrupt normally causes a complete system initialization, including the initialization of peripheral controllers, which could cause data loss if it occurred during system operation but which is necessary on system power-up.

6.7 DIRECT MEMORY ACCESS (DMA)

6.7.1 Introduction

In a system in which a large amount of data is transferred to and from the peripheral devices, programmed data transfers between the CPU and the peripherals may take a large proportion of the CPU time. In other systems where there are peripherals which can transfer data at a very high rate, there may be insufficient time available between the data transfers for the interrupt system to function. It is advantageous in these circumstances to use special hardware to allow the peripherals to transfer data directly to and from the memory. The programs running in the CPU are not interrupted every time a peripheral becomes ready to send or receive a data word. All modern computer systems allow for direct memory access. In some systems it is an add-on option whilst in others it is an integral part of the basic system design. DMA transfers are invariably used to transfer information between the memory and hard disk systems which have a high rate of data transfer. Floppy disk systems, which have a lower data transfer rate, are sometimes operated under program control (as in most CP/M systems) and sometimes under DMA control. Disk based systems are very widely used, even in personal microcomputers, so DMA is an important technique to the computer architect, although the normal computer user may be totally unaware of its existence.

6.7.2 DMA Overview

A system which incorporates a DMA facility differs in both its software and its hardware from a system without DMA. Data transfers occurring under DMA control have a high priority in the system. They often occur at the end of execution of an instruction, and may be one of the high priority functions referred to in Figures 6.2 and 6.5, having higher priority than interrupt requests.

6.7.2.1 The Software
Suppose a peripheral device is required to transfer N words of data into the memory system. The interrupt service routine for that peripheral sets up the parameters necessary for the transfer. These are:

    (a) a count of the number of data words to be transferred
    (b) the start address in memory for those data words
and (c) the location (register address) within the peripheral of the first data word.

Whether the data is transferred to memory locations with ascending or descending addresses is a matter of convention within the particular system. The service routine then sends a command to the peripheral which initiates the transfer and the CPU switches back to the interrupted program. While the CPU continues with its program, the peripheral performs its data transfers to the memory. The individual data transfers take place, as indicated in Figure 6.2, at the end of the instruction which the CPU is currently executing. It is not until all the peripheral/memory data transfers are complete that the peripheral again interrupts the CPU. The service routine then sets a flag in the software to indicate that the data is available in the memory system and at some future time the program requiring that data will be run. The service routine, therefore, initiates but does not control the data transfers.

6.7.2.2 The Hardware

In a DMA system the memory can be accessed by the peripheral devices and the CPU , not by the CPU alone as in non-DMA systems. Some hardware is required so that different devices requesting access to the memory are treated in a logical, orderly fashion. Requests for access to the memory are rather like the multiple requests to the CPU for an interrupt. The system which controls the requests for memory access is usually, therefore, very similar to the system which controls the CPU interrupt requests. Each DMA device in the system is allocated a priority, either by a multilevel DMA request/acknowledge line pair or by daisy chaining the DMA acknowledge line through the devices. Thus, when a DMA device requires access to the memory, it raises a DMA request to be granted access to the memory. Requests from the CPU for access to the memory are treated just as any other request. It is common to find that the CPU has a lower priority than the peripheral devices. In a system incorporating DMA, therefore, the CPU must be designed so that it can temporarily suspend operation if the memory is busy.

6.7.3 Types of DMA Transfer

DMA data transfers may take place in different modes in different systems or in the same system. The modes are normally chosen so that the maximum system throughput is achieved, which usually is the same as ensuring that the memory system is worked at its maximum possible rate. No device in the system is then kept waiting for longer than is absolutely necessary for access to the memory.

6.7.3.1 Cycle Stealing

This is probably the most common operating mode. In cycle stealing mode each device, including the CPU, is allowed one memory cycle at a time. Towards the end of this memory cycle the system samples the current requests for access and at the end of the memory cycle the current highest priority device is granted access. The mode is more correctly named single-cycle mode to distinguish it from other modes which allocate more than one memory cycle. The name cycle stealing arises because the cycles are assumed to be stolen from the CPU. Figure 6.10(a) shows diagrammatically the accesses to the memory by a CPU executing a sequence of memory reference instructions.

It is assumed that the operation of the CPU logic is fast compared with the memory cycle time so that the CPU causes the memory to run at almost its maximum speed. This is a realistic assumption in most systems. The memory is accessed twice by each CPU instruction, those marked Fn are the accesses for the instruction fetch and those marked On are the accesses to fetch the operand. In practice, of course, there may be more than one access for the fetch as when multiple length instructions are fetched. There may also be more than one access for the operand, as in the case of indirect addressing via the memory. Each time the CPU requires a memory access it raises a memory cycle request, also shown in Figure 6.10(a). This request is hand-

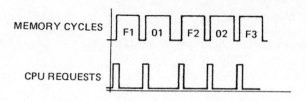

Figure 6.10(a)   *CPU only requesting memory cycles*

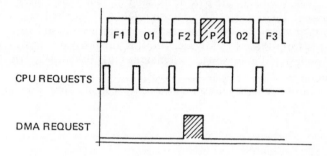

Figure 6.10(b)   *Showing cycle stolen by peripheral*

shaken by the memory access controller which issues the Request Acknowledge signal, and is removed by the CPU as soon as the request is granted. At
any time a peripheral device may also raise a memory access request which is
usually called a DMA request, when issued by a peripheral device. If the
peripheral device has a higher DMA priority than the CPU it is granted the
next available cycle as shown. The request from the CPU is maintained until
it is acknowledged.

Notice in particular that the peripheral device does not have to wait until
the CPU has completed its instruction before being granted access to the
memory. Cycle stealing is, therefore, a mode of DMA transfer which may
be, but is not necessarily, one of the higher priority actions carried out by the
CPU at the end of instruction execution, as shown in Figure 6.2. The
maximum time the peripheral must wait, if no higher priority DMA device is
in the system, is one memory cycle time. During the cycle granted to the
peripheral the CPU is inactive. If the DMA request by the peripheral occurs
while a CPU instruction is in progress rather than between instructions, the
execution time of that instruction may be increased by one memory cycle
time.

The situation illustrated in Figure 6.10(a) is, to some extent, a worst case
situation. In any normal program not all the instructions are memory reference instructions so that it is unusual to find the memory system fully
occupied by the CPU. For much of the time the memory system may be idle,
and if a peripheral requests a cycle in such a period it will be granted at once.
The fact that the cycle is granted to a peripheral is totally transparent to the
CPU if the latter does not require the cycle itself. Although it is undoubtedly

possible to devise a system in which the peripheral is granted cycles which are not required by the CPU, in practice this is not done. Peripherals are given a DMA facility because they are unable to wait for more than a very short time between each transfer without causing a system error. It is therefore not possible to make them wait the unpredictable time required for a "spare" cycle not required by the program in the CPU.

In practice a peripheral sometimes steals a cycle just as the CPU could use it, and sometimes the peripheral cycle causes the CPU to wait for less than one cycle time for access. At other times the peripheral uses a spare memory cycle. Hence the effect of the DMA facility on the execution time of an instruction is not predictable and it follows that the execution time of part or all of a program is likewise unpredictable in a DMA environment. Programs in which critical timing is necessary cannot be timed by software and run in a DMA environment. All real time measurement must be carried out by interrupting peripherals in such systems.

6.7.3.2 Burst Mode Transfers

Sometimes it is more efficient to allow a peripheral to capture sole access to the memory for a number of consecutive cycles, rather than to allow it to enter into contention with other devices over a relatively long period. In such a system, a peripheral device may obtain access to the memory and transfer a burst of data words at the maximum rate which the memory can sustain. If the peripheral cannot accept or send data at the maximum rate sustainable by the memory there is no point in using this mode of DMA transfer. A peripheral which cannot keep up with the maximum rate at which data can be transferred into or out of the memory should allow other devices to obtain memory cycles. If one device has sole access to the memory, the rest of the system is in a state of suspension while that device refuses to release the memory. This can cause a catastrophe in the system. An event in any device will be ignored by the system because the CPU cannot execute programs. However, if the main system memory is a multiple ported memory (see Chapter 1), then burst mode transfers via one port do not necessarily cause the cessation of activity in the rest of the system. Burst mode is used, for example, for fast memory-to-memory transfers between the system memory and the local memory of buffered devices, when both memories can operate at the same speed.

6.7.4 Implementation of DMA Transfers

DMA transfers are not inherently different from the data transfers between digital systems that were considered in Chapter 5. As is to be expected, therefore, they are carried out normally on a bus system very similar to the bus systems considered in Chapter 5.

Two approaches to the provision of a DMA bus are:

(a) provide a DMA bus which is totally separate from any other bus in the system
(b) use the standard I/O bus for DMA transfers.

The provision of a totally separate DMA bus is found on some mini-

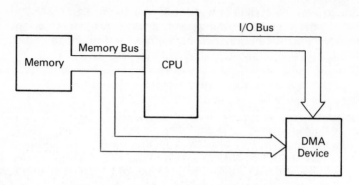

Figure 6.11   *DMA device in a 2-bus system*

computers. Generally it is an expensive solution for it requires the provision of a set of data lines, address lines, direction and control handshake lines. Further it usually implies that the memory system is at least a two-port system, one port for the DMA bus and another port for the CPU. An alternative approach, used in computer systems in which the memory is not connected to the I/O bus (see Chapter 1, Figure 1.1), is to connect DMA peripherals as devices on the memory bus, as shown in Figure 6.11. In this case the memory is a single port memory, and the DMA devices have a dual port controller, one port to the I/O bus and one port to the memory bus.

The use of the standard I/O bus for DMA transfers is the method favored by the current 8-bit and 16-bit microprocessor based systems, and by many minicomputer manufacturers. In all these systems the memory and peripherals are attached to the same bus. The bus contains the DMA request/DMA acknowledge line pair for handshaking, in addition to the lines discussed in previous chapters.

In most of the microprocessor systems, the DMA request lines in the I/O bus, often called the Halt or Wait line, causes the processor chip to suspend operation at the end of the current instructions and relinquish control of the I/O bus. At this stage the processor chip issues the DMA acknowledge (Bus Available) signal and the DMA device then performs a data transfer whilst holding the DMA request line active to prevent interference from the CPU. At the end of the DMA transfer, the DMA device relinquishes control of the bus, and deactivates the DMA request line to hand control of the bus back to the CPU, which then continues processing. It should be noted that such a system is essentially a burst mode DMA system. The DMA device forces the CPU to suspend activity and itself becomes the I/O bus controller. As noted earlier, bursts of more than a single data transfer should be used only with great care to prevent a system crash. DMA servicing in this mode is given higher priority than interrupt servicing. Hence in Figure 6.5, which shows the CPU timing cycle including the hardware interrupt routine, the test for high priority action shown immediately after the instruction execute phase but before the test for interrupt requests, is in fact a test for the DMA request. If a DMA request is present, it is serviced by the processor releasing

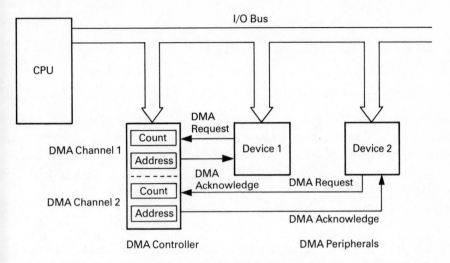

Figure 6.12   *Use of DMA controller chip*

control of the I/O bus. When the DMA is completed and control returns to the CPU, the latter then tests for interrupt requests pending and continues with the cycle shown in Figure 6.5. DMA is handled this way in the widely used Intel 8080/8086 families, Zilog Z80/Z8000 families and in the Motorola 6800/68000 families.

Some microprocessor-based systems allow an additional DMA mode which corresponds to cycle stealing. A DMA device requesting a DMA transfer may cause suspension of CPU activity during the execution of an instruction. Usually only one data transfer should take place at such times, because the microprocessor hardware does not refresh the dynamic registers within the CPU during such suspension of activity. It does perform refreshment of the CPU registers during suspended activity. Further, it is necessary for the DMA device to be synchronized to the CPU clock for such transfers, because the CPU must not be forced to relinquish control of the I/O bus while it is itself using the bus.

In the majority of microprocessor-based systems, the implementation of a DMA system is greatly assisted by using a DMA controller chip. These chips are available from a number of semiconductor manufacturers. Figure 6.12 shows the outline of a typical DMA system implemented using such a controller chip. The controller chip interfaces directly to the I/O bus of the microprocessor system. In many cases these chips provide the necessary logic for the implementation of a prioritized DMA system, in much the same way that a multilevel interrupt structure is derived from a single level system as shown in Figure 6.8. The DMA controller chip normally contains a word count register and a memory address register for each of the DMA priority levels which it controls. Hence, when the CPU acknowledges the DMA request, the DMA controller chip puts the memory address on the I/O bus lines and asserts the direction line. The peripheral device puts the data onto

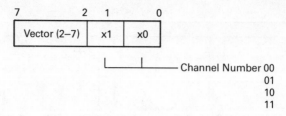

Figure 6.13 *DMA controller interrupt vector*

the data lines or reads the data lines. When the word count for a particular DMA priority level becomes zero, the DMA controller chip raises an interrupt request on behalf of the peripheral device. The DMA controller issues an interrupt vector which is used, as shown in Figure 6.4, to locate the address of the device service routine within a jump table in memory. If the controller is controlling, say, four peripheral devices, its interrupt vector will be constructed as shown in Figure 6.13. The least significant two bits of the vector are used to identify the peripheral whose word count is zero. Thus the DMA chip can issue four separate interrupt vectors. These four vectors are used to vector directly to the service routines for each of the individual devices attached to the DMA controller.

CHAPTER 7

Computer Arithmetic

7.1 INTRODUCTION

This chapter introduces some aspects of computer arithmetic which were not included in Chapter 3. Arithmetic is here considered in the context of an 8-bit machine because the problems are more acute as the machine word becomes smaller. Nevertheless, the same principles apply to all computers, even the mainframe computers.

It is a common misconception that arithmetic calculations are simple to the computer. It is true that the high operating speed of computers allows complex arithmetic calculations to be performed quickly. It is also true that, at the machine level, arithmetic is probably the most difficult task which the computer performs. This difficulty arises from the vast range of numbers with which the computer must cope. If a user wishes to apply a computer to tasks requiring large numbers of numerical calculations (number crunching applications), a machine with an architecture suited to number manipulation should be chosen.

In Chapter 3, section 3.5.2, the idea of the machine number range was introduced. The examples given showed that for an 8-bit machine the number range is $+127$ through -128. Clearly, if all the arithmetic calculations the machine can perform are to lie within that number range, the machine will find very limited application. A 16-bit word length does not substantially ease this problem because the number range of a 16-bit word is limited to $+32,767$ through $-32,768$. There is a further restriction within these number ranges, that all numbers must be *integers*, which means that fractional numbers are not permitted. To overcome these problems, arithmetic within the computer is normally carried out in one of two formats, *integer arithmetic* or *floating point arithmetic*. Floating point arithmetic is the more common and is defined below.

7.2 INTEGER ARITHMETIC

This is arithmetic performed on integers, and is used either when the number range of the calculation is within the machine number range, or when numbers are stored in two or more computer words. This latter technique is used to increase the effective word length of the machine and thus to increase its number range. Integer arithmetic is not often used because it is not often possible to forecast in advance the number range with which a particular program will have to cope.

7.3 MIXED NUMBERS

Mixed numbers are represented by two numbers separated by a point (.). The number to the left of the point is an integer and that to the right of the point is a fraction. In decimal notation mixed numbers are represented, for example, in the form 18.817, where the point is called a decimal point. The columns of figures to the right of the decimal point are weighted as negative powers of 10, and those to the left of the decimal point are weighted as positive powers of 10. Similarly in the binary system mixed numbers may be represented in the form 0101.101 where the point is called a *binary point*. The binary digits to the right of the binary point are weighted as negative powers of 2 and those to the left of the binary point are weighted as positive powers of 2. The first column to the right of the binary point thus represents 1/2, the second column 1/4, the third 1/8 and so on. The number shown therefore represents decimal 5.625 $(4 + 1 + 1/2 + 1/8)$. The sign digit convention explained in Chapter 3 still applies.

7.4 FLOATING POINT NUMBERS

In this chapter the notation P(exp N) is used to indicate P raised to the power N.

Suppose an 8-bit machine is to be applied to general arithmetic problems. Its number range must be extended so that it can perform calculations for a wide range of users. Nuclear physics applications may require manipulation of numbers of the order of 10(exp −30). Cosmic physics may deal with numbers of the order 10(exp +30). The number range of the machine should therefore encompass numbers of these magnitudes. A 128-bit integer can accommodate numbers from 1 through 2(exp 128)−1, which is a number range of the order of 10(exp 38). A 128-bit fraction can accommodate numbers from 1 through 2(exp −128), approximately 1 through 10(exp −38). Suppose 256-bit mixed numbers, consisting of a 128-bit integer and a 128-bit fraction, were used in a computer. The number range would then be approximately 10(exp +38) through 10(exp −38), which is sufficient for most applications.

Unfortunately, the representation of numbers as 256-bit mixed numbers would be very disadvantageous in the following respects:

1. The amount of memory required would be very large if a reasonable amount of numbers is stored at any one time.
2. The time taken to perform arithmetic on 32-byte (256-bit) numbers would be large, and arithmetic calculations would be very slow.
3. In the vast majority of cases, most of the 256 bits would be zeros because numbers are rarely, if ever, known to an accuracy of 1 bit in 256 (1 in 10(exp 76)). Most of the long arithmetic procedures would thus be arithmetic on zero bytes.

A 256-bit number such as that described above has the binary point in a fixed position, between the 128-bit integer and the 128-bit fraction. Such a number could equally well be represented by a 128-bit word in which the binary point is not in a fixed position. If the binary point were at the rightmost end of the word the number would be 2(exp 128) − 1. If it were at the leftmost end of the word the number would be approximately 2(exp −128). This is a *floating point* number. Binary floating point numbers are represented in the twos complement notation (see Chapter 3), in which the most significant bit is the sign bit.

In most numerical problems an accuracy of 1 bit in 128 is much too precise. In practice, only the most significant N bits of the 128-bit floating point number, excluding the leading sign bits, are stored in the computer. N is a number normally between 16 and 32, giving an accuracy of between 1 bit in 16 (1 in 65,000) and 1 bit in 32 (1 in 10(exp 10)). It is also necessary to know the position of the binary point within the 128-bit floating point number. The floating point number is represented, therefore, by two parts. The first is the *mantissa*, which comprises *one* sign bit plus the 16 through 32 most significant nonsign bits of the floating point number. The second is the *exponent*, which is a number representing the position of the binary point within the 128-bit floating point word.

For convenience, the mantissa is considered to be a pure fraction, with the binary point immediately to the right of the sign bit, as shown in Figure 7.1. The mantissa is always *left justified*, which means that the most significant bit is the first of the infinite number of sign bits (see Chapter 3), and the rest of the bits are the most significant nonsign digits. Hence, as shown in Figure 7.1, the mantissa of a positive floating point number has a 0 sign bit immediately followed by a 1. A negative number has a mantissa with a sign bit of 1 immediately followed by a 0. The binary point lies between these two bits.

The mantissa must be multiplied by 2(exp E), to give the actual number represented, where E is the exponent part of the floating point number. E is a number between +127 and −128 if the mantissa is left justified.

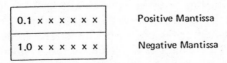

Figure 7.1 | 0.1 x x x x x x | Positive Mantissa
            | 1.0 x x x x x x | Negative Mantissa

Figure 7.1 *Mantissa in floating point numbers*

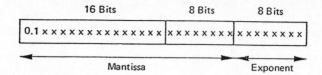

Figure 7.2   *Floating point number in 16-bit machine*

In practice, the exponent is not usually stored as a twos complement number, but as an *excess-N* number, where N is 128 in the case under consideration. In most floating point number representations in computer systems the exponent is stored as part of a computer word, not as a complete word. For example, in a 16-bit system two words may be used to store each floating point number. One and a half words may be used to store a 24-bit mantissa, and the remaining 8 bits may be used to store the exponent, as shown in Figure 7.2. If the exponent is to be manipulated using the instruction set of the machine (which it must be), it is much more convenient to consider the exponent to be a number in the range 0 through 255 than to consider it to be a number in the range −128 through +127. This is basically because when manipulation of the exponent is carried out, the exponent is extracted from the word in which it is stored by using the logical AND instruction and a mask as described in Chapter 2. Usually the exponent is the least significant part of the word, and the masking operation then leaves the most significant bits in the word, the sign bits, as zeros. These are the correct sign bits if the exponent is positive, but they must be changed if the exponent is a negative twos complement number. By considering the exponent to be always positive, its manipulation is always the manipulation of a positive number. On output from the machine in printed form, the mantissa and the exponent are both converted from binary to decimal. It is a simple matter to subtract 128 from the exponent before carrying out this conversion.

To summarize, then, floating point numbers are always written in two parts. The first is the mantissa, which is a left justified fraction whose length is determined by the precision to which the numbers are represented. The second is an exponent, written in excess-N code, where N is a number equal to half the notional word length of the mixed numbers which the floating point numbers represent.

7.5 ARITHMETIC WITH FLOATING POINT NUMBERS

Arithmetic with floating point numbers must be programmed using the instruction set of the CPU. In a small machine the instruction set rarely includes floating point arithmetic instructions. The format of the floating point representation of numbers is convenient for the manipulation of those numbers by the integer arithmetic instructions of the small computer's instruction set. In an 8-bit machine the mantissa may be a double length integer and the exponent may be a single length integer. To perform, for example, a multiplication of two floating point numbers, a program must multiply the two mantissas and add the two exponents. These are both tasks which can be carried out by relatively simple programs. For an addition of two floating point numbers, the two numbers must first have their exponents equalized. This is done by right shifting the double length mantissa of the number with the smaller exponent and incrementing its exponent at every shift until the two exponents are the same. Then the mantissas are added, and the exponent of either is taken as the exponent of the result. All these operations can readily be carried out using instructions of the types considered in Chapter 2. Arithmetic and shift instructions which operate on double length words are helpful in programming these operations.

7.5.1 Justifying

When an operation has been performed between two floating point numbers the result may not be in the standard, left justified, format. For example, if two positive numbers are added the result may have a sign bit equal to 1, apparently indicating a negative result, as shown in Figure 7.3. The result obtained must, therefore, be justified to obtain the result in standard format. In this case a right shift of one place with an increment of the exponent is required. Similarly, the subtraction of two positive numbers may require that the result be shifted left one or more places with the appropriate decrementing of the exponent. In a few small computers, and in the mainframe computers, "justify" instructions are provided in the instruction set. In most small computers these operations must be programmed with the standard CPU instructions.

0.1 0 0 1	Mantissa of 1st number
0.1 1 0 0	Mantissa of 2nd number
1.0 1 0 1	Result. Sign Bit = 1.
0.1 0 1 0 1	Required position for result

Figure 7.3 *Addition of positive numbers*

7.5.2 Accuracy of Floating Point Operations

Inaccuracies in floating point operations may arise, for example, because although the floating point numbers are effectively 128-bits long, only the most significant 16 bits are available in the computer. If two almost equal numbers are subtracted, the result cannot be accurate to 16 bits. All subsequent calculations with that result are also not accurate to 16 bits. The reader should consult a book on numerical techniques for a more profound treatment of the accuracy of numerical calculations.

7.5.3 Rounding

It will be noticed that in the example of Figure 7.3, the justify operation caused a 1 bit to be shifted out of the least significant bit position. The loss of this digit represents a loss of accuracy in the final result. If a large number of calculations is carried out, each using the result of previous calculations, the final result may be highly inaccurate. To minimize this inaccuracy—it cannot be completely eliminated—a rounding process must be employed.

Suppose two floating point numbers are multiplied together. The mantissa of the result will, in general, contain twice as many digits as each of the two mantissas taking part in the multiplication. The result will then have to be justified to the standard format. If the standard is a 16 bit mantissa, the least significant 16 bits of the result of the multiplication may have to be discarded. However, if these 16 bits represent a number with a value more than half that of the least significant digit of the 16 bits retained, the result should be rounded up. This can be done by adding 1 to the least significant bit of the result. In practice this is most easily done by adding the most significant bit of the discarded bits into the least significant end of the bits being retained.

Although the rounding procedure is simple to understand, there are pitfalls in its application. There exist many rounding algorithms, which attempt to solve the problem of when best to apply rounding so that the final result is not made even more inaccurate by the rounding procedure than it might have been without rounding! In some high level languages, such as BASIC, all calculations are carried out by floating point arithmetic programs, even if the user requests arithmetic on integers. The results are sometimes, though fortunately not often, startling. Occasionally it is possible, for example, to obtain results such as 5.999999999 as the product of 2×3. Rephrasing the statements causing the calculation can sometimes remove this anomaly. Such results are a consequence of the floating point algorithms used in the machine.

7.5.4 Floating Point Overflow

It is possible for the results of a manipulation of floating point numbers to be larger than the largest positive or negative number which can be accommodated by the machine's floating point format. This is the case when the binary point goes beyond the rightmost digit of the 128-bit floating point word represented by the floating point notation. The condition is called floating point overflow. It is analogous to the integer overflow condition detected by the overflow flag in the condition codes register. The condition is detected in the machine when the exponent becomes too large, not when the mantissa overflows. The mantissa cannot cause floating point overflow, even though its manipulation may cause the CPU overflow flag to set. The apparent overflow of the mantissa caused, for example, by the addition of two positive numbers giving an apparently negative result, is corrected by justifying, by moving the mantissa within the 128-bit word, as explained in section 7.5.1 and illustrated in Figure 7.3.

7.5.5 Floating Point Underflow

If the result of a floating point operation is a number which is smaller than the smallest number which can be represented in the floating point format of the machine, underflow is said to occur. This is not the condition when the number is a very large negative number. Underflow occurs when the exponent of the number is a very large negative number. Underflow indicates that the binary point has moved to the left of the leftmost digit of the 128-bit floating point word, which means that the number is too small to be represented in the standard, justified format. In excess-128 code, the exponent has become less than zero when the mantissa is justified. In this case the number itself is very small, very close to zero, so in the machine the result is set to zero.

7.5.6 Floating Point Number Regions

The floating point number regions are shown in Figure 7.4. The overflow regions start at the number represented by the largest positive or negative mantissa multiplied by 2 raised to the power equal to the largest exponent. The underflow regions, one positive and the other negative, are separated by the number zero. Their upper limits are at the numbers represented by the smallest mantissa multiplied by 2 raised to the power equal to the largest negative exponent.

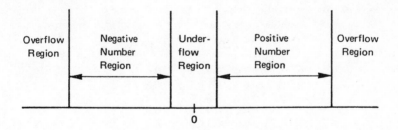

Figure 7.4   *Floating point number regions*

7.5.7 Floating Point Hardware

For applications in which much floating point arithmetic is performed, many computer system manufacturers provide, at a price, a hardware floating point unit. This is an electronic subsystem which performs floating point arithmetic on correctly formatted numbers. The floating point hardware is an integral part of the CPU in those computers in which there are floating point instructions. In those systems without floating point instructions the floating point unit is a peripheral connected to the machine I/O bus or a "coprocessor" connected to the system bus. To perform floating point arithmetic in these systems the program sends the number along the I/O bus to registers in the floating point unit, then sends the appropriate command to its command register, and waits for the result to be produced in the result registers. This gives a large saving of time in the execution of the programs.

7.6 DECIMAL (BCD) ARITHMETIC

Numerical information is often coded in Binary Coded Decimal (BCD) Code, particularly in control and data logging applications. In this coding system, shown in Figure 7.5, each of the decimal digits 0 through 9 is represented by four binary bits. The natural binary equivalents of the decimal digits are normally used, giving rise to the natural Binary Coded Decimal (NBCD) coding system. If other groups of four bits are allocated to represent the numbers 0 through 9, other binary coded decimal codes arise. it is normal practice to refer to the Natural BCD system as the BCD system, and to refer to any other BCD system explicitly by its particular name. In applications where the numerical inputs to the computer or microprocessor system are in BCD, it is often found that numerical outputs are also in BCD. Therefore it is convenient to process the numbers internally in the computer system in the BCD format. This saves the inconvenience of converting from BCD to binary on input, processing in binary, and converting back from binary to BCD on output. When the numbers being manipulated are not very large, direct manipulation in BCD code is not difficult. The instruction sets of some small machines, including microprocessors, contain instructions to assist in this manipulation.

BCD		DECIMAL
0000	0000	00
0000	0001	01
0000	0010	02
0000	0011	03
0000	0100	04
0000	0101	05
0000	0110	06
0000	0111	07
0000	1000	08
0000	1001	09
0000	1010	
0000	1011	
0000	1100	
0000	1101	Invalid Codes
0000	1110	
0000	1111	
0001	0000	10
0001	0001	11
0001	0010	12

Figure 7.5 *Some BCD codes*

```
0000   0011   BCD 3      0000   1000   BCD 8
0000   0101   BCD 5      0000   0101   BCD 5

0000   1000   BCD 8      0000   1101   Binary 13 (Invalid BCD)

                         0000   0110   Filler (6)

                         0001   0011   BCD 13

      (a)                        (b)
```

Figure 7.6   *BCD addition*

To illustrate the problems of BCD arithmetic, consider Figure 7.6(a). This shows the addition of two BCD numbers, 3 and 5, in an 8-bit machine. The result, 0000 1000, is the correct BCD representation of the sum, 08. The addition process is identical to that of the addition of two binary numbers as performed in the ALU. Figure 7.6(b) shows the result of the binary addition of two BCD numbers, 8 and 5. The binary addition gives the correct binary result, 13, encoded in 4 bits, but this is not the correct BCD representation. The result is in the range of invalid BCD codes shown in Figure 7.5. To convert the result of the binary addition to the BCD code a *filler* of 6 (0110) must be added to the least significant 4 bits, the LS BCD digit. When this is done the result, 0001 0011, is the correct BCD representation of the decimal number 13.

Conversion from the result of a binary addition of BCD numbers to a correct BCD representation is always performed by the addition of the filler of 6 to the groups of 4 bits representing the BCD digits, if the 4 bits contain an invalid code. The reason for this can be observed from Figure 7.5. If the result of a binary addition of two BCD digits lies in the region of invalid codes, the addition of 6 to the result effectively moves the result to the code six places down in Figure 7.5. This will then be the correct code because in the BCD system the six invalid codes should always be skipped. Notice that this correction is *not* required if the result of the binary addition lies in the range 0 through 9.

The above is the first of three conditions under which the filler of six must be added to the result of a binary addition of two BCD digits to yield a correct BCD result.

For the second condition consider the addition of the BCD numbers 9 and 8 as shown in Figure 7.7. The result is correct as a binary result, 17. As a BCD result it is incorrect, 11, but does not contain invalid BCD codes. The BCD codes are valid because the region of invalid codes has been spanned by the calculation. It is necessary, therefore, to detect the case when the addition spans the region of invalid codes, and to add the filler of 6 when that happens. The addition of 6 to the result of Figure 7.7 gives the correct result, 17. The hardware can detect this condition because the addition of the two binary digits gave a carry from the least significant BCD digit to the next

```
0 0 0 0   1 0 0 1   9
0 0 0 0   1 0 0 0   8
─────────────────
0 0 0 1   0 0 0 1   Result = Binary 17
─────────────────            BCD 11
```

Figure 7.7   *Binary addition of BCD 9 + 8*

BCD digit. This carry represents a 16, the 1 in the most significant BCD digit of the result and 6 which is the filler to be added into the LS digit. In machines with a decimal adjust instruction, the carry generated between the BCD digits by the binary addition of BCD numbers is used to set a flag in the condition codes register. This flag is set or cleared on all binary additions, and the decimal adjust instruction adds the filler if the flag is set.

For the third condition, suppose the result of a binary addition of two BCD digits is invalid (in the range A through F). The addition of a filler always produces a carry from the digit being filled into the next higher digit. If this higher digit is a 9, the carry will convert it into (hex) A, a code in the invalid range. The higher digit must therefore also be filled. To prevent a repetitive cycle of filling, the hardware detects the condition when a result digit is 9 *and* the previous (less significant) digit is to be filled, and adds the filler into the more significant digit at the same time.

A BCD result digit requires a filler, then, if:
   it lies in the range A through F;
   OR a carry occurred out of it during the binary add stage;
   OR it is a 9 AND the previous digit is to be filled.

BCD subtraction requires a similar adjustment of the result of a binary subtraction. The difference between addition and subtraction is that addition is, in effect, counting from a low to a higher number, while subtraction may be considered to be counting from a higher number to a lower number. When the result of an addition gives as invalid BCD code, as illustrated in Figure 7.5, #6 has to be added to give a correct result; similarly, if the result of a binary subtraction of two BCD numbers gives a result in the invalid code range, the valid BCD result is found by subtracting a correction of 6.

In some small computer systems, the decimal adjust instruction operates correctly after both add and subtract instructions; most microprocessor-based systems, however, do not make a correct adjustment after a subtraction, and care must be taken to examine carefully the specification of the decimal adjust instruction to avoid programming errors.

If (as is usually the case) BCD add and subtract instructions are not provided in the instruction set, then BCD arithmetic, if required, must be programmed using the normal instruction set; and the detecting of the conditions which call for a correction, and the applying of that correction, must be performed in the program.

If there is a decimal add instruction in the instruction set of a CPU, it causes the hardware to perform the binary addition and automatically to continue to carry out any correction necessary. If there is a decimal adjust instruction, it is used after a binary add instruction to cause the CPU to perform the correction.

BCD numbers can be represented in tens complement notation (see Chapter 3 section 3.5). For example, to decrement a two-digit BCD number, 99 (the two-digit tens complement of 1), must be added to the number. The carry from the most significant bit indicates that the BCD digit from which the carry occurred must be filled. Hence it is necessary to program the tens complementing procedure, the BCD add and the BCD subtract.

7.7 THE CONDITION CODES

7.7.1 Introduction

The condition codes are flags which set to 1 or clear to 0 automatically according to conditions in the ALU (see Chapter 2 section 2.3.3). Usually they reflect the condition of the word at the output of the ALU at the end of an instruction, because in most CPUs data transfers occur mainly through the ALU (see Chapter 1 section 1.6, and Chapter 2 section 2.1). The condition flags vary from machine to machine, but the four flags mentioned in Chapter 2 section 2.3.3,

The Zero Flag (Z)
The Negative Flag (N)
The Carry Flag (C)
The Overflow Flag (V)

are present in most computers. Some of their uses are considered in this chapter.

From machine to machine there are considerable variations in the types of instructions which affect the condition codes flags. For example, in some machines instructions which cause straightforward data transfers from one register to another or from a register to a memory location, do not affect any of the condition flags. In other machines such transfers affect all the condition flags. Careful study of the detailed specification of each individual instruction will reveal that some instructions affect all the flags, some instructions affect some flags but not other flags and some affect no flags. It is very easy, when writing assembly language programs for an unfamiliar machine to assume, incorrectly, the affect of the instructions on the condition flags.

7.7.2 The Zero Flag

The Zero (Z) flag sets to a 1 if the result of an ALU operation is zero, otherwise it clears to a 0. Most instructions causing a data transfer through the ALU affect the state of the Z flag.

In the instruction set there is usually a conditional jump instruction, "jump if the result of the previous instruction was zero". This type of instruction (jump on zero), tests the state of the Z flag and causes a jump if the flag is a 1. Variations such as "jump on nonzero", "jump to subroutine if zero" (or nonzero) and "return from subroutine if zero" (or nonzero) all test the state of the Z flag and cause a jump accordingly. Instructions of the type "jump if the content of register R is zero" usually cause a transfer of the content of the register through the ALU to set up the flags, and then cause a jump according to the state of the Z flag. Notice that conditional jump instructions use, but do not normally change, the state of the flags.

The Z flag is used in conjunction with the other flags as described in the following sections.

7.7.3 The Negative Flag

The Negative (N) flag, or Sign flag, reflects the state of the most significant bit of the output from the ALU at the end of an ALU operation. It is assumed, whether it is true or not, that the word on the output of the ALU represents a twos complement number. Hence if the sign bit of the number is a 1, the N bit sets to 1, otherwise it clears to 0.

The flag is used for conditional jump instructions in much the same way as the Z flag is used (see section 7.7.2 above). The tests made are, of course, for negative or non-negative (positive), rather than zero or nonzero. This flag is also used in conjunction with other flags as described in the following sections.

7.7.4 The Carry Flag

The Carry (C) flag sets if there is a carry out of the most significant bit of the ALU during an arithmetic or logical operation. It also sets when a subtract operation assumed a borrow from the bit of higher significance than the MSB of the word.

In many computers, the shift instructions, right, left and circular, cause the bit shifted out of the word to be shifted into the carry bit. This is useful when manipulating multiple length operands as described in section 7.7.7 below.

7.7.5 The Overflow Flag

The Overflow (V) flag is used for different purposes in different circumstances and in different computers. The overflow flag sets to 1 when the result of an arithmetic operation produces a result which is outside the number range of one machine word.

In some computers this flag cannot be cleared to 0 by the ALU hardware when it subsequently detects a number within the range of a single word. This type of V flag is usually used in conjunction with an interrupt enable bit in the condition codes register. The overflow interrupt enable bit is a mask bit, logically ANDed with the V flag. When the result of the AND is a 1 an interrupt is requested. This enable bit acts in exactly the same way as the interrupt enable bit in the status register of a peripheral device (see Chapter 6 section 6.2.3.6). Normally interrupts of this type, called *internal interrupts*, or *traps*, have a higher priority than interrupt requests from the peripherals. The standard interrupt priority system used by the computer directs the CPU to the overflow interrupt service routine which takes whatever action has been programmed. This type of overflow flag is very useful when arithmetic calculations are being carried out because it provides almost instant action if the numbers go out of range.

In other computers, the overflow flag sets to 1 as explained in the previous section, but clears to 0 when a subsequent arithmetic operation causes a result which is within the machine number range. This type of overflow flag is not normally linked to the interrupt system, but is useful in the detection of jump conditions, where it is necessary to know the conditions caused by the previous instruction in the program.

The best computer systems have both types of overflow flag. Both do exist in some computers, although they are often not both explicitly available for the use of the programmer. The uses of the overflow flag are described in the following sections.

7.7.6 Other Flags

Some computers have flags to indicate conditions such as the parity of the last operand transferred in the machine, floating point overflow and under-flow flags and other special flags which are helpful in the particular system.

Other computers appear not to contain even the four Z, N, C, V flags. However this may be a rather misleading appearance. The flags are explicitly available for the use of the programmer only in those machines in which they can be changed by instructions in the instruction set. These are instructions of the type "set V", or "clear C", or "transfer the content of register R to the condition codes register". Such instructions are absent from some instruction sets, which do, however, contain instructions of the type "jump if the content of register R is zero". Although there may be no Z flag available to the programmer in such a machine, such a flag does exist in the hardware. It is available for the use of the hardware in the execution of the conditional jump instruction. It is not mentioned in the manufacturer's literature for the user, but it will be found in the engineering drawings for the CPU.

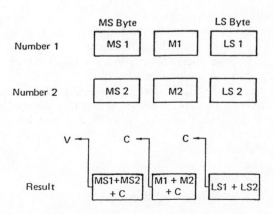

Figure 7.8 *Triple length addition*

In yet other computers the Z and N flags are replaced by, or coexist with, flags which indicate the relative magnitudes of the two operands entering the ALU. These are the Greater Than ($>$) or Less Than ($<$) flags which set to 1 or clear to 0 on combinations of Z and N as explained below.

7.7.7 Carry, Overflow and Arithmetic Instructions

In small machines, arithmetic calculations frequently require operations to be carried out on words which are two or more machine words in length. The programming of multiple length arithmetic, as it is called, can be considerably eased if the add instructions and the carry and overflow flags have the right characteristics. Consider the addition of two triple length numbers as illustrated in Figure 7.8. There will exist no triple length add instruction in the CPU instruction set, so the addition must be programmed using the ordinary single length add instructions. The addition will be carried out in three steps:

Step 1. Addition of the least significant (LS) bytes, which should set the carry flag as appropriate.

Step 2. Addition of the middle bytes, plus addition of the carry generated in step 1 above. This addition should also set the carry flag as appropriate.

Step 3. Addition of the most significant bytes plus addition of the carry as generated in step 2. This addition should set the overflow flag if the result of the 3-byte addition exceeds the number range of a 3-byte word. This is the same condition as the normal overflow condition applied to the addition of the MS bytes of the 3-byte word plus the carry from step 2.

In many computer instruction sets there are a number of different add instructions which assist the task of programming the steps 1 through 3 above.

Step 1 requires an instruction:
Add A to B. Do not add in the carry flag.
        Set or clear the carry flag.
        Overflow is irrelevant.

Step 2 requires an instruction:
Add A to B. Add in also the carry flag.
        Set or clear the carry flag.
        Overflow is irrelevant.

Step 3 requires an instruction:
Add A to B. Add in also the carry flag.
        Set or clear the overflow flag.
        Carry is irrelevant.

These different add instructions appear in the instruction sets of the mainframe computers, and some are included in the instruction sets of some small computers. Often, however, in small machines the programmer must write programs which test the conditions of the overflow and carry flags as appropriate, and use conditional jumps to instructions which perform the addition of the carry when necessary.

Similar requirements exist in multiple length subtraction, in which case the carry flag sets when a borrow from the next more significant byte is assumed. The middle and most significant bytes are then subtracted using instructions which subtract the bytes and the carry flag.

7.7.8 The Flags in Justify Operations

In machines in which justification must be programmed, the flags can be used to detect the end of the justify operation. Suppose a positive number is to be left justified, it can be shifted left until it becomes negative. Shifting it right one place then leaves it in justified format. The exponent is decremented by one for each left shift, and incremented by one for the right shift.

7.7.9 The Carry Flag and Multiple Length Shifts

Multiple length operands require logical manipulation in exactly the same way as single length operands. In many computers the shift instructions (see Chapter 2 section 2.3.2) act as if the carry flag were part of the word being shifted. The bit which is lost from the machine word in a single shift appears as the carry bit, whether the shift is to the left or to the right. Circular (rotational) shifts occur with the carry interposed between the ends of the word being shifted. These arrangements are very helpful when double or multiple length shifts have to be programmed. For example, suppose a double length left shift of one place is being programmed in a computer system in which the word length is 4 bits. One method is illustrated in Figure 7.9. This method uses the left circular shift instruction in which the carry flag

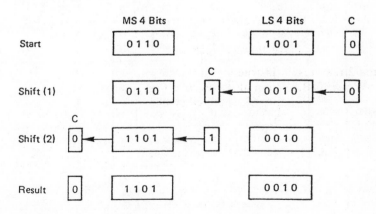

Figure 7.9 *Double length left shift*

is interposed between the end bits of the word being shifted. Three machine instructions are required for every single bit shift of the double length operand:

1. Clear the Carry flag to 0.
2. Circular left shift 1 place on the LS word. This shifts the carry bit (0) into the LS end of the LS word. It simultaneously shifts the MS bit of the word into the carry bit.
3. Circular left shift 1 place on the MS word. This shifts the MS bit of the original LS word from the carry into the LS bit of the MS word. It simultaneously shifts the MS bit of the original double length word into the carry bit, but that is irrelevant to the double length result.

This example illustrates that an instruction set may be designed to facilitate the programmer's tasks, even though the instructions required by the programmer are not provided directly. One of the major differences in programming at assembly language level on the mainframe computers and on the small computers, is the availability of a very wide selection of instructions on the mainframe machines. Only a very limited set of instructions is available on the small machines.

7.7.10 Arithmetic (Signed Number) Comparison

When manipulating numbers, it is a common requirement to wish to compare two numbers and to take action according to which is the larger. Conditional jumps such as "jump if $A > B$" or "jump if $A < B$" are often included in computer instruction sets. The comparison of two numbers is carried out by subtracting one number from the other and setting the condition codes according to the result. Many instruction sets include a

A	B	A−B		N	V		Z		
100	80	+20	A>B	0	0	N'.V'=1	0	(N'.V').Z' =1	(N EXOR V)'.Z' =1
−80	−100	+20	A>B	0	0	N'.V'=1	0		
80	−100	+180	A>B	1	1	N.V=1	0	(N.V).Z' =1	
100	−80	+180	A>B	1	1	N.V=1	0		
100	100	0	A = B	0	0	N'.V'=1	1	(N'.V').Z =1	Z=1
−80	−80	0	A = B	0	0	N'.V'=1	1		
80	80	0	A = B	0	0	N'.V'=1	1		
−100	−100	0	A = B	0	0	N'.V'=1	1		
80	100	−20	A<B	1	0	N.V'=1	0	N.V'=1	N EXOR V=1
−100	−80	−20	A<B	1	0	N.V'=1			
−80	100	−180	A<B	0	1	N'.V=1	0	N',V=1	
−100	+80	−180	A<B	0	1	N'.V=1	0		

Figure 7.10   *Results of comparison of numbers*

"Compare" instruction which performs the subtraction of one operand from another and sets up the condition codes according to the result, but does not deposit the result in a memory location or in a register. This leaves the two operands unaltered.

The $A > B$ and $A < B$ conditions can be derived from the settings of the N and V flags, provided that the V flag is not the type which stays set once it has been set. The V flag used for this purpose must set to 1 or clear to 0 automatically on the result of each arithmetic operation. Figure 7.10 is a table of the results obtained when two numbers A and B, of magnitude 100 and 80 (decimal) respectively, are subtracted in an 8-bit ALU. The number range of this machine is $+127$ through -128 (see Chapter 3), so that a result of magnitude 180 gives overflow. The results shown should be related to Figure 7.11, which shows the four machine number regions from which the combinations of N and V shown in Figure 7.10 are derived. Note that in the overflow regions the sign detected by the machine is opposite to the sign of the correct result.

The results shown in Figure 7.10 can be stated in more general terms as:

1. The result of the subtraction $A - B$, where $A < B$, is a negative number. This number, as detected in the ALU of a computer system, appears to be either:
(a) negative AND in the machine number range; or
(b) positive AND in the machine overflow range.

These conditions apply to all numbers in the machine, and can be stated in terms of the machine condition code settings as:

$A < B$ if $N.V' = 1$ OR $N'.V = 1$

i.e. $A < B$ if N XOR $V = 1$
(see Chapter 2 section 2.2.2.3 for the definition of the EXCLUSIVE-OR function).

2. The result of the subtraction of two numbers $A - B$, where $A > B$, is a positive number greater than zero. This number as detected in the ALU of a computer system appears to be either:

(a) positive AND in the machine number range and nonzero; or
(b) negative AND in the machine overflow region.
In this case the number cannot be zero.

These conditions can be stated in terms of the machine condition code settings as:

$A > B$ if $N'.V'.Z' = 1$ OR $N.V.Z' = 1$

i.e. $A > B$ if $(N$ XOR $V)'.Z' = 1$

The condition when $A = B$ can be detected when the subtraction of B from A causes the Z flag to set to 1. Hence:

$A = B$ if $Z = 1$

In some machines hardware is used to detect the "greater than" and "less than" conditions and to set flags accordingly. These machines provide "jump if greater than" and "jump if less than" instructions in the instruction set. Where these conditional jumps are required but not provided in the instruction set, the conditions must be generated and tested by software.

7.7.11 Logical (Unsigned Number) Comparison

It is often convenient to compare two bit patterns which do not represent numbers. For example, it may be that a program is searching a table of 8-bit ASCII characters for one particular character. In this case the bit patterns can be treated as if they are all positive numbers with the first sign bit in the 9th bit position. Even in an 8-bit machine each word can then be considered to contain a number between 0 and 255 decimal. If two such numbers are compared by subtracting one from the other, they are essentially 9-bit numbers in an 8-bit machine. The negative and overflow flags in the 8-bit machine do not reflect those conditions for the 9-bit words. In this context, therefore, the V and N flags provided in the 8-bit machine are irrelevant.

If a positive number B is subtracted from another positive number A, the result is either positive (including zero) or negative, but cannot give overflow. A positive result indicates that $A = B$ OR $A > B$ (see section 7.7.10 above), and a negative result indicates that $A < B$. When these numbers are 9-bits long, the conditions must be deduced by interpreting the settings of the 8-bit machine's flags. This is in fact a simple matter when Z and C flags are present in the computer.

Consider the case when $A < B$. The result of the subtraction $A - B$ is a negative 9-bit word. In the 8-bit machine the ninth bit is, of course, not present. However, since the ninth bit in both the original words A and B was a 0 (they are both positive) the only way in which the ninth bit of the result can become a 1 is for a carry to occur between the eighth and ninth bits. This carry causes the C flag of the 8-bit machine to set to 1. Conversely, only if no carry occurs from the eighth bit to the ninth bit will the 9-bit result be positive. Hence:

if $C = 1$ then $A < B$; *and*
if $C = 0$ then $A > B$ OR $A = B$

The distinction between $A > B$ and $A = B$ can be made by including the state of the Z flag. Clearly, when $A = B$, Z will be set to 1 as a result of the $A - B$ subtraction, but if $A > B$ then Z will be cleared to 0 by the subtraction. The condition when the ninth bit is 1 and the other 8 bits are 0s, which would also set Z to 1, cannot occur because that would be a result of -256 which is out of range because B is a maximum of $+255$. The full conditions are then:

$A > B$ if $C = 0$ AND $Z = 0$, i.e. if $C'.Z' = 1$
$A = B$ if $C = 0$ AND $Z = 1$, i.e. if $C'.Z = 1$
$A < B$ if $C = 1$

It is not necessary for a subtraction and interpretation of the flag settings to be performed for the detection of these conditions. It is possible to use a purely logical comparison of the two 8-bit patterns. The principle of this method, but not the logical gating required, is described below.

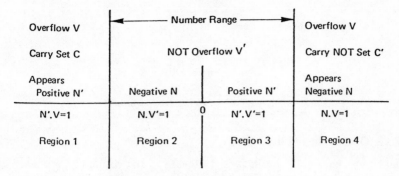

Figure 7.11   *Machine number regions*

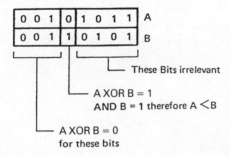

Figure 7.12   *Logical detection of A < B*

Suppose two 8-bit words, A and B, are compared bit by bit, commencing with the most significant bit of each word. If the two words are identical, the corresponding bits of each word are identical. In this case the EXCLUSIVE-OR of the corresponding bits of each word is zero for every bit position. If A and B are not identical, as in Figure 7.12, then in at least one bit position in the words the corresponding bits are different, a 1 in one word and a 0 in the other. Taking the most significant bit position in which this situation occurs, the 1 is in the word which represents the greater number. A priority detecting circuit, similar to that used for detecting the highest priority interrupt request in a multilevel interrupt system (see Chapter 6), can be used to ignore the comparison of lesser significant bits of the words. Figure 7.13 shows the block diagram of the logical system which performs this comparison. The system has the two 8-bit words as its inputs. Three outputs, of which only one is a 1 at any time, are used to indicate the conditions A > B, A = B and A < B. Such circuits are available as standard integrated circuit packages which can be purchased from semiconductor vendors.

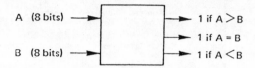

Figure 7.13   *Logical comparator*

7.7.12 Other Uses of the Flags

When the meaning of the flags is irrelevant in the context of a particular program, that program may use them for any purpose, for flagging any conditions. They can be used, for example, for passing information from one subroutine to another. Suppose a program is reading ASCII characters from a teletype, and that it is desired to process only characters in the range A through Z. One method is to write a subroutine to test whether the character is in the required range. The subroutine sets the V flag (say) if the character is in range and clears the V flag is the character is out of range. It then returns to the main program which contains as its next instruction a "jump if V clear" instruction. All the flags may be used in this way provided that there exist instructions to set, clear and test them.

CHAPTER 8
Memory Management Techniques

8.1 INTRODUCTION

The current developments in technology are making available very large memory systems at very low cost. As a result of these developments, the techniques for addressing large memories, which have hitherto been available only on mainframe computers and large minicomputers are becoming available on microcomputers and are very common on even the smallest minicomputers.

The most recent small computer systems have a computing power equal to that of mainframe computers of a few years ago, and consequently are being applied in environments in which considerable computing power is required. Such environments often bring with them two important requirements:

1. A large memory system is required to hold the large amounts of data which the systems must access.
2. Security of data is required between tasks which the system must perform. Hence if data relating to two tasks exists in memory, it must be impossible for the program which accesses one data set to access the other data set by accident due, for example, to a programming error.

These requirements imply that in systems in which large memories are used it is normal also to find some form of memory protection, such that programs are allowed access to some parts of memory but not to other parts. Schemes which allow such a system to be built are usually called *memory management* schemes.

There are two essential features of any memory management scheme:

1. Firstly, the memory is considered to be divided into a number of blocks, the block size depending on the particular system.
2. Secondly, one or more blocks is allocated for the use of a particular software module or task. Some protection method is required to prevent the software accessing memory outside its allocated blocks. Further, protection may be extended to allow only certain types of access so that,

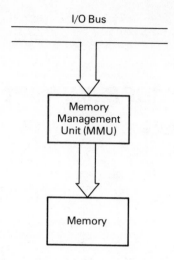

Figure 8.1   *Memory management hardware system*

for example, a particular software task may be allowed to read a particular block of memory but not to change the content of that block of memory.

Memory management schemes rely on both hardware and software for their operation. A hardware memory management unit (MMU) is connected between the memory and the other devices in the system. The MMU contains a number of registers which specify its management functions. The MMU hardware appears as a peripheral to the system, and the memory management software sets up the registers of the MMU. For a system in which the memory is attached to the I/O bus, the hardware configuration is shown in Figure 8.1.

8.2 MEMORY BANK SWITCHING

The simplest method of memory management is probably bank switching. The memory is divided, say, into 8 banks of memory, each bank being 64K bytes, requiring a 16-bit address to address a location within the memory bank. When a particular software task is running, the computer system uses as its memory one particular bank of memory. When a new task is run, the system switches to another bank of memory. Hence no task can access the memory which belongs to another task. The MMU contains a bank selector register which holds the number of the memory bank currently in use. To switch memory banks requires that the system outputs the new memory bank address to the bank selector register. Memory bank switching is most often used in systems in which the CPU produces a 16-bit address, giving a maximum 64K byte addressing space, but in which 64K bytes is insufficient for the application. Figure 8.2 illustrates a bank switched memory system.

The bank selector register is used as an address extension register to extend the 16-bit effective address produced by the CPU hardware.

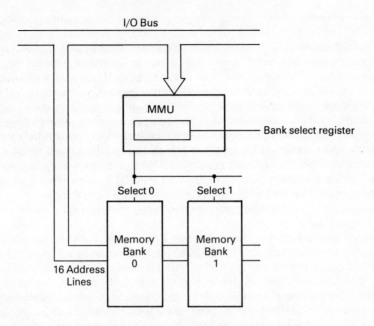

Figure 8.2 *Memory bank switching system*

8.3 VIRTUAL MEMORY SYSTEMS

An increasing number of computer applications are coming into being in which very large software suites are required to run. For example, a single application may comprise a data base management system, in which there is a relatively small volume of code which accesses a very large volume of data. The total size of such a system may be many millions of bytes *(megabytes)* and it may well be uneconomic to install such a large amount of memory on the computer system. Another typical example is a system which is required to run many different software tasks. Such a system may be controlling an automatic industrial system, consisting say of a number of machines. There may exist a software task designed to run each different machine. As each machine requires attention so the system will run the particular task which drives that particular machine. In total, the amount of software may be very large but at any instant it may be necessary for the system to be able to access only a small portion of the overall software. That small portion will be whatever is necessary to run a particular task to drive a particular machine. Such a system is called a *multitasking* system. A third example is a system to which is attached a number of terminals, or VDUs, so that the system may be used simultaneously by a number of people. Each user of the system may be performing different jobs. That is, one user may be editing a file, another may be running a BASIC program, a third may be interrogating a database and so on. Such a system is called a *multiuser* system. It is often convenient to organize such a system so that each user has access to a particular software task at any instant, and the system may contain separate tasks to operate other devices such as printers which will also be attached to the system. Such a system, which consists of a number of tasks which will be run when required according to the needs of the peripheral devices, and which can be used by a number of users is called a multiuser, multitasking system.

In systems such as these, in addition to the user tasks there must always be a number of tasks which are designed to operate the computer system in a satisfactory manner. This suite of tasks is collectively known as the *operating system* and is designed to run the user's tasks as and when required. Examples of common operating systems, although not necessarily multiuser or multitasking operating systems, are CP/M, UNIX, CPM/86 etc. A discussion of operating system functions is outside the scope of the present discussion, but one of the functions the operating system performs is memory management.

In all systems such as those described above, a common characteristic is that the total software code and data space required by all the tasks which may be run in the system is very large and it is uneconomical to install in the system sufficient memory for all the tasks and all the data required to be present at any one time. In practice, therefore, the code and data space for the tasks is maintained on a backing memory, also called *secondary storage*, such as a disk, and the tasks are brought into main memory *(primary storage)* by the operating system memory management software as and when required. As a result, a programmer writing a task does not decide where that task will reside in memory. In fact the task may be run from memory in certain locations, be suspended by the operating system, and then at a later time be put back into memory at different locations for the continuation of its run. Hence although the programmer must organize the code and data in a logical way the programmer does not organize the physical locations in memory into which that code and data will be loaded and run.

Suppose a software task consists of 16K bytes of code and 8K bytes of data, being therefore 24K bytes overall in size. This task can be considered to be 16K of code from memory locations 0 to 16K-1 and 8K of data in memory locations from 16K to 24K-1. Hence all memory address references within the program will be references to memory locations between 0 and 24K. This 24K address space is called the program *logical address space*, or the program *virtual address space*. The task is said to occupy 24K bytes of virtual memory. When the task is actually run in the computer system it will be loaded into memory locations which are different from 0 to 24K and the memory management system will ensure that all address references within the program are translated into their correct addresses for running in the computer system. The memory addresses required by the system when the task is actually running in the system are the addresses of the actual physical memory in which the task is loaded. Thus the memory management system translates the logical addresses in the task into the physical addresses required to access the actual memory locations occupied when the task runs. The range of addresses required to access the code and data for the task when it is in memory is called the *physical address space* of the task.

8.3.1 Address Translation

In the simplest case translation of the logical address to a physical address can be carried out using a base register. Suppose the 24Kb task referred to above is loaded into memory locations from 32K up to 46K, then a base register can be loaded with the number 32K. All memory accesses can then be achieved by adding the content of the base register to the logical address generated by the program. The function of the operating system would be to load the task into memory locations 32K upwards, then to load the memory management base register with the number 32K and transfer control of the computer to the task. Although memory management systems are in practice more complex than this, in principle this is the way in which they achieve the required logical to physical address translation. Figure 8.3 illustrates address translation by a MMU which contains a base register and a hardware adder.

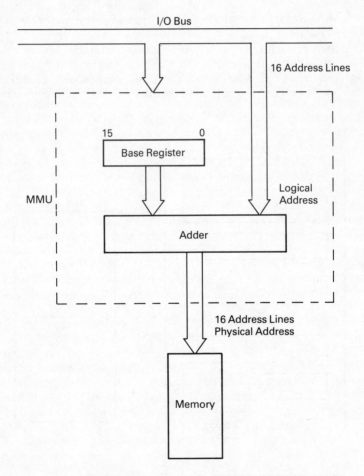

Figure 8.3 *Use of a base register in MMU*

8.3.2 Memory Management Functions

The example above, of a task of 24K bytes does not present a difficult memory management problem because the physical memory will usually be more than the 24K bytes required for the task. Hence the memory management unit may consist of no more than a simple base register. Consider now the case when the software task and its data space are very large. The modern microcomputers and most minicomputers can generate logical addresses of 24 bits or more. Hence the logical address space available to a task is upward of 8 Megabytes (8Mb). Suppose then that there exists a task which occupies a few Megabytes. The logical addresses generated within the task will span that few Megabytes. Although memory is not very expensive it is still not economical to purchase and install sufficient memory to cope with the needs of very large tasks. Consequently in such cases the physical memory will be less than the logical memory required for the task. The task cannot then exist in its entirety in physical memory at any instant. None the less it is still possible to devise a memory management system which will allow the task to be run.

The details of such schemes will be discussed later, but for the moment consider a simple system which will illustrate the need for the memory management unit to perform certain functions. Suppose that both the code and data in the task are larger than the available physical memory. Then we

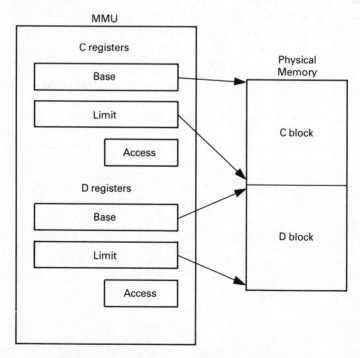

Figure 8.4   *Management of two blocks of memory*

can conceive of dividing the available physical memory into two halves and allocating a base register for each half. Some of the task code could be loaded into one half of the memory, which we will call the C half of the memory, and this could be loaded into the other half of the memory, the D half of the memory, and be managed by the D base register. The relevant parts of the system are shown in Figure 8.4.

8.3.2.1 Memory Limits

Consider just the problem of managing the C part of the memory, which is similar to the problem of managing the D part of memory. When the task starts to run the code will execute progressively through the memory locations until ultimately an instruction fetch will be required for an instruction which has not been loaded into the physical memory. The memory management system must detect this event and request that the operating system loads into the physical memory the required code. The operating system must suspend the task, load the C section of physical memory with the next block of code and then cause the task to resume. The memory management hardware must, therefore, be sufficiently intelligent not only to know the base address in physical memory of the code section but also to know the upper and lower limits of the logical addresses of that code. In addition to the base register, the memory management hardware contains a limit register or limit registers, plus the necessary hardware to compare the contents of those limit registers with the logical addresses being generated by the software task. When the hardware detects that the logical addresses are out of range it raises a high priority interrupt, or *trap*, in the system and the interrupt service causes the operating system to be invoked to perform the memory reload.

8.3.2.2 Access Rights

Consider now one particular case of another important function of memory management systems, that of allocating *access rights* to the physical memory. Suppose we have the same system as that just described, that is half the available physical memory is used by the task code and half by the task data. The code is managed by the C base register and its associated limit registers, and the data is managed by the D base register and its associated limit registers. Suppose further that the task is properly written, at least insofar as the code is never modified. During the instruction fetch part of the CPU instruction cycle memory accesses will always be to the part of physical memory managed by the C register. Apart from the case of immediate operands, which we will ignore for the moment, all memory accesses which occur during the instruction execution part of the CPU instruction cycle will be to physical memory locations managed by the D register. If, due to a programming error or some other reason, an instruction fetch is attempted from that part of memory managed by the D register, then the program is attempting to execute data as if it were code and a program error has occurred. If the memory management hardware monitors the instruction cycle of the machine such an occurrence can be detected. A high priority interrupt can be raised and the operating system can suspend the task and inform the task owner of the error. Similarly if access is attempted to the section of physical memory managed by the C register during the execution part of the CPU instruction cycle, then the software is attempting to use its own instructions as data and this also constitutes an error condition. Again, the memory management hardware can raise an interrupt in the system and the operating system can take appropriate action. The memory management hardware is thus allowing access to the physical memory only when such access is logically correct. Such access rights can be refined to cope with a number of other conditions, including the case of immediate operands. For the latter, allowing memory read operations from either the C or D physical address spaces during the execution part of the CPU instruction cycle, but inhibiting memory write operations in the C physical address space during that time achieves the objective. In this case the C address space has become read only; writing to this space is prohibited. The D address space is read-write, so that data may be read from the D address space or written to that address space.

As shown in Figure 8.4, the MMU requires a set of registers for each block of memory managed. The register set for each block consists of registers to perform the memory management functions described above.

8.3.3 Paging

The remainder of this text will consider a computer system in which the word length is 16 bits and in which all logical addresses are 24 bits long. This is purely for clarity of the descriptions, and the techniques described apply equally to systems with other word lengths and with other logical memory address lengths.

In a paged memory management scheme, see Figure 8.5, both the logical address space and the physical memory are divided into blocks. These blocks are of arbitrary length but in any particular system all blocks are the same length. Typically a block is between 16 bytes and 4K bytes. Each of these blocks is called a *page*. A page is simply a block of memory address space. For the purpose of discussion we will consider a system in which the page length is 1K bytes. To access any byte within a page in this system requires 10 address bits. The 24 bit logical address generated by the system can therefore be considered to be divided into two parts. The least significant 10 bits comprise the address of a byte within a page. The most significant 14 bits specify a page number within the logical address space.

Suppose the computer system contains 1Mb of physical memory. Physical memory addresses will then be 20 bits long. The least significant 10 bits of the physical memory addresses will be the address of a byte within a page in physical memory. The most significant 10 bits of the physical addresses will be the page number of a page in physical memory. Physical memory consists of 1K pages each containing 1K bytes.

One function of the memory management unit in this system is to translate the 24 bit logical addresses into the 20 bit physical addresses. Assuming that the memory is connected to the I/O bus of the system, then the inputs to the memory management hardware will be the 24 logical address lines in the I/O bus and the outputs of the memory management hardware will be the 20 physical address lines which connect to the actual memory hardware. Since pages in the logical address space and in the physical address space are the

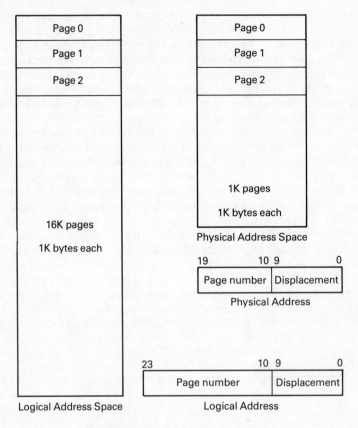

Figure 8.5 *Page addressing*

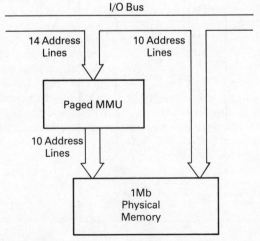

Figure 8.6 *Paged MMU hardware system*

same size, each requiring 10 address lines, the least significant 10 physical address lines are identical to the least significant 10 logical address lines. The memory management unit does not therefore intercept those address lines physically, so that the 10 least significant address lines from the I/O bus are connected directly to the memory hardware. This system is shown in Figure 8.6. The address translation function of the memory management unit (MMU) is thus the translation of the 14 bit logical page numbers into the 10 bit physical page numbers.

Address translation is performed inside the MMU by hardware. Inside the MMU there are a number of pairs of registers, effectively one pair for each physical memory page. Each register pair consists of a 14 bit logical page register and a 10 bit physical page register. The logical page register contains a logical page address and the physical page register contains the start address in physical memory at which the page is loaded. These registers are loaded by the operating system when it loads a page into the physical memory. Hardware in the MMU compares the 14 MSBs from the I/O bus (the logical page address) with the 14 bits in the logical page register. If these are identical then the MMU hardware outputs the 10 bits in the physical page register to the memory hardware. The access to the memory hardware is therefore to the correct physical memory location. If none of the MMU logical page registers contains a number which matches the logical page number on the I/O bus an interrupt is raised and the operating system takes

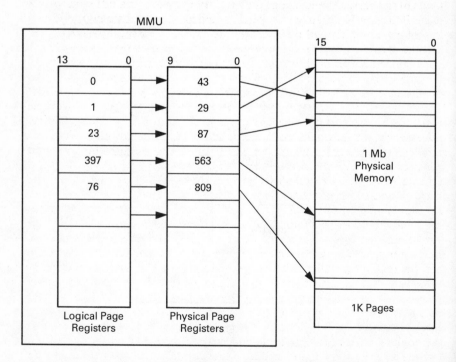

Figure 8.7 *Page address translation registers*

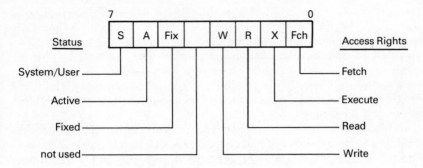

Figure 8.8 *Typical page status register*

appropriate action. Figure 8.7 shows this system. Notice that the logical pages may be loaded into physical memory in any order.

The limit function of the MMU is also performed by these two registers. The content of the 10 bit physical page register corresponds to the base register, that is the C or D register, of the earlier discussion. The logical page register also inherently sets the upper and lower limits of the logical addresses which are currently available in the physical memory. If the software running in the CPU tries to access memory locations outside the limits of the current logical page then it is trying to access a different logical page. If the new logical page has been loaded into physical memory, the new logical page number will be in another of the MMU logical page registers and the MMU will perform the required address translation. If the page is not loaded, then none of the MMU logical page address registers will contain the new page number and the MMU raises an interrupt which calls the operating system to load the new page.

The provision of access rights to the page is implemented by a further register, the Page Status Register as shown in Figure 8.8. 3 bits of status information are shown in this figure but different systems contain different numbers of status bits. Figure 8.8 shows only four access rights bits used which are fetch access, execute access, read access and write access. A typical scheme would be for the operating system to set to a logic 1 the bits corresponding to the access allowed. Hence if the page were to be used only for the fetching of instructions and for the reading of immediate operands the fetch bit would be set to a 1, the execute bit would be set, the read bit would be set and the write bit would be cleared to a 0. This would allow the reading of instructions during the fetch phase of the CPU instruction cycle and the reading of immediate operands in the execute phase of the instruction cycle, but would inhibit the writing of data into the page during any phase of the instruction cycle. The page is, therefore, a page of read only memory. If the page were a page of data the fetch bit would be cleared to inhibit the fetching of instructions from the page. The execute bit would be set to allow access to the page during the execute phase of the instruction cycle. The write bits would be set to allow both reading and writing of data within the page. Figure 8.9 shows the operation of the access rights function

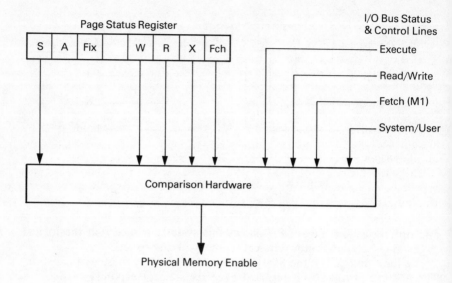

Figure 8.9   *Useage of status information*

in more detail. Each access rights bit in the status register is compared by hardware within the MMU with the logical state of the control lines in the I/O bus. The I/O bus is assumed to contain status lines indicating the instruction fetch and execute phases of the CPU instruction cycle, which is normal in microcomputer systems. The read only and read/write bits are compared with the read and write lines in the I/O bus, which may in practice be a single line—the direction line. Thus access rights to the physical memory are enforced by the MMU hardware by monitoring the status of the system as specified by status lines in the I/O bus. If the system attempts a memory access the MMU allows that access only if the logical page number *and* the system status is as specified in the registers in the MMU. Should these conditions not be met the MMU raises an interrupt request and the operating system takes the necessary action.

The paging system as described so far would work only in a system in which there was a single task. Consider the case of a multitasking system in which two tasks are currently active. Assume there are sufficient page registers in the MMU, and therefore sufficient space in the physical memory, for some pages of both tasks to be loaded in physical memory simultaneously. Some of the MMU page registers would correspond to one task, say task 1, while others would correspond to task 2. Suppose that by coincidence logical pages 1 and 2 or task 1 are loaded in physical memory together with logical pages 2 and 3 or task 2. Further suppose that task 1 is currently running. If task 1 is running in page 1 there is no problem, but suppose it runs into page 2. Within the MMU there are two logical page registers which contain the logical page number 2. The system must therefore unambiguously select the page register for task 1. This can be done by using one of the bits in the page status register to indicate whether that particular page is active or not. When the operating system activates a task, in this case task 1, it sets the "active" status bit in those page status registers in the MMU which belong to the task, and clears the "active" status bit in all other MMU page status registers. Consequently the only page registers which the MMU uses for memory accesses are those registers which manage the parts of physical memory allocated to the task which is actually running in the system. Other pages belonging to other active tasks may be loaded in physical memory, but cannot be accessed by the running task. The task currently running in the system cannot, therefore, corrupt or access code or data belonging to another task.

There are further complications. Suppose the memory management system detects a memory violation attempt by a user task and raises an interrupt request. This causes the operating system to run. The operating system is a collection of tasks, and because there has been a memory protection violation the operating system will normally have to reorganize the physical memory. This in itself will require access to the memory both for the fetching of instructions and data for the operating system tasks and for the loading and unloading of pages belonging to the user tasks. Memory accesses by the operating system for its own code and data will, of course, be routed through the MMU. Operating system tasks will be paged in the same way as the user tasks. It is possible that page 2 of an operating system task will be loaded at the same time as page 2 of one or more of the user tasks. The situation now is that before the operating system has had time to change the "active" status bit in the MMU page registers for the user task which gave the violation the MMU will be presented with a request for access to logical page 2 of the operating system. One further status bit in the page register is therefore necessary to give unambiguous access to the operating system page 2 even though the user task page 2 has active status. This is the "system/user" bit where the system is assumed to be the operating system. Only the operating system is allowed access to system pages, and a request by the operating system to the MMU will be granted, in the circumstances described, unambiguously to the correct page of physical memory. When a switch to the operating system occurs a "system" status bit in the I/O bus becomes active giving an unambiguous comparison from which the MMU can select the physical page for execution of the operating system code. Figure 8.8 shows the system/user bit as one of the standard status bits.

Figure 8.8 also shows the "fixed" status bit. This status bit is required by the operating system to indicate that the particular page in memory must not be exchanged for a page in secondary storage. Fixed pages may be used for a number of purposes, one of which is to contain the operating system code and data for the task which responds to MMU violation interrupts. That part of the operating system which manages the MMU hardware must always be available in memory. Temporarily fixed pages are also used for the data area for peripheral devices which DMA data to and from memory even when the task requesting the DMA is suspended waiting for the DMA to complete. Many memory management systems provide other status bits to assist the operating system to implement efficient algorithms for determining which pages to swap from physical memory into secondary storage.

8.3.4 Segmentation

Memory segmentation schemes have certain characteristics in common with memory paging schemes. A memory segment is a block of memory and is managed by a memory management scheme which is partly hardware and partly software. The status bit system for segments is much the same as that described above for pages and will not, therefore, be described again.

In spite of similarities between paging and sementation schemes, segmentation is fundamentally different from paging. Memory pages, as described above, are separate contiguous blocks of memory. Memory pages do not overlap one another. Memory segments are also separate blocks of memory, but segments may overlap one another. In a paged system, the program counter may be incremented so as to move the system from one page into the next page. In a segmented system it is not possible to move from one segment into the next segment by incrementing the program counter. Thus each memory segment is inherently selfcontained in spite of the fact that it may overlap another segment. A major difference between paging and segmentation systems is that paging is transparent to the programmer. Paging is handled totally by the operating system and the MMU hardware and the person writing the applications program has no knowledge that it is occurring. With segmentation this is not so. Since it is impossible to increment the program counter to move from one segment to another, the programmer is involved in the organization of segments. A program is written with explicit segmentation directives embedded in the code and the programmer consciously organizes a software task into a number of segments. How this is done is up to the programmer, but it may for instance be convenient to put all the code into one segment, and to put different types of data into different segments. If software is written in assembly language for a segmented system there are segmentation directives within the language. The programmer is responsible for setting up and organizing the contents of segments, but the handling of these segments within the MMU and the hardware of the computer need not be understood by the programmer. Handling of segments by the memory management system is transparent to the programmer.

In a segmented system the logical address consists of a segment number and an address, a displacement, within the segment. Considering the 24 bit logical address system used as our previous example, if this were a segmented system the 24 bit address may be partitioned as shown in Figure 8.10. The 8 most significant bits of the logical address form an 8 bit segment number. The least significant bits of the logical address form a 16 bit displacement within the segment. Each memory segment is then 64K bytes long, because the displacement address is 16 bits long. There are 256 such segments possible in the system because the segment number is 8 bits long.

The MMU for a segmented system contains a number of segment register sets very similar to the page register sets in the MMU of the paged system. These segment registers contain for each segment, the segment number, the base address of the segment and the segment status bits. For the moment, assume that the physical memory is 16Mb, requiring a 24 bit physical address. A register set for a segmented MMU is shown in Figure 8.10, from

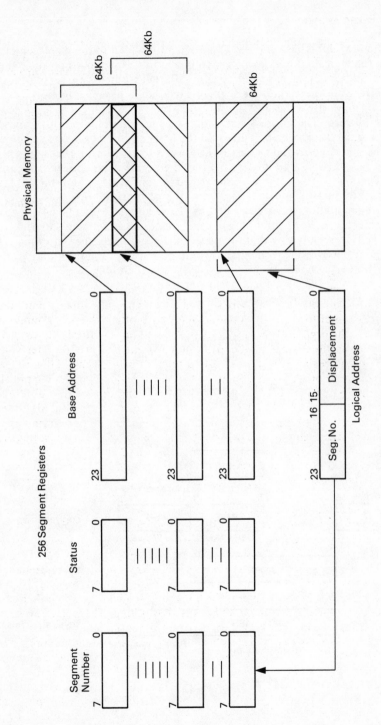

Figure 8.10 *Segmentation scheme*

which it can be seen that the segment base address is a 24 bit physical address.

In the MMU the base address of a segment is added to the displacement part of the logical address, which is 16 bits in this example, to produce the physical address. If the base addresses of different segments are set to be less than 64K bytes apart, then the segments overlap in physical memory. This condition may arise if the least significant 16 bits of the segment base address are not all zero. The address translation mechanism, addition of the base address to the displacement, will cause the higher addresses in one segment to be the same physical addresses as the lower addresses in another segment. Hence the MMU can be used to overlap the segments as shown in Figure 8.10. This was not the case with the paged system MMU where the MMU produced the most significant 10 bits of the physical address.

The segmentation so far described has fixed length segments, 64K bytes per segment. It is, however, not very usual to require all segments to be 64K bytes long. Remembering that the programmer organizes the data which is loaded into the various segments, it would be normal for a programmer to specify that a segment should not exceed a specified length. For example, suppose part of the data for a particular task consists of some fixed data tables and the programmer specifies that these tables shall be the only data to occupy a particular segment. The fixed size of the tables predetermines the size of the valid data area within the segment. Program references which access that particular segment and which attempt to access memory locations outside the valid data area are erroneous, and should cause the system to indicate an error. This can be done if it is possible to limit the size of the segment. The MMU then traps if an access is made to a segment at an address that is outside the bounds of the segment. Further, it would be very

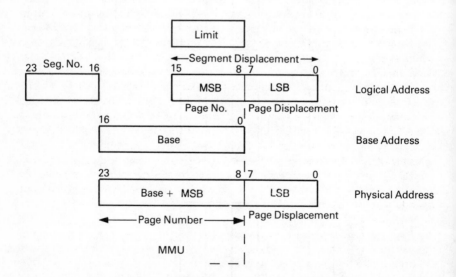

Figure 8.11   *Address translation – segmented MMU*

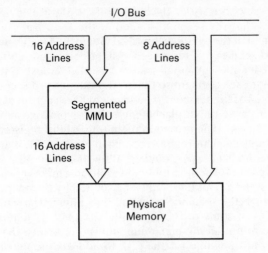

Figure 8.12   *Segmented MMU hardware system*

wasteful of available memory if a 64K byte segment had to be used to contain a very small data set. The ability to vary the segment length improves the efficiency of memory utilization.

Variable size segments are possible if each segment consists of an integral number of relatively small pages. Suppose each segment is an integral number of pages each of which is 256 bytes long. The 16 bit displacement in the logical address can then be regarded as an 8 bit page number and an 8 bit address of a byte within the page, as shown in Figure 8.11. Since a page is the smallest block of memory handled by the memory management system, segments are now constrained to start on page boundaries. The segment base address register in the segmented MMU is not now 24 bits long but 16 bits long, corresponding to the 16 most significant bits of the 24 bit physical memory address. The least significant 8 address lines of the I/O bus bypass the MMU and are connected directly to the physical memory hardware, just as were the least significant 10 lines in the paged system described above. This arrangement is shown in Figure 8.12. The output from the segmented MMU is a 16 bit address which corresponds to the start address of a page in physical memory. It is thus a 16 bit page number. This 16 bit page number together with the 8 bit page displacement form the 24 bit physical memory address.

If there is less than 16Mb of memory in the physical memory, the most significant physical memory address lines will not be used. To ensure that the 24 bit address does not exceed the limits of the physical memory available, the operating system must know how much physical memory is installed. The memory management software then ensures that the segment base address of all loaded segments is within the bounds of the physical memory available. It also ensures that the segment loaded at the top of physical memory is wholly contained in the available physical memory. An alternative is the use of a combined segmented and paged system described later.

In a variable length segmented system, the MMU must contain a segment limit register for each segment so that a trap can occur if access is requested outside the limits of the segment. The segment base register acts as the lower limit register because the displacement is always positive and added to the base register content. The provision of an upper limit register is, therefore, additionally required. This register, shown in Figure 8.11, is an 8 bit register containing the highest page number allowed within the segment. Any attempt to access a higher page number results in a memory violation trap to the operating system. This limit register is loaded by the operating system at the time at which the segment is loaded into physical memory.

If the lengths of some of the segments in a task, as determined by the programmer, are not all the maximum allowed length (64Kb in the example), then it is not possible for the task to address the maximum possible memory which could be addressed by the 24 bit output from the MMU. Suppose all the segments were specified to be the minimum size, 256 bytes. Then a task which uses the maximum number of segments—256 as determined by the segment number bits in the logical address—has available in the logical address space only 256 segment of 256 bytes each, a total of 64K bytes. This limitation is set by the segmentation scheme, not by the limitations of available physical memory or by the number of address bits available in the logical address space. In practice, of course, a programmer designs the software to be segmented into segments of sufficient number and size as to accommodate the task being written.

In some circumstances, it is not possible at the time of writing a task, to ascertain the segment size required. For example, if a task uses a stack for the storage of input data, as is often done in the case of compilers, the size of the input data is unknown at the time of writing the task. It is normal practice to allocate one segment for the stack and therefore this segment could be allocated the maximum available size to accommodate a large set of data if necessary. This is not a very satisfactory arrangement, and it is better to use an operating system which can increase the size of the segment at the time the task is running to allow maximum utilization of the physical memory. Thus the task writer allocates a small segment for the data stack. When the task first runs, the number in the segment limit register (specifying the number of pages in the segment) is that specified by the task writer.

When the task fills its stack segment with input data, the MMU traps to the operating system with a memory violation attempt. The segment status register contains a status bit indicating that it is a segment which can be expanded by the operating system if it overflows. The operating system then allocates more space for the stack segment by increasing the number in the segment limit register for that segment. Since the limit register contains the number of pages in the segment, the segment has been expanded. The operating system then reloads the segment into physical memory, allocating sufficient pages to accommodate the larger segment size. The segment has therefore been automatically increased in size to accommodate the data it is currently handling. Such a segment is said to have a dynamically variable length.

Variable length segments allow the physical memory available to be used very efficiently so that tasks are allocated only as much physical memory as they require, allowing the maximum number of tasks to be loaded in physical memory at any instant and minimizing the amount of swapping of tasks between the primary and secondary storage. This swapping of tasks is a relatively slow process, as the secondary storage is usually a disk system. Task swapping activity is very low in a system which is not working hard, that is in a system in which very few tasks are active. As the system becomes busier, with more tasks becoming active, there is a need for the operating system to swap tasks more frequently. The situation is, therefore, that as the system becomes busier and has less idle time it is required to spend more time on its own internal organization. Proportionately less time is then available for the external tasks which the system is designed to perform. A point can soon be reached when the system is overloaded because it is spending so much time organizing itself that it has insufficient time available for the external tasks. Any mechanism, such as minimizing the space allocated to tasks in physical memory, which minimizes the swapping between primary and secondary storage can therefore bring considerable improvements in the work throughput of the system. Segmentation schemes can be a considerable help in such systems.

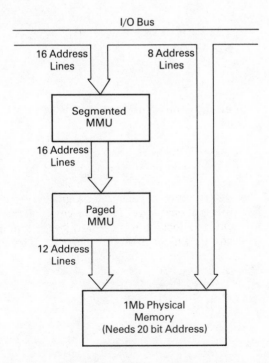

Figure 8.13 *Segmented and paged system*

8.3.5 Combined Paging and Segmentation

The output from the segmented MMU described above was assumed to be a 16 bit page number. Together with the 8 least significant address lines from the I/O bus which were considered to contain an 8 bit page displacement, the output from the segmented system is a 24 bit memory address. If there is less physical memory installed than can be addressed by 24 bits (16Mb), then this 24 bit address can be used as the 24 bit logical address input to a paged MMU handling pages of 256 bytes. Thus a memory management system consisting of segmentation organized by the programmer and implemented by a memory management system transparent to the programmer may be superimposed onto a transparent paging system to give a segmented and paged system, the outline of which is shown in Figure 8.13.

Segmented and paged systems have been implemented on large computer systems, but at the time of writing the author is not aware of any such systems in microcomputers, although some microcomputer memory management schemes are almost segmented and paged. Most small systems at present use either paging *or* segmentation, but not both.

Postscript

The reader who has completed a study of this book may choose to study further in one or more of a number of directions.

The small-computer specialist still has many topics of study. For example, the engineer has the problems of designing electronics systems in which microprocessors are used as embedded components. This requires a decision on which functions to implement in hardware and which in software. A good understanding of both areas is required for a proper decision to be reached. The newer and all embracing subject area of Information Technology is also one in which a balanced view of hardware and software is necessary. The software engineer will also find a challenge in designing software to take full advantage of the newer 16/32-bit microprocessors with their capability for multiuser and multitasking operations. Programming such machines will in many cases require an understanding of the more advanced hardware facilities of such machines.

Such systems are rapidly encroaching upon application areas previously reserved for medium or large scale conventional systems. To provide effective service to users, they will have to adopt many of the mechanisms previously restricted to mainframes, albeit in a form suitably modified for the new generations of supermicros and superminis.

The large system specialist has much to learn from and about smaller systems. For instance, the availability of Read-Only Memory designed originally for microcomputers has led to the use of ROM to store the essential parts, the kernels, of Operating Systems. Recovery from software and hardware faults is thereby made easier and quicker, and the system operates more quickly in normal mode. Large systems are also using peripherals, controllers and terminals furnished with their own programmable intelligence in the form of microchip processor and storage, which have to be programmed to perform the necessary functions of system integration. Most mainframe manufacturers now actively market their own or bought-in microcomputers for dual purposes—as intelligent workstations linked to the central processor or as stand-alone microsystems, as the user selects. The design of systems with distributed intelligence, and even of systems in which the central processor is replaced by a closely or loosely linked network of smaller computers, is one of the most challenging tasks in modern computing.

Small Computer Characteristics

This appendix presents a survey of the characteristics of some popular small computer systems expressed in the terminology of the text rather than in the terminology used in the manufacturer's literature.

The purpose of the survey is to emphasize that there are certain common properties of computer systems as described in the earlier parts of the book, regardless of whether the system is described as a minicomputer, microcomputer, personal computer etc. in the marketplace. It is also intended to reveal the architectural differences beween apparently similar systems. It must be stressed that the appendix is not intended to be a comparative study of the computer systems described, and the systems are not all described to the same level of detail. The information given is presented in the same sequence as the related topic is dealt with in the chapters of the text. Six computer systems are discussed, chosen because they are the market leaders in the different sectors of the small computer market, and also because they cover the complete range of small computers as defined in Chapter 1:

VAX minicomputer
PDP-11 minicomputer
6502 microprocessor
Z-80 microprocessor
M68000 microprocessor
Intel 8086/8088 microprocessor

The latter two entries illustrate the significant developments in commercial microprocessors.

These are all designed and manufactured in the USA.

A.1 THE DIGITAL EQUIPMENT CORPORATION PDP-11 COMPUTERS

The PDP-11 is a family of small computers that now range from the MicroPDP-11, through the LSI-11 microcomputers to the original and more recent PDP-11 minicomputers. The family has grown over 15 years and has encompassed every change in electronic technology with virtually the same architecture. The PDP-11 is the original, archetypal and most widely used 16-bit computer.

General Features

Word length 16 bits, address width 16, 18 or 22 bits. Maximum memory size 2M words of 16 bits (4M bytes). Registers—all 16 bits long:

Six GP Registers
Instruction Register
Program Counter
Stack Pointer
Status Register
Memory Management Registers (up to 8).

Instruction Set

The basic instruction set contains 81 instructions. It can manipulate integer data in 8 and 16-bit format. There is also an optional Floating Point Instruction Set that can process floating point numbers in single-precision (32-bit) and double-precision (64-bit) form; and an optional Commercial Instruction Set can manipulate Character Strings and Decimal Strings (numeric and packed).

Data Transfer Instructions
These instructions move data between registers and memory, or between two registers. Single address instructions operate on a word in memory. The 1 1/2 address instructions move data between memory and a register, with the result routed to either the register or memory location. The 2 address instructions transfer between two memory locations. The Mode subfield in the address field of the instruction (see Figure A1) may be used to specify a register reference instead of a memory reference.

Arithmetic and Logical Instructions
There are single, 1 1/2 and 2 address arithmetic and logical instructions. The logical operations AND, OR, EX-OR and NOT are provided. These instructions operate on data in the registers or in memory.

Jump Instructions
Fifteen conditional and one unconditional jump instructions are provided. Most of them use relative addressing.

Subroutine Entry
The PDP-11 architecture contains a stack which is part of the main memory. The subroutine entry instruction is a 1 1/2 address instruction which causes

the content of the specified register to be pushed on the stack and the link address to be stored in that register. The PC is then loaded with the memory address specified in the instruction, which causes the jump to the first instruction in the subroutine. The Return instruction causes the PC to be loaded from the specified register, and the register to be loaded from the top of the stack.

Shift Instructions

Left, right and circular shifts are provided. These instructions are in single address memory reference format, and can act on the contents either of a memory location or a GP register. The carry flag is used as an extension of the register whose contents are being shifted. Each shift may be from 1 to 15 positions.

Flag Instructions

One instruction allows the Zero, Negative, Overflow and Carry flags to be set or cleared according to the state of a field in the state of a field in the instruction.

Miscellaneous Instructions

Halt, No-op and Wait instructions exist, and a number of special Trap instructions which are useful in error diagnosis. The Commercial Instruction Set contains 27 instructions which perform arithmetic, moves, conversions, searches and comparisons on character and numeric strings. The Floating-Point Instruction Set performs arithmetic and conversions on floating-point numbers.

Instruction Set Coding Structure

The coding of the instructions in the basic instruction set is as shown in Figure A.1. There are five major coding levels. Level 1 is coded by a 3-bit field (bits 14–12); level 2 by a single-bit field (bit 11); level 3 by a 4-bit field (bits 15, 10, 9 and 8); level 4 by a 2-bit field (bits 7 and 6); and level 5 by a 3-bit field (bits 2, 1 and 0). In every case the escape field to the next lower level is all zeros in the current coding field.

The Level 1 instructions are 2-address instructions. In most of these bit 15 is used to indicate the address of a word or that of a half-word (leading byte in a word). The 3-bit opcode field is:

```
bit 14  13  12
     0   0   0   Escape Code to level 2
     0   0   1   Copy
     0   1   0   Compare
     0   1   1   AND
     1   0   0   Special Function
     1   0   1   OR
     1   1   0   Add or Subtract (depends on bit 15)
     1   1   1   Not used
```

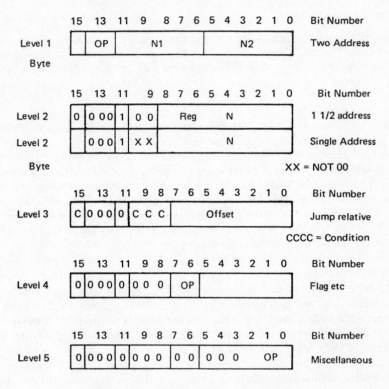

Figure A1 *PDP-11 instruction coding*

Level 2 instructions, coded by bit $11 = 1$, are divided into subgroups:

bit 10 9
0 0 1 1/2 address instructions
0 1 Single address instruction
1 0 Single address instruction
1 1 Not used

Level 3 instructions, for which bits 14–11 are all zero, contain the conditional jumps, coded by bits 15, 10, 9 and 8. There are fifteen conditional jumps and the escape code to the next level (0000).

Level 4 instructions are coded thus:

bit 7 6
0 0 Escape to level 5
0 1 Unconditional jump
1 1 Swap bytes
1 0 Flag instructions or Return, decoded by bit 5

Level 5 coding uses the three least significant bits to code the miscellaneous instructions.

Addressing Modes

The memory reference instructions contain one or two address fields each 6 bits long. Three of these bits are a GP register address and the second three are Mode bits. In 2 address instructions the two operands may be addressed by different techniques.

Direct Addressing

Memory addresses in the PDP-11 are normally held in one of the GP registers and a field in the 16-bit instruction contains the address of the register containing the memory address. In this sense memory addressing is indirect via the registers. There are no immediate mode addressing or direct addressing instructions in the PDP-11. However, the PDP-11 programmer can write instructions in the assembly language which appear to be immediate mode or direct addressing instructions. This is because the use of special registers in the CPU in the calculation of memory addresses gives the appearance of these addressing modes.

Indirect Addressing

The normal mode of addressing in the PDP-11 is indirectly via one of the GP registers. The manufacturer's literature generally refers to this mode as direct addressing. Two level indirect addressing is provided in which the first level is via a GP register and the second level is via the memory location whose address is in the GP register.

Multiple Length Instructions

Double length (32-bits) and triple length (48-bits) instructions are included in the instruction set. If the instruction is single address of 1 1/2 address the Mode and register 6-bit field can indicate that the operand is in the location next to that of the instruction code. The manufacturer refers to this mode of addressing as Immediate mode addressing because if the instruction is considered to be double length then the operand is part of the instruction. The 6-bit mode/register field is explicitly coded in this case as:

Mode bits = Indirect addressing via the PC, autoincrementing the [PC]

Similarly triple length instructions can be used when the instruction code is a two address format and the addressing mode for both operands is indirect via the PC, autoincrementing the [PC] after each memory access. Multiple length instructions are mandatory when indexing.

Indexing

Any of the GP registers may be used as an index register. When indexing is required the instruction is always double or triple length. The second word of the instruction is taken to be the address field for the first operand. The content of the GP register specified as the index register is added to this to obtain the effective address. If two operands are to be obtained by indexed memory reference the third word of the instruction is taken to contain the address of the second operand, to which the content of the GP register specified as its index register is added to obtain its effective address.

Notice that indexing is not used in the PDP-11 to increase the addressing range of the address field of the instruction but purely as a convenience to the programmer.

Relative Addressing
Relative addressing may be specified by explicitly coding the indexed addressing mode, and using the program counter as the index register. It is of interest to note that the PDP-11 assembler uses relative addressing as the normal addressing mode both for jumps and for data addressing. This is possible because the relative addressing offset is 16-bits long (the content of the second word of the double length indexed instruction). Thus the whole of the 64K memory is accessible using this mode of addressing. The use of relative addressing as the normal mode allows the code produced by the assembler to be loaded into memory at any position without modification. Such code is called position independent code.

Autoincrementing and Autodecrementing
These can be specified for use with indirect addressing via the registers in which case the content of the register is incremented after the memory access or decremented before the memory access. This allows the programmer to use any GP register as a stack pointer. There is no mode for autoincrementing or autodecrementing an index register content after indexing.

Combined Indirect and Indexed Addressing
All indexed addressing is combined with indirect addressing via the registers. Additionally it is possible to specify indexing of the second level of indirect addressing in which case the memory is accessed via the GP register to recover an address which is added to the content of the index register before the memory is accessed for the operand. Hence only preindexing of the indirect address held in the memory is possible.

Input/Output

The PDP-11 family supports I/O buses with 16, 18 or 22 lines in its various models.

The standard I/O bus connecting peripherals and memory to the processor is the UNIBUS, which contains 18 address lines and 16 data lines, along with control lines which include a pair of SYNC lines for handshaking and a R/W direction line. UNIBUS was the first data bus in the industry to enable devices to send, receive or exchange data without processor intervention or intermediate buffering in memory. Peripheral data and status registers have addresses in the top 8K of addressable memory. The earlier LSI-11 microprocessors contained an I/O bus with 16 address lines, shared with the data lines in the interests of economy. Later LSI-11 models extended the number of address lines to 22. Finally the largest PDP-11 processor was designed with a 22-bit memory bus to which were attached a UNIBUS via a special 22–18 bit translation unit (the UNIBUS Map); one or high speed MASSBUS controllers controlling a high-speed MASSBUS for disk and tape devices; and a cache memory placed between the processor and main memory.

Interrupt Handling

Interrupts are multilevel and hardware vectored. A device wishing to interrupt the processor asserts the interrupt request line and puts its vector on the data lines. The vector does not include the least significant two bits because bit 0 in the PDP11 address is used to address a byte within a word, and the interrupt vector points to a double word in the memory. As the word address must be even, bit 1 is not required either. The double word pointed to by the interrupt vector is normally in the low end of the memory system. The first word of the double word contains the address of the start of the device service routine, while the second word contains a Processor Status Word (PSW) to be used while the routine is running. This determines which devices can interrupt the service routine, as explained below. On receipt of an interrupt request the processor pushes both the current Processor Status Word (PSW) and the link address on to the stack, then loads the Processor Status register and the PC from the locations pointed to by the interrupt vector.

Interrupt Priority Allocation

In the PDP11 a device is not allowed to request an interrupt unless it is the master device on the I/O bus and is therefore in a position to initiate a data transfer on the bus (see chapter 5). Only one device at a time can ever be in this state and consequently only one device will ever be allowed to raise an interrupt request at any instant in time. The situation of simultaneous interrupt requests can therefore never arise and a device raising an interrupt request is assured of an immediate response by the processor. Hence a device wishing to request an interrupt AND in a state to do so, puts its interrupt vector on the I/O bus data lines and uses the interrupt request line as the SYNC for the vector. This SYNC is acknowledged by the processor on a separate interrupt acknowledge line. Interrupt priorities in this system are determined indirectly by a priority system for allocating mastership of the bus.

Requests for mastership of the bus are made on one of eight levels, each level consisting of two lines, a request line and the corresponding acknowledge line. The latter is daisy chained through all the devices on a particular level (see Figure 6.7). For this purpose the CPU is also a device on the bus, but its priority level is not permanently fixed. The CPU priority level is determined by a field in the Processor Status Word, and this field can be changed by program. Only those devices on a priority level higher than that of the processor can be allocated control of the I/O bus and are therefore able to interrupt the processor.

Direct Memory Access

In this minicomputer system, a device requiring a DMA transfer requests use of the I/O bus on a special DMA request line (called NPR—Non Processor Request). This is the highest priority request for use of the bus and is granted at the earliest opportunity by the issuing of an acknowledge signal (called NPG—Non Processor Grant). The earliest time at which the device takes charge of the bus is immediately at the completion of the current bus cycle, if there is one in progress. It is given immediate access to the bus if the bus is idle when the request is made. One bus line (SACK—Selection ACKnowledge) is provided in the system so that the device may, by holding a signal on that line, retain use of the bus for more than one cycle for burst mode DMA transfers. Once the device is in control of the bus it can obtain memory cycles as they become available. The device is not required to send a signal to the CPU to disable the CPU bus drivers. The CPU has to contend for the bus when it requires its use. The CPU may, therefore, be held up for any period of time waiting for the bus to become free. DMA devices always have higher priority than the CPU for use of the bus.

Memory Management

As described above, there are three levels of address width current in the PDP-11 family; 16 address lines, which can address 64K bytes of memory, UNIBUS's 18 lines which can address 256K bytes, and 22 lines which can address 4M bytes. Instructions executed by the processor can however in each case linearly address only 64K bytes of address space in a 16-bit word. To overcome this disparity a Memory Management Unit is implemented which, when activated, will treat a 16-bit address in an instruction not as a physical value in the range 0 to $2**16 - 1$, but as virtual address subdivided as follows:

Page No/Block No/Byte Displacement
(3 bits) (7 bits) (6 bits)

Thus a program can be mapped into 1–8 pages, each page consisting of up to 128 blocks of 64 bytes. Each of these pages may be physically located anywhere in the address space afforded by the specific I/O bus or in the area of memory attached if this is lower than the maximum. The physical addresses of pages allocated to a program are held in one of two or more sets of eight 32-bit page registers; the virtual page number in the instruction is the entry number in that table, which returns a page address that is 12 or 16 bytes long. The block and byte displacement are then applied to the physical page address to give the actual instruction address.

This facility enables the computer system to process more than one user program in memory at any one time, each program being allocated its own pages in the page table. Similarly, in the appropriate models, there is a separate mapping of the 18-bit addresses carried from a UNIBUS device into a 22-bit memory address. The UNIBUS Map registers are allocated in the top 8K bytes of memory which is always reserved for UNIBUS.

A.2 THE DIGITAL EQUIPMENT CORPORATION VAX COMPUTER

The VAX computer was designed to be compatible with and extend the capabilities of the PDP-11 family. The VAX family now ranges from the MicroVAX to the multiprocessor 11/785 system which can be described as a "supermini" rivaling traditional mainframes in power and facilities.

General Features

Word length 16 bits, internal address width 32 bits, external address width 24 or 30 bits. Maximum virtual memory 4 gigabytes. Maximum connectable memory 8M bytes. Sixteen 32-bit general purpose registers are provided, including the Program Counter, Stack Pointer, Argument Pointer and Frame Pointer, all four of which have a special significance in certain instructions but are otherwise usable in the normal way by a programmer. There are also many other special purpose or privileged instructions not accessible by a program at least in the User mode. The larger VAX systems contain a cache memory; interleaved memory via two memory controllers; and a prefetch instruction buffer which allows the next instruction to be fetched and decoded while the current instruction is executing.

Instruction Set

The VAX instruction set is an extension of the PDP-11 instruction set, and contains over 300 different instructions. A VAX instruction consists of an opcode (1 or 2 bytes), and up to 6 operand specifiers. Each operand specifier may consist of an Addressing Mode (4 bits, see below) and up to 2 Register numbers (4 bits) and addresses, data or displacements (32 bits).

Data Transfer Instructions
Both Data Transfer and Arithmetic and Logical Instructions can manipulate the following data types:

Integers, represented as bytes, words, longwords (32 bits), quadwords (64 bits), or octawords (128 bits);
Floating Point Numbers, represented as 4, 8 or 16-byte formats;
Packed Decimal Strings, represented as 2 digits/byte, up to 16 bytes/string;
Numeric Strings, represented as 1 digit/byte, up to 31 bytes/string;
Character Strings, represented as 1 character/byte, up to 64K bytes/string.
Bit Fields, represented as up to 32 bits/field.

Data can be transferred between registers or register and memory. Data can also be converted from one format to another, as appropriate.

Arithmetic and Logical Instructions
Arithmetic can be performed in floating point, decimal or BCD format. There are some special instructions such as POLY—evaluate Polynomial, and CRC—Cyclic Redundancy Check.

Jump Instructions
There are two groups of jump instructions—Branch on Condition (16 instructions), and Branch on Bit (6 instructions). There are also 6 Loop and 6 Loop and Case instructions.

Subroutine Entry and Exit
Both subroutine and procedure calls and returns are provided, and a Change Mode which is equivalent to a software interrupt.

Flag Instructions
There is a group of instructions which can set or unset bits in operands or in the Status Register.

Miscellaneous Instructions
There are sets of instructions to process bit fields and queues, and some privileged instructions executable only in one of the nonuser modes— Kernel, Executive or Supervisory. There are also PDP-11 compatibility instructions executable by the VAX processor—almost the complete PDP-11 instruction set.

Addressing Modes

VAX Addressing Modes can be divided into two classes—those which use the GP registers 0–14 and those which use the Program Counter. Of the thirteen general register modes, eleven are similar to PDP-11 modes, plus the Indexed and Literal modes.

Literal Mode
A 6-bit field in the instruction can be interpreted as an integer or floating point number.

Indirect Addressing
The specified GP register contains the operand ("Register Mode"); or the register contains the address of the operand ("Register-Deferred").

Autodecrement Mode
The contents of the specified register are first decremented by the size of the operand and then used as the address of the operand. The size of an operand is the number of bytes in the data type specified by the instruction.

Autoincrement Mode
The contents of the specified register are used as the address of the operand and then incremented by the size of the operand. If the register is the PC, this is called "Absolute Mode".

Autoincrement-Deferred Mode
The contents of a register are used as the address of a memory location containing the address of the operand and are then incremented by four. If the register is the PC, the mode is known as "Immediate".

Displacement Mode
The value stored in the register is used as the base address, to which a byte, word, or longword is added to give the effective address of the operand.

Displacement-Deferred Mode
The value stored in the register is used as the base address of a table of addresses, to which a byte, word, or longword is added. The resulting sum is the address of a location that contains the actual address of the operand.

Indexing
All of these modes except Register Mode can be modified by an index register. In an indexed addressing mode, one register is used to compute the base address of a data structure, and the other register is used to compute a displacement from the base address. The processor first finds the base operand address, using any one of the above addressing modes except the Register Mode; takes the value stored in the index register and multiplies it by the given operand size; and adds the result to the base address to give the effective address of the operand.

Relative Addressing
This is used with the PC specified as the register, followed by a byte, word or longword displacement which is added to the contents of the PC (i.e. the address of the next instruction) to give the operand address. This mode is useful for writing position-independent code.

Relative-Deferred Mode
This is similar to the Relative Mode except that the sum of the contents of the PC and the displacement is the address of a location which itself contains the address of the operand.

Input/Output

The VAX processors employ the UNIBUS and MASSBUS (larger models only) bus structures developed for the PDP-11 family. The largest processor also has a highspeed 32-bit wide Synchronous data path linking the processor(s), memory controllers and UNIBUS/MASSBUS adapters. The UNIBUS adapter may permit up to 15 buffered paths as well as the direct path between a peripheral and memory or processor. When a UNIBUS device wishes to interrupt the processor for service, it issues a Bus Grant request on one of four I/O lines. The processor responds with a Bus Grant signal, unless it is already processing a request from a device of higher priority or a device of the same priority bus nearer the processor electrically. One word or byte is transferred in one Read/Write cycle. DMA requests arrive on a separate line, the Non-Processor Request line, and receives immediate attention. The device receives a NP Grant signal and one byte is transferred. The MASSBUS adapter permits block transfers of up to 64K bytes between memory and attached high speed peripherals. The program initiating a MASSBUS transfer supplies the starting (virtual) address for the block of data to be transferred which is then mapped into a physical address (see below), and the number of bytes to be transferred. The MASSBUS adapter contains a 32-bit data buffer into which two 16-bit words are assembled before transmission on the 32-bit wide system bus.

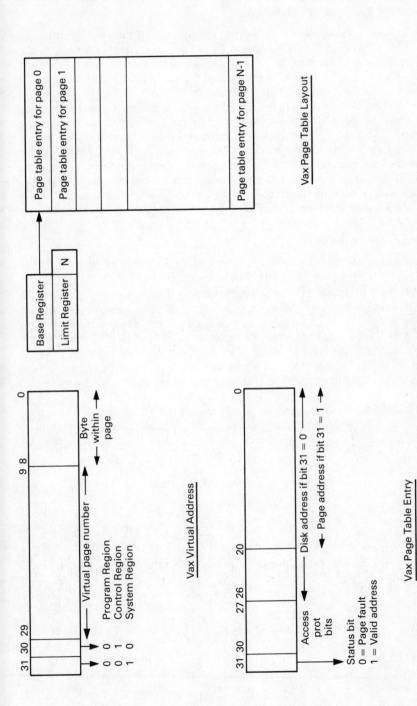

Figure A2 *Vax memory management architecture*

Interrupts and Interrupt-Handling

The Processor recognizes 31 levels of priority −1 to 16 for use by software, 17–24 for hardware interrupts, and 25–31 for other features such as the Interval Timer. Interrupt levels 21–24 correspond to the four UNIBUS lines. Except for the UNIBUS interrupts, the interrupting device supplies a vector from the System Control Block, which directs the processor to a memory location containing the address of the appropriate interrupt service routine. The processor has a lower but floating priority than contending devices, but raises its priority to the level of the interrupting device during the execution of an interrupt service routine. Non-UNIBUS hardware can provide 16 separate vectors for each priority level. An interrupt service routine operates in the Kernel Mode and is terminated by a Return instruction which reloads the interrupted program's Status Register and PC from the stack onto which they were pushed at the time of the interrupt.

Memory Management

Physical memory is divided into I/O Address Space and Memory Address Space. UNIBUS and MASSBUS device registers and the UNIBUS Map (see below) are located in the I/O Address Space, which is the top megabyte of addressable memory. Memory is allocated to programs in pages of 512 bytes; the pages allocated to a program need not be contiguous in memory, and only a subset of the pages of a program need (and in the case of a very large program can) be resident in memory at any one time. A physical address is therefore treated as a page address (15 or 21 bits), and a page displacement within page. The leading 1 or 4 bits identify an address in I/O space.

Virtual address space consists of all possible 32-bit addresses that can be exchanged between a program and processor to identify a byte location in memory—$2**32$—1 or 4 gigabytes. It is divided into Process space, used by user programs (further subdivided into a Program Region and Control Region), and System Space used by nonuser mode routines. All memory references to this virtual space are treated as virtual addresses and mapped into the physical space that is available. A virtual address consists of a 2-bit field selecting the region, a 21-bit virtual page number and a 9-bit displacement. The page number is used as an index into a page table in which there is an entry for each page of a program. If that program page has been loaded into a physical page, its entry contains the starting address of the page of memory allocated to it; if not, it will contain the identification of the disk sector on which it is stored. The page table entry also indicates its status and access protection codes. Figure A.2 shows the layout of virtual addresses, page tables and page table entries.

Three page tables are provided, controlled by Base and Length Registers, one for each area of virtual address space. When a virtual address reference is issued by a program, the status bit of the selected page table entry is examined, and if it indicates a loaded page, the byte displacement from the virtual address is added to the page address to give the actual memory address. If it indicates a page that is not loaded, a page fault interrupt is signalled which will cause the memory management software of the operating system (itself known as VMS) to load that page of the program from disk into memory, if necessary writing the code currently occupying that page back to disk first. There is also an Address Translation Buffer used to store commonly-referenced virtual-actual address translations, in order to reduce the time taken in page table lookup. Similarly, UNIBUS-generated addresses of 18 bits are translated into physical addresses via the UNIBUS Map. 9 bits are used to index a UNIBUS Map (a set of 32-bit registers in main memory), returning a 15-bit page address, and 9 bits are used as a byte displacement. The MASSBUS adapter similarly generates a physical address from an 8-bit reference into the MASSBUS Map and a 9-bit displacement which is added to the retrieved 15-bit page address.

A.3 THE MOS TECHNOLOGY (MOSTEK) 6502 MICROPROCESSOR

The 6502 is the microprocessor at the heart of most of the popular personal/ home/hobby microcomputers—Apple II, Commodore PET, BBC Micro—and must therefore be the single most widely used 8-bit microprocessor.

General Features

Word length 8 bits, address width 16 bits.
Maximum memory space 64K bytes.
An 8-bit primary accumulator (the A register); two index registers (X and Y); a Program Counter (not usable as a GP register); Stack Pointer and Status Register are provided.

Instruction Set

There are around 60 instructions types, 1, 2, or 3 bytes long. There are only 8-bit instructions—16-bit operations have to be performed using two 8-bit operations.

Data Transfer Instructions
The 6502 has a full set of data transfer instructions of the 1 1/2 address type. The contents of the A, X and Y registers may be transferred to and from memory with LD and ST opcodes with the register label appended e.g. LDY. There is no direct loading for the S register. Interregister operations are provided in the Transfer group (TAY = transfer the contents of register A to register Y). There are no 2 address instructions. There are also two stack Push and Pop instructions, for the A register and Status register, in which the stack pointer is also updated.

Arithmetic and Logical Instructions
A restricted set of arithmetic functions is available. Addition/subtraction is with carry only. A special decimal mode is available, via the decimal flag, which allows direct addition and subtraction of BCD numbers. Increment and Decrement operations are available on memory and on registers X and Y but not A.
    The logical functions are AND, ORA and EOR. A BIT instruction ANDs a memory location and the A register.

Jump Instructions
There are 8 conditional and 1 unconditional jump instructions. They are single address instructions using relative addressing.

Subroutine Entry and Exit
The subroutine entry instruction is a single address memory reference instruction, causing the contents of the PC to be pushed on to the stack. Return from the subroutine causes the PC to be reloaded from the stack. There is also a Break instruction which is equivalent to a software interrupt, and a corresponding Return.

Shift Instructions
Right and Left shifts are provided, but of 1 bit position only. They operate on the contents of a memory location or the A register. There is a Left Rotate instruction, and on newer models a Right Rotate.

Flag Instructions
There are seven flags used singly and in combination to produce the conditions for the Jumps. There are special instructions to set/clear four of the flags; they are otherwise set/cleared on the result of a normal arithmetic or logical operation, or by the Compare instruction.

Miscellaneous Instructions
There is a NOP instruction. No I/O instructions are provided, as the 6502 supports only memory-mapped I/O.

Addressing Modes

Immediate Addressing.
The operand follows the opcode, both one byte long.

Direct Addressing
There are two forms of direct addressing. In the first, known as Page Zero addressing, the address of the operand follows the opcode as a single-byte number. It can address any of the first 256 locations of memory. These locations, known as Page Zero, are commonly used as a variable storage area.
The second form is known as Absolute addressing. The complete address of the operand follows the opcode as a 2-byte number, low byte first. It thus allows access to any location in memory.

Indexed Addressing
The address of the operand is formed by adding the contents of the byte(s) that follows the opcode—the offset—to the contents of one of the two index registers. Several indexed modes are available:

Page Zero—the address of the operand is a page zero location formed by adding a single-byte offset to the contents of the X or Y register. Absolute—the address of the operand is the sum of an absolute 2-byte offset and the specified index register contents.
Indexed X Indirect—the address is contained in a 2-byte number located on page zero, pointed to by the sum of the offset and the contents of the X register.
Indirect Y Indexed—The address of the operand is the sum of the contents of a 2-byte number located on page zero and the contents of the Y register.

Relative Addressing
The effective address is the sum of an offset and the contents of the PC. This is used only in the Jump instructions.

Instruction Set Coding Structure

The addressing mode appears within the opcode itself in most instructions, in a 1, 2, or 3-bit field according to the number of alternatives relevant. In

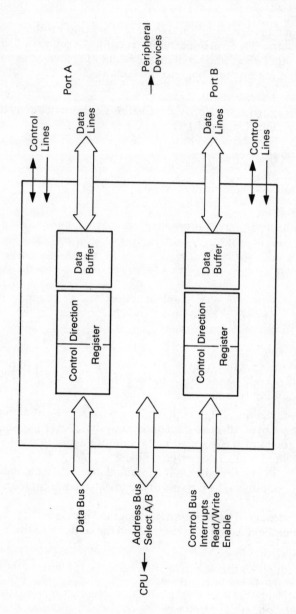

Figure A3 *The 6520 programmable input/output chip*

some register instructions the register is also coded in bits 7–8, leaving the first three bits to indicate the instruction type.

Input/Output

Peripherals and memory are connected to an I/O bus containing 16 address lines, 8 data lines, a Read/Write direction and a Ready line. The 6502 permits only memory mapped I/O, so that there are no I/O lines. Data transfers are initiated and synchronized solely by the use of the Ready signal, which halts the processor at the end of a cycle and inserts wait cycles into the on-board system until the peripheral or its controller can transfer data to/from the bus, according to the direction indicated on the Read/Write line.

Like all microprocessors the 6502 family includes interface chips which sit between the peripheral/controller and the I/O bus. The 6520 is a typical programmable input/output interface (see Figure A.3). It contains two external input or output ports each with 8 parallel data lines and two control lines for handshaking with external devices. Each port can be set to Read or Write by setting a bit in the Direction Registers. There is a Control Register for each port that is also program-set, and a Data Buffer for each port to stabilize the data for output. A more advanced version of the 6520 is the 6522 Versatile Interface Adapter or VIA for short. This allows each of the 16 external lines to be configured separately, and contains two programmable timers and a serial-parallel and parallel-serial converter. It is this adapter in particular that makes it possible for low-cost microcomputers to be interfaced to so many different types of external signals.

Interrupts and Interrupt-Handling

There are two interrupt lines, one for normal interrupts and the other for higher priority nonmaskable interrupts. A normal interrupt may be masked (ignored) if the interrupt–enable flag is not set. A nonmaskable interrupt (e.g. a power failure) or an enabled normal interrupt causes the processor to save the contents of the PC and S register on the stack, and fetch the contents of two fixed memory locations. The content of these two words is the starting address of the interrupt service routine, which is user-provided and has to poll all the attached devices to discover the source of the interrupt signal before it can service the call. The interrupt flag is software-controlled and is reset by the Return instruction, which also reloads the PC and S register from the stack. There is also a software-initiated interrupt facility in the Break instruction which has the same effect as a normal hardware-initiated interrupt.

Memory Management

Memory is assumed to be allocated in pages of 256 bytes. Page zero is used in page zero addressing—see above—and page 1 is dedicated to the stack. Memory references are relocated to pages 2+, by treating the 16-bit address as an 8-bit page number and 8-bit displacement. The page number can be incremented by 2 to give an address that is always in user memory space. Data transfers across page boundaries take up an additional machine cycle.

A.4 THE Z-80 MICROPROCESSOR FROM THE ZILOG CORPORATION

The Z-80 and subsequent variants Z-80A/B is by far the most commonly used microprocessors in 8-bit microcomputers designed and sold for business use, and is still to be found in new microsystems currently being introduced to the marketplace. It is also often found in conjunction with the M68000 (see next section) in 8/16 bit dual processor microsystems.

General Features

Word length 8 bits, address width 16 bits.
Maximum memory space 64K bytes.
There are sixteen 8-bit GP Registers arranged in two complementary sets each including a primary Accumulator and a flag register. Only one set can be active at a time, but the sets are switch-selectable. In each set, pairs of the 8-bit registers are used together to hold a 16-bit physical address or to hold an operand for double-precision arithmetic.

Also available are two Index Registers, generally used to hold base addresses for instructions in indexed mode, but also otherwise ready for use as GP Registers; a Stack Pointer and Program Counter.

Instruction Set

The instruction set contains 158 instructions, 1–4 bytes in length. It supports both 8- and 16-bit operations, and block moves and I/O commands provide efficient movements of data within the system, which accounts for its effectiveness in commercial computing.

Data Transfer Instructions
8-bit and 16-bit data transfers are allowed between register and memory and between registers. Block transfer instructions provide for repeated transfers of one byte from a starting address/to a starting address until a byte counter is decremented to zero. Stack Push and Pop, and interregister Exchanges are also available.

Arithmetic and Logical Instructions
8-bit and 16-bit arithmetic can be performed in various addressing modes. 8-bit operations include the logical operators AND, OR and XOR. The A register must always be used as the location of the first operand. There is also a 16-bit instruction allowing the Z-80 to perform BCD addition and subtraction.

Jump Instructions
There are two unconditional and five conditional Jump instructions, and both conditional and unconditional subroutine Calls and Returns, using the stack to hold the return address.

Shift and Rotate Instructions
1-bit and 4-bit Shift and Rotate operations are permitted on register or memory operands, in just about every possible shift configuration.

Flag Instructions
There is a BIT, TEST, SET and RESET group of instructions which operate on one of the bits in an 8-bit register and separate instructions to set the complement, carry and interrupt flags.

Input/Output Instructions
The Z-80 instruction set contains two special input/output instructions IN and OUT with several variations, between registers and any one of 256 input and output ports. Single-byte or multiple-byte transfers can be effected. Alternatively these instructions can be ignored and devices addressed in memory. Similar in structure to the Block I/O are a set of Block Search instructions, which examine memory locations from a starting address and compare its contents with the contents of the A register, terminating the search when the two values match or when the byte count is decremented to zero.

Other Instructions
The Z-80 is strong on processor control instructions, with three interrupt mode instructions (see below) and Returns/Restarts.

Instruction Set Coding Structure

The first two digits of a one-byte opcode differentiate the instruction type as follows:

    01 – Load
    10 – Arithmetic and Logical Instructions
    11 – Jump
    00 – Relative Jumps

with the remaining six digits containing up to two sets of three bits representing either register or condition codes.

In two- or three-byte instructions, a value in the first byte of:

    11011101   refers to index register X;
    11111101   refers to index register Y;
    11101101   refers to an operation in which register indirect addressing employs a linked pair of the 8-bit registers;
    11001011   refers to a Bit/Set/Reset instruction, with the byte following decoded thus:

    00 – Rotate
    01 – Bit selection
    10 – Reset
    11 – Set
    followed by a 3-bit bit-code.

Addressing Modes

Immediate Addressing.
The single-byte operand follows the opcode.

Immediate Extended
The operand is a 2-byte number that follows the operand.

Implied Addressing
The location of the operand is in one of the registers which is named in the opcode itself.

Extended Addressing
The address of the operand follows the opcode as a 2-byte number, low byte first.

Indexed Addressing
The address of the operand is formed by adding a single-byte offset that follows the opcode to the contents of one of the index registers X or Y.

Register Indirect Addressing
The address of the operand is held in a specified pair of the GP registers.

Register Addressing
The operand is held in a specified register.

Relative Addressing
The address of the next instruction is formed by adding a single-byte offset immediately following the opcode to the contents of the PC (jump instructions only).

Page Zero Addressing
The location of the next instruction is 1 of 8 prespecified page zero locations, selected in a single-byte Restart Instruction.

Bit Addressing
A single bit position may be specified within an operand.

Input/Output

Memory and peripherals are attached to the I/O bus which contains 40 lines including 8 data lines and 16 address lines. Among the control lines are:

IORQ which indicates that an address on the low 8 address lines is a valid input or output port number;
MREQ which indicates that a 16-bit address is a valid memory location;
RD and WR indicate the direction of a transfer;
BUSRQ and BUSAK are the bus request signal from an external device and the bus grant from the processor respectively.

After a BUSAK the processor is locked out during a DMA operation. A BUSRQ takes priority over other interrupts. One byte is transferred during a single cycle, and a Wait signal can be used to delay the completion of the operation.

Along with other microprocessors, the Z-80 family contains a set of interface chips, including an I/O bus adapter to the industry standard S100 bus to which a large number of peripheral devices can be attached.

Interrupts and Interrupt-Handling

There are two interrupt signals—the nonmaskable interrupt and the normal interrupt. The NMI has priority over all states other than a Reset and Bus Request. The normal interrupt will be ignored if the interrupt flag is not enabled by the Enable Interrupt instruction.

The NMI causes the contents of the PC to be pushed on to the stack, and executes a Restart to a fixed location in page zero of memory which must contain the first instruction of an interrupt service routine.

A normal interrupt can operate in three modes, selectable by an Interrupt Mode instruction.

In mode 0 a Restart opcode is placed on the data bus to save the PC and then jump to a fixed location in page zero to start the execution of an interrupt service routine.

In mode 1 the processor does this automatically, jumping to a fixed memory location.

In mode 2 the processor saves the PC and the user supplies the address of the first instruction of a service routine as follows: the contents of the Interrupt Vector register supplies the first eight (most significant) bits (i.e. the starting address of the Interrupt Vector Table), and the interrupting device supplies the eight least significant bits (i.e. the displacement to a specific entry in the table). Each device is connected to the normal interrupt line in a prioritizing scheme in which the implicit priority is set by two additional signals. These allow the interrupting device to signal its relative displacement along the bus away from the processor, which corresponds to the position of its entry in the Interrupt Vector Table.

A.5 THE MOTOROLA M68000 MICROPROCESSOR

Designers of 16-bit microprocessor sets had an interesting and fundamental design choice. They could either make their architecture compatible with the earlier 8-bit designs or they could use the advantage of greater density and integration of circuitry to their greatest advantage by building more extensive registers and new instruction sets. Compatibility means that software can be transferred to the new 16-bit microprocessor with little or no change, even though the performance improvement may thereby be compromised. The designers of the M68000 microprocessor opted to pursue the objective of designing the best 16-bit micro that current technology permitted, and it is the verdict of both the business and consumer microcomputer manufacturers that they have succeeded in that objective, since the M68000 is to be found within a large proportion of the top range multiuser micros, and also in the Sinclair QL system (but see below).

General Features

Word length 16 bits, bus registers and system bus and all operations are 32 bits wide. The external (I/O) bus has 23 address lines and 16 data lines, but a version has been announced with 32-bit address and data lines, making it a true 32-bit microprocessor. There is also a version, used in the Sinclair QL, which uses only 8 of the 16 or 32 data lines. Maximum memory linearly addressable is 16M bytes (4 gigabytes in the 32-bit version). Maximum attachable memory is 4M bytes.

Registers—all 32-bit:

  8 Data Registers
  8 Address Registers
  2 Stack Pointers
  Program Counter
  Status Register (16-bits)

All 16 user registers and the PC may be used as index registers; the address registers for base addressing, and the data registers for byte, word and longword (32-bit) operations.

The M68000 has a prefetch queue, into which instructions are loaded during idle bus cycles and decoded before execution by the processor.

Instruction Set

Instructions are from 1 to 5 words in length. The first word carries the opcode and an address mode and register mode pair. Following words contain either up to 2 immediate operands or up to 2 effective address data for source and destination memory locations.

Five basic data types are supported: bits, BCD, bytes, words, longwords. There are 56 instruction types, each of which can, with few exceptions, operate on bytes, words and longwords in perfect symmetry, and most of the instructions can use any of the addressing modes described below. Combining instruction types and variations, data types and addressing modes gives over 1,000 useful instructions from such a small but powerful basic set.

Data Transfer Instructions
The Move instruction allows data transfers between register and memory and between registers, and the effective addressing modes applicable permit the manipulation of both data and addresses. There are also several special data movement instructions: to move multiple registers, to exchange registers, move peripheral data, and several stack operators.

Arithmetic and Logical Instructions
The arithmetic operations include the four basic Add, Subtract, Multiply and Divide, and Negate and Compare. There are signed and unsigned variations, and operations on extended and mixed size numbers. The logical operators provided are AND, OR and EOR. There are also Add, Subtract and Negate BCD numbers instructions available.

Jump Instructions
14 conditional and one unconditional Branch instructions, and subroutine Jump, Branch and Return instructions.

Shift and Rotate Instructions
Shift operations in both directions are provided by both arithmetic and logical Shifts and Rotates. All such operations can be performed in registers and memory. All operand sizes are supported and allow a shift count of 1–8 bits in the instruction or 1–64 bits specified in a data register.

Flag Instructions
The Set instruction can set and reset any one of the 16 condition codes conditionally.

Other Instructions
There is a large set of system control instructions some of which are privileged instructions invalid in user mode (see below). No special I/O instructions are provided except Move Peripheral Data (with source-destination operands).

Addressing Modes

Immediate Addressing
The operand is located in the word that follows the opcode.

Absolute Addressing (Long and Short)
The absolute address follows the opcode either as a two-word or one-word number.

Direct Addressing (Data/Address Register)
The operand is located in the specified data/address register, or in the status register.

Indirect Addressing
The address of the operand is contained in the specified address register.

Indirect Addressing with Postincrement
As above, but when the operand is fetched the contents of the specified address register are automatically incremented by the size of the instruction i.e. by 1, 2, or 4 according to the length of the operand fetched in bytes.

Indirect Addressing with Predecrement
The address of the operand is formed from the contents of the specified address register decremented by 1, 2, or 4 according to the size of the operand.

Relative Addressing
The address of the operand is the sum of the contents of the specified address register or the PC and a single-word displacement that immediately follows the opcode.

Indexed Addressing
The address of the operand is the sum of the contents of a specified address register or the PC, and the contents of a specified index register, and an 8-bit offset contained in the word that follows the opcode.

Instruction Set Coding Structure

In the opcode (see Figure A4), bits are used as follows:

bit	function
15–12	instruction type
11–9	register number (if relevant)
8	to/from memory indicator
7–6	operand size
5–3	addressing mode
2–0	register used in addressing mode (if relevant)

In an indexed addressing mode, the second word is organized as follows:

bit	function
15	data (0) or address register (1)
14–12	register number
11	sign extended index (0) or longword value (1)

in index register

10–8	unused
7–0	offset.

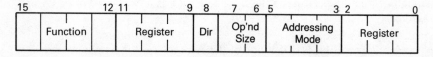

Figure A4   *The structure of the M68000 opcode*

Input/Output

Memory and peripherals are attached to the I/O bus. The M68000 memory maps its I/O ports, so that there are no special lines. The bus contains 23 address lines and 16 data lines and a full complement of control lines. An attached device requests control via a Bus Request. At the end of a cycle the device responds with a Bus Grant, to which the device replies with a Bus Grant Acknowledge. The device then sets the direction line, and two signals that indicate the size and location on the bus of the data about to be transferred.

The addressed device then places data on or removes it from the line, and indicates completion by a Data Transfer Acknowledge signal. The processor inserts wait signals until this signal is received, up to a maximum elapsed time, at which point a Bus Error signal is generated to abort the operation. Logic is therefore required in the device to complete the operation correctly.

There are also three control lines that enable the earlier 8-bit M6800 devices to be accessed over the I/O bus.

Interrupts and Interrupt-Handling

The M68000 runs in either Supervisory or User state. In the latter certain privileged instructions may not be executed. System exceptions may be internally or externally generated. External exceptions (= interrupts) place a preassigned priority level on 3 Interrupt Priority lines, coded in the range 0-7. If the priority level of the interrupting device is greater than the current priority level, the processor saves the contents of the Status Register and restarts processing in the Supervisory state. The three function lines are set to high values, and the interrupting device then provides either a vector number from which the processor finds the relevant Vector Table entry, or it can request autovectoring, in which case the starting address of the interrupt service routine is found in a fixed position in the Vector Table for that priority level.

Memory Management

The M68000 can directly ('linearly') address 16M bytes of memory on its 23 address lines. The three function lines are used to supply a segment indicator, for four segments: supervisory program, supervisory data, user program and user data. This effectively gives a 24-bit address space. Subsequent versions of the M68000 have progressed beyond this level of memory management. The M68010 treats the 24-bit address as a virtual address, which is translated into a physical address by a Memory Management Unit. Memory is allocated in page of 64K bytes, and an address is partitioned into a page number (8 bits) and a byte displacement within page (16 bits). A page table is used to hold the starting address in memory of each loaded page of a program, and the page number from the virtual address is used to index the page table. If a selected page has already been loaded into memory, the byte displacement is added to the indicated page address to provide the physical address of the reference. If the page is not loaded, the access is suspended until the page has been loaded from the virtual memory maintained as an image in backing storage. The M68010 provides hardware support for this process as a page fault exception, which causes the processor to store the PC and status register on the stack before initiating the page load routine, after which the program's registers are reloaded and the suspended instruction continued.

The M68020 operates as the M68010, but provides a full 32-bit address space supporting 4 gigabytes of virtual address space. The 32-bit addresses are mapped into real memory by the Memory Management Unit, which takes the leading 16 bits as a page table index and 16 bits as a byte displacement. The physical address of the segment is found from the indicated page table entry, to which the byte displacement is added to give the actual memory location sought.

The M68020 also provides a cache memory for holding current address translation information; and a co-processor interface for a floating point processor. New data types, addressing modes and 32-bit instructions bring its overall performance up to and beyond that of a large VAX computer.

A.6 THE INTEL 8086/88 MICROPROCESSOR

The Intel 8086 and 8088 are probably the most widely used of the current generation of 8/16 bit microprocessors. They are to be found in the smaller versions of the IBM Personal Computer (the larger models contain the extended versions of the 8086 discussed at the end of this section), and in the popular Sirius and Apricot microsystems. They were designed to be reasonably compatible with their 8-bit predecessor, the Intel 8080, in the interests of software conversion.

General Features

Word length 16 bits, system bus width 16 bits, external bus width 16 bits (8086) or 8 bits (8088) for data, 20 bits for addresses.

There are four GP registers, which can be treated either as four 16 bit registers or two sets of 8-bit registers. Each can be used as a primary accumulator, but they may have a special significance in some instructions. There are also ten special purpose registers, some of which can be used as index registers or for other addressing purposes:

Stack Pointer	Status Register
Base Register	Instruction Pointer
Source Index Register	Code Segment Register
Destination Index Register	Extra Segment Register
Stack Segment Register	
Data Segment Register	

Instruction Set

There is a large and sophisticated instruction set of 91 instructions, with variations for the various addressing modes, 8 or 16 bit operands, decimal integer arithmetic etc.

Data Transfer Instructions
It is possible to move data between registers and memory with Move instructions, and between registers with the Exchange instructions. There are 3 Push and Pop instructions operating on the stack, and a special Movep for moving peripheral data.

Arithmetic and Logical Instructions
A wide range of such instructions is provided: Add/Subtract with/without carry, signed/unsigned Multiply/Divide, in register–register or register–memory addressing modes. There is also a BCD Carry instruction to facilitate BCD arithmetic. The logical operators supplied are OR, AND, XOR and NOT.

Jump Instructions
There are 5 unconditional and 15 conditional Jumps, and 3 Loops. There are 4 Calls/Returns and a software interrupt Trap/Return.

Flag Instructions
The Compare instruction and 7 flag Set/Clear instructions are provided to manipulate flags not otherwise set on the result of arithmetic operations.

Shifts and Rotate Instructions
Three Shifts and four Rotates can reposition data in registers or memory, one or many bits at a time.

Other Instructions
String transfer instructions, processor control (Halt/Wait/Lock/Nop) instructions and special I/O instructions are also provided.

Addressing Modes

The large number of special registers facilitates a large variety of addressing modes. The 8086/88 uses a segmented addressing scheme, in which the address of an opcode or operand is formed by a combination of the contents of a register and a 16-bit offset. The base addresses are stored in the four segment registers, and the offsets may be stored in the memory location following the opcode or in any of the other special purpose registers or one of the GP registers. The address is formed by shifting the contents of the named segment register 4 places left and then adding the offset. Instruction addresses are always formed by the addition of the code segment register and the instruction pointer, which acts as the PC for the system. Instructions may use a combination of the index registers, the contents of memory locations and the segment registers to form an operand address.

The other interesting feature of the 8086/88 which affects the operation of the addressing modes is that the processor is internally divided into two asynchronous functional blocks, the execution unit or EU, which performs the operations specified by instructions, and the bus interface unit or BIU which fetches the opcodes and operands and stores the operands. The BIU maintains an instruction queue in which it keeps the next 6 or 8 bytes needed by the EU, and the instruction pointer points to the next instruction to be fetched by the BIU.

Immediate Addressing
The operand follows the opcode.

Direct Addressing
The operand address follows the opcode in memory.

Register Addressing
The operand is in a named register.

Indirect Addressing
The operand address is contained in the named register.

Based/Indexed Addressing
The operand address is the sum of a displacement following the opcode, and the contents of the B register or Base register (Based Addressing); or of the

Source or Destination index register (Indexed Addressing); or of both (Based Indexed Addressing).

String Addressing
The string operands use the index registers to point to the start of the source and destination locations.

I/O Addressing
I/O ports can be memory or I/O mapped. Memory mapped ports can be accessed using any memory addressing mode; I/O mapped ports can be accessed in Immediate Mode (using an 8-bit port number in the opcode) or in Indirect Mode (using the Destination Index Register).

Input/Output

Memory and peripherals are attached to the I/O bus, which contains multiplexed lines for use by both address and data in the same cycle. What is thereby saved in space on the bus is compensated for by greater space in the control lines.

Bus requests are made on the HOLD line, and acknowledged by the processor with a HOLD Acknowledge signal;

A RD or WR line is set to indicate direction of the forthcoming transfer;
M/IO is set to indicate whether a memory location or I/O port is involved;
DEN enables the external bus buffers;
READY inserts delays to permit the insertion of data to/from the data lines.

After a byte is transferred, the processor recognizes the resetting of the HOLD line to regain control of the bus. If the 8086 is configured in 'maximum' mode, i.e. in a multiprocessor configuration along a high-speed Multibus bus, then some of the control lines are redesignated as 3 status lines and 2 prioritized bus grant request and acknowledge lines, in the interest of resolving contention for the bus. A LOCK line is also defined to delay relinquishing control of the bus.

The usual family of interface chips is provided for the usual construction of a full processor/memory/peripheral interface system on a single board. A noteworthy development of the 8086 is the 80186 (also known as the iapx 186), in which no fewer than 20 such chips have been integrated into a single processor chip which requires only memory to complete a single-board system. This gives up to five-fold improvement in performance at ultimately a lower cost; and at the same time 10 extra instructions have been added to the standard 8086/88 instruction set, and in some cases extra hardware has been provided to perform functions implemented in microcode on the 8086.

Interrupts and Interrupt-Handling

As usual, there are two interrupt lines, for normal and nonmaskable interrupts. The NMI signal saves the flag register on the stack and fetches the NMI vector from a fixed position in the Interrupt Vector Table, starting the interrupt service routine from the address continued in the vector. The NMI has a lower priority than some software interrupts and exceptions. The INTerrupt Return instruction is used at the end of the service routine to reload the registers and restart execution of the interrupted program.

The regular interrupt saves all the registers and outputs the interrupt acknowledge signal. The interrupting device must place the vector number on the data bus. This is used to find the appropriate entry in the Interrupt Vector Table, and the service routine is started. The IRET then reloads the registers and restarts the interrupted program.

There is also an INTerrupt command which has the same effect as a normal interrupt generated by software or hardware, with a fixed position in the Vector Table.

The 8087 Numeric Processor

The 8086 family of chips contains a numeric processor chip that interfaces to the 8086/88 as a 'co-processor'. This processor can handle seven data types (3 sizes of integer, packed decimal and 3 sizes of real numbers), which it internally processes in a common 80-bit format with a guaranteed accuracy of 18 bits. All 8087 instructions (the 8086 instruction set plus 68 floating point arithmetic instructions) have a unique 5-bit prefix, and all instructions fetched by the BIU are placed in both processors' prefetch queue. The host processor only calculates the address of an operand for an 8087 instruction, and the 8087 takes over the address, fetches the data and performs its operations in parallel with the host processor. The 8087 may require additional accesses to memory, in which case it will issue a Bus Grant request as if it were a standard peripheral. Internally the 8087 has a special set of 80-bit registers as intermediate accumulators, in addition to the normal 8086 register set.

Memory Management

The 8086/88 employs segmented addressing—a memory reference is treated as a 16-bit segment address and a 16-bit offset. Segment addresses are stored in the appropriate segment register, the offset in any other register or in memory immediately following the opcode. A physical address is generated by shifting the contents of the named segment register four places left and then adding the offset. Segments are logical address concepts, and may overlap in memory.

The 80286 (iapx 286)

The 80286 is the latest product in the 8086 family (at least until the emergence of the 80386 which will be a true 32-bit processor). It offers three advantages over the 80186: firstly there is a further increase in integration, secondly there is a significant enhancement in parallel operations, and thirdly the memory management functions are expanded primarily in the interests of multiuser processing. It provides 24 address lines in the I/O bus thus permitting the physical addressing of up to 16M bytes of memory, and a virtual address space of 1 gigabyte for each task.

The 80286 processor is constructed of four parallel and independent units; bus interface unit, address unit, instruction unit and execution unit. Each of these units can operate in parallel, so that for instance the instruction unit takes instructions placed in a queue by the BIU, decodes them and places them fully formatted in an instruction queue awaiting execution in the EU. Finally the address unit performs the address-translation and access-protection functions (see below) using its own high-speed cache to hold currently-used mapping and protection data.

The enhanced Memory Management Unit is also integrated into the processor chip. Each user has access to up to a gigabyte of virtual address space split between shared and private use areas. Shared use areas are for the storage of common data, files, library routines and the operating system itself. The private use area is for individual application programs. A virtual address on the 80287 is composed of the same two 16-bit elements as on the 8086. Fourteen bits of the contents of the named segment register are used to select an entry in a programs global or local descriptor tables. The descriptor table entry contains the base address of the segment in physical memory (if it is already loaded), to which the 16-bit offset is added to give the physical address required; the size of the segment (up to 64K bytes); and its access rights. If a segment is addressed that is not present in memory, an access exception is signalled to the processor to cause the access to be suspended until an exception handler can allocate memory to that segment and load it into physical memory. Within a task's virtual address space, there is a four-level protection scheme, on top of the protection of one user's space from access by another. The Address Unit (see above) implements the protection scheme by signalling access-violation exceptions to the processor.

Bibliography

The following books will provide further reading on Compute. . ...itecture. The list is intentionally not long in the hope that the reader may be encouraged to search for the books listed. A brief indication of the content of each book is given. The books listed contain references to a much larger reading list for the person who wishes to study the subject in depth.

GENERAL

Baer, Jean-Loup, *Computer Systems Architecture,* Computer Science Press, 1980. Comprehensive and complete treatise on computer architecture 'from microprocessors to superminicomputers'.

Eckhouse, Richard H. Jnr. and Morris L. Robert, *Minicomputer Systems: Organisation and Programming (PDP-11)* (2nd Edition), Prentice-Hall 1979. Gives a good appreciation of the hardware and software of minicomputers, particularly the PDP-11.

Gear, C., *Computer Organisation and Programming* (3rd Edition), McGraw-Hill, 1980. Covers architecture and programming, particularly for IBM and DEC systems.

Hamacher, Carl V. et al., *Computer Organisation* (3rd Edition), McGraw-Hill, 1984. Deals with the design and components of all types of compute.

Healey, Martin, *Minicomputers and Microprocessors*, Hodder and Stoughton, 1976. Covers the same ground as the text's Chapters 1–6 but : more detail. Recommended further reading.

King, Tim and Knight, Brian, *Programming the M68000,* Addison-Wesley 1983. A comprehensive guide to programming the M68000, concentrating on the architecture as seen by the programmer.

Leventhal, Lance A., *Introduction to Microprocessors: Software, Hardware, Programming,* Prentice-Hall, 1978. A wide coverage of 8-bit microprocessors.

Lewin, Morton N., *Logic Design and Computer Organisation,* Addison-Wesley, 1983. Builds up from gate structures and logic operators into processors and programs. Highly recommended for a bottom-up approach.

Mano, M. Morris, *Computer System Architecture* (2nd Edition), Prentice-Hall, 1983. Deals with architecture in depth. Recommended continuation from this text.

Osborne, Adam, *An Introduction to Microcomputers,* Volume 1, Osborne/McGraw-Hill, 1980. An authoritative treatment of micro-computer fundamentals.

Tanenbaum, Andrew S., *Structured Computer Organisation* (2nd Edition), Prentice-Hall, 1984. Recommended continuation text, software-biased but with a cover of hardware and architecture.

Witting, Phil, *Fundamentals of Microprocessor Systems,* Chartwell-Bratt, 1984. Comprehensive and up-to-date treatment of microprocessors.

SPECIFIC

Barden, William Jnr., *Z-80 Microcomputer Handbook,* Prentice-Hall, 1978

Digital Equipment Corporation, *PDP-11 Architecture Handbook,* 1983–4

Digital Equipment Corporation, *VAX Architecture Handbook,* 1981

E1-Asfouri Souhail et al., *Computer Organisation and Programming: VAX-11,* Addison-Wesley, 1984

Ferguson John and Shaw Tony, *Assembly Language Programming on the BBC Micro,* Addison-Wesley, 1983

Gorsline George W., *Sixteen Bit Modern Microcomputers: the Intel I8086 Family,* Prentice-Hall, 1984

Intel Corporation, *iapx88 Book,* 1983

Intel Corporation, *iapx186/286* Handbook, 1984

Motorola Inc., *M68000 Microprocessor Users' Handbook,* 1982

Poe, Elmer C., *The Microprocessor Handbook,* 1983

Zaks, Rodney, *Programming the Z80* (3rd Edition), Sybek, 1982

Zaks, Rodney, *Programming the 6502* (4th Edition), Sybek, 1983

Exercises

1. Use any computer system to which you have access, and write the following programs for that system using assembly language.

(a) Accept a string of ASCII characters from the console keyboard. A string is a sequence of characters terminated by a carriage return character. Store the string in a table in memory. Output the string of characters in legible form on a VDU display. Characters should be formed on a 7×5 matrix and be readable by people. Your program will have to access a second table in which is stored the patterns of dots and spaces to be used for every character of the alphabet, 5 sets for each character to be shown legibly.

This gives good practice at manipulating codes, and at using the indexing and/or indirect addressing capabilities of the system you are programming.

(b) Write a program to print out all 8-bit three-spaced code sets. (see Parity Coding, chapter 3).

(c) Write a program which uses the ASCII code SI (Shift In) — hex 0F — control + O (see Figure 3.5) as the upper case shift character, and the ASCII code SO (Shift Out) hex 0E — control + N — as the lower case shift.

Type in messages from a VDU or other keyboard with all characters in the same case. Store them in memory in the correct case as determined by the depressing of the SI and SO keys. At the end of each line display the characters stored in memory.

(d) Look up Booth's Algorithm for the multiplication of two numbers. Write a program to implement it.

2. Describe the different addressing modes typically found in minicomputers and microcomputers in terms of their appearance to the programmer and their implementation as data transfers between registers. Explain how they can be used to increase the addressing range of the machine instruction.

3. Two alternative methods of programming data transfers between a CPU and a peripheral device are:

(a) by executing a program loop to examine a 'ready' status bit;

(b) using an interrupt system to interrupt the CPU when the device is ready.

If a cassette tape reader can transfer 1000 characters per second explain why it is more efficient in terms of CPU utilization to connect the cassette reader to an interrupt driven system. Estimate the efficiency of utilization of the CPU when the cassette reader is used in systems (a) and (b) above. State clearly any assumptions you make.

4. A 16-bit minicomputer system has a multi-level interrupt system with 8 interrupt levels. Explain how the interrupt priorities of the peripheral devices can be resolved by hardware to give each device a unique priority in the system.

If the priority is fully vectored, explain how the hardware may cause a jump to the interrupt routine of the highest priority interrupting device.

5. What is meant by the term *effective address*? A computer system uses:

Indirect addressing

Indexing

Relative addressing

Double length memory reference instructions

Explain carefully how the effective address is obtained in each case.

If this computer system has a CPU with eight addressable general purpose registers, including the Program Counter, devise one set of memory reference instruction format(s) which could provide all the addressing modes above.

6. A 16-bit minicomputer system has an Input/Output instruction format as shown in Figure A.1. Given that:

(i) The I/O bus contains 16 'data' lines and a few control lines;

(ii) Peripheral command and data information are transferred along the I/O bus on the 'data' lines;

(iii) All information transfers on the I/O bus are controlled by a handshaking protocol.

Explain carefully with the help of a flowchart or waveform diagram (see Figures 5.7 and 5.8), the sequence of events which occurs when the CPU executes an OUTPUT instruction. You must specify the functions of all the necessary lines in the I/O bus system and show how they take part in the output data transfers.

7. For each of the topics (a) through (g) below, define the topic and, where appropriate, explain its structure, uses, important parameters and the benefits and restrictions conferred on the system in which it is used.

(a) Random Access Memory

(b) Read Only Memory

(c) Interleaved Memory

(d)   Multiple Ported Memory
(e)   Memory Access Time
(f)   Memory Cycle Time
(g)   Stack Organized Memory

8. Compare and contrast the instruction set of the Digital Equipment Corporation PDP-11 minicomputer with that of the Motorola M68000 microprocessor (or any two computer systems with which you are familiar). Your comparison should cover at least the following topics:

(a)   The richness of the memory reference instruction set;
(b)   Memory addressing techniques available in the system;
(c)   The methods of subroutine entry and return and their effects on the programming techniques available;
(d)   Shift instructions;
(e)   Jump and branch instructions;
(f)   The arithmetic and logical instructions.

Where appropriate, your answer should include comments on the interaction of the architecture and the instruction set.

9. By referring to a unit cube diagram (see Figure 3.6(a)), explain the structure of a single parity bit error detecting system.

10. Explain, with the use of suitable diagrams, the difference between the signed magnitude numbering system and the twos complement numbering system. Give reasons for the choice of the latter in computer systems.

11. Discuss and distinguish clearly the functions of the Carry Flag and the Overflow Flag.

12. Explain with the help of suitable diagrams how one word of information is passed between two devices in:

(i)   a system in which synchronization is single-ended;
(ii)   a system in which handshaking is used.

Discuss these two synchronization methods.

13. Data transfers along a computer Input/Output bus occur selectively to one of many devices attached to the bus. Explain two methods which could be used for device selection. Describe the functions of any special bus lines which these methods require.

14. In a computer system in which the peripheral devices can interrupt the CPU each peripheral has a unique priority. Explain how that priority may be determined:

(a)   Entirely by software;
(b)   Entirely by hardware;
(c)   By a combination of hardware and software.

15. Why is the nesting of interrupts desirable? What are the *necessary* requirements of a system which allows nesting of interrupts? Explain two methods for realizing these requirements.

16. Explain, with the help of suitable diagrams, a method of implementing programmed data transfers between a 16-bit word CPU and an optical character reader. It should be assumed that data are transmitted in parallel to and from the CPU accumulator. Explain clearly how program control is exercised over the data transfers.

17. What is meant by the term 'floating point number'? Explain carefully how a floating point number may be represented by a fixed point mantissa and an exponent. Discuss the uses of this representation in a computer system.

18. A CPU contains four condition code flags Z, N, C and V (see chapters 3 and 7). Show how these flags may be used to derive the conditions $A < B$, $A = B$, $A > B$ for conditional jumps, where A, B are the two words at the input to the ALU. What special conditions, if any, attach to the setting and clearing of the flags in this context?

19. Why is floating point arithmetic normally used in computer systems? Explain carefully its advantages over integer arithmetic and the limitations in its use.

20. A 16-bit computer system contains a BCD add instruction and a tens complement instruction, which act on the contents of the GP registers. If the 4-BCD-digit content of two registers are added, derive conditions for the detection of overflow in the system.
(Not in the main text—condition is 1 through 9 in MS digit).

21. Why is it sometimes necessary to add a filler of 6 to the result of a binary addition of two BCD digits? Derive the complete set of conditions for the addition of this filler.

Index

This highly acclaimed textbook for students of computer science and electronic engineering has been thoroughly revised. It provides a complete, straightforward introduction to the basic structure and workings of small computers – minicomputers, microcomputers and microprocessor systems.

"I found this book both technically informative and also very interesting to read. Each section of the book is well set out and the explanations are well augmented with clear diagrams. . . . I recommend this book for anybody who wants to know more about small machine architecture, as a fine introduction to the subject."
DATALINK*

"Almost every aspect of small-computer structure and operation is covered in a manner that is both concise and enlightening . . . a very competent and lucid work."
ELECTRONICS & POWER*

"Likely to prove popular with students, who will find packed into its pages a surprisingly large amount of information."
INTERNATIONAL JOURNAL OF ELECTRICAL ENGINEERING EDUCATION*

*Reviews of the First Edition

Prentice/Hall International

0-13-044736-6